10 Principles
FOR
Spiritual Parenting

10 Principles

FOR

Spiritual Parenting

Nurturing Your Child's Soul

Mimi Doe with Marsha Walch, Ph.D.

HarperPerennial
A Division of HarperCollinsPublishers

HarperCollins books may be purchased for educational, business, or sales promotional use. For information please write: Special Markets Department, HarperCollins Publishers, Inc., 10 East 53rd Street, New York, NY 10022.

FIRST EDITION

Designed by Elina D. Nudelman

Library of Congress Cataloging-in-Publication Data

Doe, Mimi.
    10 principles for spiritual parenting : nurturing your child's soul / by Mimi Walch Doe with Marsha Fayfield Walch. — 1st ed.
      p. cm.
    Includes index.
    ISBN 0-06-095241-5
    1. Child rearing—Religious aspects.   2. Parenting—Religious aspects.   3. Children—Religious life.   4. Parents—Religious life. I. Walch, Marsha Fayfield.   II. Title.   III. Title: 10 principles for spiritual parenting.
HQ769.3.W36   1998
649' .1—dc21   97-35123

98 99 00 01 02 ❖/RRD 10 9 8 7 6 5

Contents

Acknowledgments

Special thanks to Connie Clausen and Megan Newman for their wonderful guidance.

Mimi Doe:

To my husband, Tom—I cherish our life together. And to our daughters, Whitney and Elizabeth—your light-filled spirits have brought me such joy, wisdom, and fulfillment. You fill my heart with love. I am grateful to Brenna and Megon McDonough, my sisters of the soul. I am blessed with dear friends who nourish my spirit—Tracy Heffernan, Jenny Breining, Chrissie Bateman, Jane Turner Michael, Leli Sudler, Garland Waller, Lucy McBride, Emily Lania, LuAnne Pryor, Meredith Gabel, Lynn Shipway, Marty Doe, and the many others who have crossed my path thus far in my journey. I thank all the children and adults I have been privileged to work with and who have shared so much.

Marsha Walch:

I am blessed with children who support, inspire, and teach me more than I could ever have taught them. I am forever grateful to them and to my husband, who always believed I could do anything, and who inspired me to try. I thank all the children, friends, relatives, and patients who have opened their hearts and souls to me. I thank friends like Helen Caire, Janet Balch, Jane Byrne, Sheryl Leon, DeAnn Viator, Connie Dodson, and many others who have given me their time and knowledge, and who have shared their parenting experiences. I thank too my brother, Bob Fayfield, who in remembering his childhood brought mine back.

Introduction: How to Use the 10 Principles for Spiritual Parenting

Every good thing that is pink or red is God's love, it's God's valentine to me, like a sunrise or a sunset or a rainbow. (Age four)

When you're ready to go into the body, if you've passed all your tests, you get to decide if you want to remember heaven or if you want to forget it. (Age nine)

Children are spiritual beings. They naturally have what many of us spend years trying to reclaim. What if instead of working on one's "inner child" as an adult, we remain in the light of our intrinsic spirituality and retain our childlike wonder and faith? There is a way to do that. If we recognize and honor our children's innate spiritual connection they may never have to lose it.

Look at the colors around Lillie. I can see pinks and yellows, oh look, I see them with my inside eyes all around Lillie. (Age six)

We know more about nutrition than did past generations. We've identified learning disorders and new educational techniques. We give our children every advantage we can afford, and some we cannot. We organize, direct, enroll, coach, and transport our children to and from lessons, games, practices, social events, doctor's appointments, and schools. We are trying to be good parents and give our children all they need to develop into well-rounded and successful adults. We may, however, be missing the very core of our children's being: their spirituality.

Spirituality is the base from which grow self-esteem, values, morals, and a sense of belonging. It is what gives life direction and meaning. Spirituality is a belief in the existence of a non-physical power greater than oneself. It is the consciousness that relates us directly to God, or whatever we name as the source of our being. When we use the word "God," we mean God, Goddess, Divine Spirit, the Universe, All That Is, Higher Power. We refer to this Higher Power as "He." You may choose to replace our word with "She," or any other word you find comfortable. These children have figured out their own way of distinguishing what "sex" God is:

God is an "It" because "It" is more than just a girl or a boy. (Age six)

Girls are made in God's image so when girls think of God She's a girl and when boys think of God He's a boy. When we all think of God together—God is both girl and boy. (Age five)

Spirituality involves an awareness of a sacred connection to all creation, and a choice to embrace that connection with love. Our children's spiritual natures are reflected by their unbounded creativity, vivid imagination, and joyful, open-ended approach to life. Spirituality is not the dogma of organized religion, although organized religion provides a great deal to nurture a child's soul. Not something to be taught to a child, spirituality is already there.

I talk in my sleep, that's when I'm talking to my angel.
(Age four)

All children begin life with an innate sense of wonder about their world. They are naturally intuitive and open. God is as real to them as Mommy and Daddy. We, as parents, can foster this precious state of being with our words, actions, and attention. Where there is wonder, there is spirituality. The ordinary becomes the extraordinary when we live life as a prayer, a soulful journey, when we endow our daily routine with magic, when we stop the chaos of daily life and celebrate the small moments. We affirm and acknowledge children's true state of being when we join them in their celebration of life. As we bring spirituality into our roles as parents, we consciously acknowledge the divinity present in ourselves and our children.

Spiritual parenting can offer the everyday spirituality that nourishes the child's soul. If the soul is the Divine in each of us, then to honor and strengthen this essential part is to honor God. When we acknowledge ourselves first and foremost as spiritual beings we can parent our children as the true divine individuals they are.

What if you were told you had a sacred contract to help your child unfold into his full spiritual self? Or if you were certain that living in a manner consistent with your spiritual ideals was the greatest gift you could give your child? What if you knew your life was a sacred prayer your child took as the formula for a spiritual existence? Chances are we would all make a commitment to becoming parents who feed our children's innate spirituality.

The more you can think of yourself as a channel through which God coparents your child, the more you will do what is right and centered in each decision you face. The more you see your children as the powerful spiritual entities they are, the more they will mirror that back to you. You will create a home where your children will be free to explore and follow what they know to be true: their inside visions.

Lessons they learn from the outside world, which may discourage their natural creativity, can be counteracted when, with you, they are allowed to be free, joyous, curious—and *spiritual*—beings. Think of your child as an infinite Higher Self housed in a small body. View him as a being who needs time to accept and understand life in the physical plane. You can offer your child's Higher Self a sheltered start in a supported beginning.

Parenting with spirituality is not a rigid, complicated, esoteric project. It is natural, comfortable, and adaptable to any healthy family, whatever its makeup or situation. The understanding, compassionate parent is a spiritual parent. Nurturing the natural visions, experiences, sensations, and dreams of your child keeps the door open for unlimited joy and spiritual aliveness for you both.

> *I want to find ways for my sons to get in touch with their spirituality. I get so caught up in my busy world that I forget how to do it myself.* (Mother of two)

Parenting from this perspective isn't a radical life choice, but rather an easy and natural way to interact with children. Spirituality is in our routine lives with our children, the ordinary miracles. The everyday events—dinner conversations, lighting candles, creating comfortable rituals, performing daily chores—have the potential to be sacred moments. Think of your child's mind recording each event of her life—soaking up the ambiance of her environment. These experiences become lodged in her subconscious and her soul. You can't choose your child's memories, but when you embrace a spiritual approach to parenting you increase the odds that her recollections will enrich her life and soul.

Take a moment to reflect on the times with your child that are locked in your memory: the extraordinary moment when he was born, the first time she rode a bike by herself and was free to go to a friend's house without you, the day you built a sand castle at the beach with no phone ringing—just the two of you. Think back to the morning he walked into kindergarten without looking back, the day she was asked to write about her hero and wrote about you. Remember the way it feels when her warm hand is tucked safely in yours. These are the moments you hold in your memory that nourish your soul and cause you to treasure your child. They keep you going. These unplanned, glittering instants are possible every day when you bring your attention to the enchantment waiting to enrich your soul and the soul of your child.

Be aware of the difference between your child's behavior and his soul. One mother told us, "I won't make the mistake again of assuming just because my son knows a million sports statistics and only eats peanut butter, pizza, and crackers, that he is not strongly connected with spirit." Children are beautiful, open spirits housed in human form. Living a spiritual life doesn't imply that they are little gurus who sit with crossed legs and chant all day. Kids wear their spirituality openly, and it flows through the ups and downs of growing up. We humans are far from perfect. We come close to perfection, however, when we freely express our spiritual natures—when our actions and souls are in harmony. It is the merging of children's innate, spiritual knowing with their outward actions that we wish to encourage. Let's support and honor our children when they live an authentic life with their behavior in line with their inner wisdom.

> I like my daydreams where I can meet with all the animals. I think that is what heaven is all about, talking to the animals. I try it in life sometimes and I think I can really understand what the animal is thinking. I believe that kindness to animals is what God would like the world to be about. I take care of my cat every day. Sometimes I feel so tired and my cat jumps up on me to get her breakfast. I know she needs me or she'll be hungry, so down to the kitchen I go. I try to treat people the same way I treat animals, but it is harder sometimes with people. (Age six)

Being a spiritual parent won't guarantee your kids will never fight, you will never lose your temper, or things won't fall apart. But being grounded by a spiritual awareness, a belief in the Divine, helps children and parents alike approach these negative experiences in a new way. To trust that we have the guidance we need and the potential to use our imaginations to modify our reality is to trust in spirit. The ability to create magic out of the ordinary, to feel a connection to all of life, and to make each day a new beginning enriches the soul. Parenting and living life in this way is a richer, vaster, more bountiful reality than we may have ever thought possible.

To be a spiritual parent means to prioritize your life. God sits high on your list, and therefore your own soul and the souls of your children are paramount. Living within a God-centered framework makes troubles less overwhelming and gives purpose and meaning to life. Judgment is replaced by acceptance. The child is as he ought to be—perhaps with smoothed edges. He is as his spirit dictates. The spiritual parent allows his child to be who he is and revels in this uniqueness. The spiritual parent provides fertile ground for her child to grow roots that will center and anchor her for life. She gives her child a blank canvas to fill with the colors of his soul—a palette of experiences to draw on throughout his years.

Let yourself be touched by the beauty of children. See the reflection of your own essence in these wise, creative beings.

I am an art teacher in a public school and use my classroom as a forum to connect with kids about spirituality. It isn't done blatantly, but we speak openly about the kinds of things they are experiencing. Most are having prophetic dreams, have psychic experiences, and some are seeing auras. This is rather frightening for some of them and they are anxious to connect with people who understand that they aren't going crazy. They are also anxious to hear that other kids are having the same types of experiences. If you are a teacher or a parent I think the key is to connect. Don't be afraid to say what you believe in. (Age thirty-four)

HOW TO USE THE 10 PRINCIPLES

We have organized this book into ten chapters, each focusing on one of the ten principles that serve as the framework for raising a spiritual child. These principles aren't meant to be used one after the other, but rather to weave throughout the days and nights with your children. When you become familiar with the principles you may be drawn to a certain one for a while, then find as circumstances change you are incorporating ideas from another. Spiritual parenting, like spiritual growth, isn't a logical, quantitative process, but rather an evolving, fluid endeavor. With the ten principles you have an approach with specific techniques to help guide and support you through your rippling journey of parenting.

Each chapter is an individual nugget with techniques, ideas, and tools. There are no "tasks," only "offerings." Pick and choose—try the ones that resonate with you. Also, you will find children's thoughts and ideas, and those of their parents. We have gathered these words from people in our own lives and from the many children and adults with whom we have worked.

Affirmations

At the end of each chapter we offer Affirmations for both you and your child. These simple positive self-talk messages can help cultivate an ongoing awareness of the ten principles for spiritual parenting we present. Try to use these affirmative words to replace the old, perhaps limiting messages that run through your mind. We believe that what we think creates our reality, and so it is important that your Affirmations have emotional force and meaning behind them. Compose your own if ours don't feel comfortable. Write Affirmations on index cards and post them where you are apt to see them—the bathroom mirror, the car dashboard, the refrigerator. Say them out loud, or read them to yourself and allow the meaning and the truth of the words to fill your consciousness.

Affirmations for children are a great way to reverse "I'm such an idiot" or "Dummy" into "I believe in me" or "I do my best." Try them with your child. You can read the Affirmation first and let your child repeat what you have said or, if old enough, your child can use the Affirmations any way he wishes. Saying, "I let go of the day and drift away" works like magic for a five-year-old having a hard time falling asleep. Many children quickly pick up and use Affirmations. One seven-year-old girl had been using Affirmations with her parents for about a month. One day she came home to tell her mother:

> *Jane was having trouble with reading workshop at school today. I told her to try using Affirmations. Jane laughed at me and thought it was a strange, weird word. She had never tried Affirmations, can you imagine? I told her how to try it by saying "I can read this easily." She tried and she said it really worked.* (Age seven)

Insight Building

Also at the end of each chapter we have included an Insight-Building Exercise. These exercises will help you to keep the principle alive day to day. The purpose of these exercises is to help you tap into your inner self and gain insight. They are meant to give you a deeper awareness and understanding of your own spirituality; your own needs, hopes, and goals as a parent. They also enable you to focus on some specific area of your family's life and to let other concerns drift to the edge of your consciousness for the moment. Use these activities for enlightenment with the assurance that guidance will come to you—maybe not immediately, but it will come. Be open to subtle, and sometimes not so subtle, answers.

Children's Guided Journeys

Children's Guided Journeys, one for each principle, are a child's version of the Insight-Building Exercise. This journey or meditation is meant to be read to your children as they relax and use their rich imaginations to follow your words. These simple visualizations, when used consistently, will help your children in many ways: Their creativity will be awakened, they will go to sleep more peacefully, they will develop a deeper sense of focus and concentration, they will feel more centered. Guided Journeys are another tool to use with your children to help them remain connected to spirit. Feel free to make up your own journeys and adapt them to themes that interest your child. Perhaps she loves trains—how about a visualization where she is the engineer of a magical train? Maybe she is fearful of the dark and this train glows and has huge floodlights affixed to every side. As she steers the train she illuminates the landscape. You get the idea. As children become familiar with Guided Journeys they may choose to invent their own and travel their imaginative paths by themselves, as did this eight-year-old:

> *I think there is a place that kids who don't have love escape to. I think it has good smells and is fun, like a grandma's house. Angels help kids get there. I've seen lots of other kids in that place.* (Age eight)

Parent Check-In

We have created a number of Parents' Check-In Questions for each principle. These are questions for you to ask yourself as you check on your progress and probe a little deeper into your consciousness. Asking yourself specific questions may help reveal new ideas and insights. We all have a wealth of wisdom within, and questions can quickly access this guidance. Simply write or say the first thought that comes to mind after you ask yourself the question. Some of the questions may affect you more than others—use them in a way that feels comfortable.

Children's Check-In

We've also given you Children's Check-In Questions in each chapter. These are provided as a resource for you to begin conversations with your child to check on his inner life. Often the question is the key that opens the door to communication. One mother asked her ten-year-old what he thought spirituality meant. His reply—"Spirituality means not punching in church"—was the beginning of an ongoing dialogue between mother and son. He went on to ask, "Mom, do we have to go to church to see God?" One question opened the door to another—perhaps lurking for some time waiting for the opportunity to be expressed.

We write this book as a mother and daughter who believe that our great privilege and duty as parents is to nurture the natural spirituality of our children. In *10 Principles for Spiritual Parenting* we share practical ways to do just that. We will encourage you on your journey of spiritual nurturing and ask you to open your imagination and bring your heart and mind to the joyful responsibility of loving your child. We are traveling the road with you, Mimi as the mother of two young children, and Marsha as the grandmother of those children and mother of four adults. We never stop loving our children, but as we grow and change, so too does the balance of who is nourishing whom. We are grateful for our close relationship as mother and daughter and as dearest friends. Writing this book has been the most joyful of journeys for us, and through our work we continue to give thanks for each other.

It is our hope that each of you will find our view of spiritual parenting attractive and compelling, yet adjust and adapt it to fit your life and your children. There is no higher calling than to be a parent who guides his child lovingly to her soul's destiny. You will be overwhelmingly rewarded by sharing in the development of your child's intrinsic wisdom, imagination, and *spirit*.

So, welcome to our thoughts and our ten principles. We give them to you with the genuine hope that you and your child will open to the spirituality within you both. As one child told us:

Life can be heaven on earth when things are going straight and I'm feeling hooked up with my parents.
(Age five)

THE PRINCIPLES

KNOW GOD CARES FOR YOU

I get a warm feeling around my heart. That's how I know God cares for me. (Age seven)

Most children have clear ideas and images of God. They easily acknowledge that there is a sacred Higher Power. Our role as parents is to reinforce our children's natural acceptance of this Higher Power, by recognizing and supporting their unique understanding.

I think God is a blaze of light—a powerful force that is in my eyes and heart. (Age nine)

God's place is filled with all of the colors of the world mixed together. God brings that place to me sometimes and it makes me really happy. (Age six)

I envision "God" as a gigantic web of diamonds connected by gossamer threads of consciousness, slowly turning, created and fueled by infinite compassionate

love, of which we (and all that we know) are a part.
Usually I call "God" the "cosmic glue." (Age seventeen)

Children's true identities are expressed when they are connected with their inner guidance—God within them. This is their spontaneous, creative, innate way of being. As they grow older they often become focused on the external, physical world as their only reality and look outside themselves for happiness. As many of us have come to realize, the real fulfillment in life comes from our connection to the power of the universe, the power of God, and when we drift from this union we feel a great, often unnamed void. Our goal in this book and in our work is to help you help your children maintain that connection so they'll never have to experience this void.

Sometimes I sing "Oh Dear Lord" from Godspell when
I'm on the playground because I don't have any best
friends, so that song keeps me company. I feel friends in
my heart but don't see them in my eyes. (Age five)

We explore God the same way we explore the spirit of another person—we spend time in God's presence, we watch our world for signs of God's spirit, we attempt to bring God's light into our decisions and actions, we read about others who are journeying closer to God, and we talk with those in our lives who are also seeking a close connection to spirit.

We grow up with God. He is with us when we aren't invited to the slumber party or when we are sitting in a "time-out" chair, when we wake up, and when we are dreaming. He won't leave us if we are naughty or fail to measure up to someone else's standards. God loves us even when we fail, especially when we fail, because God is our courage to try again. Nothing in our past, present, or future can keep God's steadfast love from us. When children know and trust in the ever-lasting and unconditional love from their spiritual parent, God, they will find healing, understanding, direction, peace, and support. What more could we ask for our children than to have them tuned into the source of all that is good?

Making a Connection

Children experience God in many ways. The relationship changes as they grow and evolve. To some children God is a white-bearded old man who judges them from heaven, while others hold a childhood image of God as an invisible pal. As children grow older their innocent acceptance of a loving God can become jumbled. They become accustomed to prizes, rewards, and goodie bags as symbols of affection and may begin to wonder where the wizard is in this God.

If we can bring our children's attention to a loving, constant, and available Source, perhaps they can feel a more comforting connection. An integral key to making this connection is to become aware of God's always available presence within. When children see themselves as part of this holy force, they understand God's power is inside them—they are divine, sacred beings.

I think that God is the sun because it is so powerful and always there when you wake up. It soaks into you and you don't even notice. (Age four)

When we witness children's naturally joyous and exuberant natures we glimpse the "wizard" at work—the shimmering White Light that fills us with great love. What a gift it is to see our children bring that love to one another. A family we know has two daughters, and the younger was having a hard time adjusting to her "big girl bed." She was worried she might fall out. One night the older sister tiptoed into her room and reassured her by telling her not to worry because "God puts a cover over the earth at night so we won't fall off." The frightened girl was calmed.

To easily illustrate the light of God, use a flashlight. The flashlight is an ordinary-looking object that becomes bright and sends out a beam of light when it has a battery inside. We are like the flashlight, dark and plain, until we plug into the magical power of God's light; then we are brilliant and shining. We can see where we are going, and everyone can see us coming. With God as our battery we work—we are charged and we send out our own beams. We light up our world.

Remind kids of God's power—God is the ultimate "Super Hero." When we link with the power of God we have amazing courage. For us, as for the Cowardly Lion in *The Wizard of Oz*, courage is always there; we just need to acknowledge it. It is exciting and empowering for kids to know they have immediate access to the Divine Mind, the creative Power of God. They can draw as much power from this source as they wish. People aren't the power; we are only an avenue through which the power flows. Just as cars use gasoline to run, we can fill up with God's energy and soar through our lives.

We have talked about God as a protector. I try to let my daughter know that the power within her is the light. I have tried to make God neither male nor female. God is within her, and even at the age of five she has some control over her life. (Mother of one)

GOD CARES FOR YOU

God's caring for us is a double blessing. The Creator "cares" for us both by "loving" us and by "taking care" of us. When children know they are loved and cared for they can navigate life with pleasure and peace—they have all the security they need and are never alone. Children seem to know this intuitively. They have an intimate, cozy, and personal relationship with God. It is our joy as parents to nurture this acceptance.

I think God keeps the angels in her tummy. (Age three)

Children's ethereal experiences are as diverse and individual as the children themselves; their ideas are not fixed when it comes to describing God, angels, spirit, heaven, or death. They express many variations of the same theme, and each perception seems to provide them with comfort.

God is a white puff like a cloud—often invisible. (Age six)

Oh, I see my grandpa all the time and he's really happy. He rides around the universe all day on a huge beautiful white horse. He smiles at me. (Age eight, speaking of his recently deceased grandfather)

My angel has wings as bright and golden as the sun. My angel's dress is as beautiful as a sunset and my angel's voice is as clear as glass, like my mom's voice. (Age eleven)

I think that heaven is where broken TV sets get fixed. (Age five)

When children believe in a caring universe and a caring God they can better cope with life's many unexplained situations. Their lives will be filled with glorious pleasures, heartbreaking

losses, and everyday ups and downs—hair tangles, sisters who
hurt their feelings, horses with noses as soft as velvet, delicious
ice cream, a mom who is cranky, food that is scarce, people
who die. They will look to us for explanations. How do we
answer our children's questions about these events?

*Should we tell our child that God is taking care of us
when hundreds of children are being hurt and killed
each day?* (Father of two)

*Why did God invent tummy aches and how can I get
Him to take this one away?* (Age five)

Many times we, the parents, are without answers ourselves,
but when we teach our children that God wants the highest
and the best for us, we help them understand they are not
floundering alone. We begin to formulate answers to life's
tough questions from a God-centered awareness. What a relief
to know we have an always available resource for insight into
our children's questions as well as our own. As our children
grow older we can teach them the idea that there are no acci-
dents and all things happen for a reason. Let's look for the
lessons that can be learned through both good and bad experiences and not focus on the "why." We may never know the
reason in this life, but no doubt the universe is unfolding as it
should and God is establishing divine order. We can assure
children that all people have been given the gift of choice and
God gives us grace and courage to move through the results of
our choices.

*Peer pressure is so intense in my daughter's school.
When she's feeling left out or different I remind her
that she's never alone. We came up with a little poem*

she uses, "There is not a spot where God is not."
(Mother of two)

I want my children to be comfortable talking to God. That's really the number one thing I want for them.
(Mother of three)

Give your child examples from your life of problems that were really blessings in disguise. It may look bleak now, but God has a larger plan. Marsha looks back at a lifesaving blessing:

I really didn't want to move our family away from the home and town I loved. I dragged my feet about it, but moved anyway. Several months later our former home, our neighbors, and our town were destroyed by a hurricane. That move saved our lives.

When it looks like a door is closing in your child's life, point out the wonderful possibilities waiting to come in. There is divine order with God, and we have to trust that this apparent closing is making way for the good.

We moved last summer and I had to leave my old school. I cried about that. I'm in the new school now and I have a really nice teacher and we get to use computers in our classroom. I guess it turned out all right.
(Age eight)

In the beginning we are lifelines for our young children; they depend on us for their survival and they look to us for all the answers. But the reality is, we don't have all the answers and never will. It is important to encourage children to turn to God for their wants and needs, rather than to rely on Mom or Dad as sole providers. It's key that our kids learn that no one has answers to all the questions, but God will guide us—if we ask. This is a gradual learning process from infancy, when children depend on their parents for their very lives, until, as adults, they are able to become independent. During that process the loving parent nourishes the child's body and soul, while assisting him to find his own path. The greatest gift we can give our children is to lovingly and gently shift the lifeline from us to God.

> I ask God questions all the time. My parents don't know as much as God. I don't hear a voice answer me, but usually I just kind of feel the answers. Today I asked if my life was a dream and why does my funny bone hurt when I bump it? Oh, and why numbers never stop and why are dinosaurs bigger than me? (Age six)

> Dear God, was I ever an alien? If we really change into something when we die I want to change into a squirrel. (Age seven)

Because detecting God's voice is a subtle experience, it is important to spend time discussing with your children the ways they might hear this voice. Some children may be afraid to ask questions because they expect an almighty shout from on high to boom out an answer. Other kids might anticipate God's answers to come with a blinding light. In most cases this doesn't happen! Instead, responses and insight probably creep quietly into their souls. We can assure children that the quiet voice of God is within their very being. If we point out that they can't "see" themselves growing, or "hear" their blood flowing, but yet know these things are indeed happening, they will also understand that, though they might not see anything, God is deep inside their souls. They simply need to ask for help, trust in God, and help will come in some way. Remind children to listen carefully; God will speak to them in a way that is perfect for them to understand, in a loving and kind voice, not one that is frightening or stern. This voice will come through a subtle knowing, an inside feeling, an intuition, a serendipitous situation. God's love often comes to us through other people, animals, friends, teachers. Help your child to see the examples of God at work in his life. Coincidences, perfect timing, and luck are all God at work. When you get the phone call you need, or find the perfect book to help you understand something, or run into a friend with the name of a doctor who helps heal you, that's God at work in your world.

As my father lay dying in the hospital my children prayed for God to be with him. What we saw was God working through the kind, loving people who cared for my dad—a gentle touch or a loving gesture helped ease his pain. He was treated with dignity and respect, and we saw God at work. My kids realized that God didn't make their Poppy better, but God worked through others to ease Poppy's pain. (Mother of two)

All of us can listen and hear the loving sound of God offering us help for our weaknesses and struggles. We shouldn't be surprised if it comes through the voices of our children. God speaks to us constantly—we must trust the guidance and live a life based on it. When we do, we feel God's deep caring for us.

We turn to God for the most ordinary help. We ask for assistance finding lost library books and for the safety

of our pets. God is always giving us great gifts. (Mother
of three)

*I recall carrying a lot of anger nicely dumped on a
handy individual who had never been a favorite of
mine. As time moved on this became a terribly heavy
load, consuming a disproportionate amount of my
time. "God," I said, "I'm ready to give this up now,
please help me." No bolts of light . . . no great burst of
awareness, but in time I realized I seldom thought of
the guy, and when I did it was without rage. A miracle?
I don't think so. My guess is that was God's answer and
I would have saved myself a lot of pain had I asked
sooner.* (Mother of four)

A connection with God gives children a sense of confidence
and power in a life ruled by adults. In this world where most
children don't have a voice, we can guide them to the power of
God's availability and to the knowledge that God always hears
them, no matter how small their sound. He is always available,
never at work or on the phone or taking care of the baby. Let
your child know that "God always has time just for you."
"You have a direct phone line into God's ear." "If you have a
need, turn to God."

Remember the ancient words "Seek and ye shall receive"?
Incorporate them into your thinking and teaching. Your child
can turn her needs over to God. She can seek by asking for
divine guidance and receive by staying open to God's miracles. Of course God will give her answers—all she has to do is
ask. Give your child examples of times when you turned your
thoughts and prayers toward God and gained understanding
or acceptance. Point out situations when God has answered
requests or brightened a dismal day. Explain to your child

that, contrary to the worldview of scarcity and lack, there is abundance available for the asking. Things fall into place easily and effortlessly when we turn to the Divine Light within us and let it guide our lives; there is no need for struggle. If our children only knew how much love there is for them, they would never again feel alone or worried. Remind them, and yourself, of the amazing presence that walks with us at all times.

> *I tell my kids that God is in their hearts and they can talk to Him anytime they want.* (Father of four)

> *When I get really scared I convince myself that there is no such thing as a Divine Energy or a God. I feel like I am floating around this crazy earth all alone. I have to fall back on my habits during those freak-out times. I do yoga or take a long walk in the woods, and slowly the warmth of a loving presence returns. It's like I have to get out of my head and back into my heart to feel that connection.* (Age seventeen)

Tapping the Power of Prayer

When children see God as a source of love, and discover prayer as a way to connect to that source, they have found a lifelong tool for comfort. Check out this concept with your child. Does she see God as a source of comfort? Does she know how to reach that source? Does he use prayer? How? What is prayer to him?

> *Prayer is when I talk to God and I feel all the light come to me. It is when I can hear in my mind an idea for how to solve my problem.* (Age ten)

If I haven't prayed it's like a telephone that's not hooked up. I get on the phone but nobody's there. (Age seven)

Children can use prayer as a way to speak their thoughts and feelings directly to God. They can practice being quiet and listening for His response, remembering it may come in a surprising way. One of God's ways to reach us is through our ideas and inspirations. So we talk to God in prayer and we listen to His answers by getting quiet and paying attention to the ideas that come. Help your child to trust his intuition. Help him understand that his internal voice is a way for God to give him direction. Direction may come through someone else's words or actions; it may visit your child through nature, in a sparkling sunbeam, or in the beauty of music or art. A violin's weeping or an ocean's thundering may be God's sounds, for there is no limit to the manifestations of this Divine Presence.

In an age when even our youngest children can work voice mail, calculators, computers, and bank machines, it is often difficult to encourage them to remain alert to the subtle and mysterious ways God speaks. If together you open your "inside eyes" for this rewarding spiritual quest, you both will be blessed with grace and miracles. Foster your child's conscious connection with God through prayer each day, reminding her it isn't the words that matter but rather her intention. Help her fine-tune her awareness of God's subtle and comforting voice.

I often pray for courage to handle life's surprises. I've started to say these prayers or chants in front of my kids so they can also call on the power of the universe for support during tough times. At breakfast this morning I said, "We have all we need to get through the day. God is with us always and gives us the courage to be strong, honest, and the best that we can be." I feel a great support from this kind of prayer and I hope the children will too. (Mother of two)

You may need to reevaluate your relationship with prayer before becoming comfortable using prayer as a family.

I found no solace from the rote prayers of my child-hood. The meaning of prayer, for me, is filled with old associations. I guess I need to re-create my concept of prayer. (Father of three)

Faith in a Steadfast God

When I need to feel God I just curl up on my bed and hug something real tight. (Age ten)

When she turns to a trusting God, a child can share thoughts, worries, or experiences she might not be able to discuss with her parents or friends. For kids, there is a certain wonderful safety in knowing "God won't tell." They can open to God and trust in the ideas they receive. God is flexible and can become anything a child might need at any given time. This personalized Divine Spark meets kids exactly where they are each moment.

God can transform Himself into anything I need Him to be. He could be right here in this bottle of teriyaki sauce if I needed Him to. (Age eight)

My five-year-old son and I have a candle that we light to see the flame just like the flame of Almighty love that is always inside of us. He loves this ritual. He also loves blowing it out. (Mother of one)

Faith in a caring God gives a child strength and guidance. This trust becomes their secure life jacket in the frenzied ocean of life. God is reliable, always on time, always present, never gets tired, and is never too busy. When they know God cares for them, children feel connected to something bigger than their own lives.

I tell my parents about God. I say, "There is something there." But they don't believe in Him. I know God made me and loves me and I wish my parents would too. (Age ten)

We can release some of our parental worries when we know our children are loved by the Almighty, who works beyond what we can do on earth. As we release our children into God's embrace we can envision them blessed and at peace, guided by God wherever they go and in whatever they do.

God is the Supreme Parent; we are His spiritual children. As we parent our children God is lovingly parenting us. We can always turn to God with our concerns and allow a gentle peace to ease our anxieties and quiet our fears. When we are feeling overwhelmed with responsibilities it is a great comfort to know that we can turn to a Higher Power—the perfect parent to us and the ideal partner in our parenting.

Knowing God cares allows us to move through our world wrapped in love. It also does other wonderful things:

- Children can be assured that God cherishes them at all times, not just when they are being "good" or "praying." God does not punish us by making bad things happen in our lives.

God is with us.
God is here.
If you need help
God is always near. (Age six)

• As we connect to our children with deep love, so too do we connect to God. It's a divine circle. When we love God our children feel it and the spirit of God within us blends with the spirit of God within them. We can keep the energy of that circle flowing and allow it to create an even greater link between us, our children, and God.

Once we link with our inner strength—the voice of God within our souls—we experience incredible peace and assurance. Let's give ourselves this comfort and secure it for our children.

WAYS TO ACCEPT GOD'S LOVE

It is vital that we acknowledge God's role in our own lives. When we explain how we *feel* about God our children can better understand our impressions—they *get* feelings. We can be open with our ups and downs as we grow closer to God. When we focus on what God *does* instead of *who* God *is*, it becomes easier to share our experiences.

I get so scared to go to sleep at night. I always worry about robbers coming to our house. I hear weird sounds and just know it is someone breaking in. Mom said God can take care of me and protect me. She told me God helps her take away fear. It makes me feel safer when I picture God's light blocking the door of my bedroom so robbers can't get me. (Age ten)

Link the feeling of God with your child's feelings of love. "How much do you love me? Well, God loves you even more than that. God is that feeling inside when you love someone or something or the safe feeling you have when your hand is in mine." Children *know* God, they just don't always have the vocabulary to express that knowing.

Engage your child in conversations about God and be open to what piques his interest and curiosity. Aim for a balance between sharing your beliefs and eliciting your child's ideas. Children are usually quite open and pleased to discuss spiritual concepts. Of course, there are children who find talking about God complicated, ambiguous, and frustrating.

> *I get confused about just what God is. Everyone tells me different stuff.* (Age six)

Go gently, listen, and remember to show, not just tell. Ask your children for their ideas, instead of giving them only your opinions. When your children have questions about God, turn the question around and find out what they imagine God to be. Allow children's imaginations to soar as they express their images of the Almighty—as they reach into their radiant inner selves and share their descriptions. Be careful not to correct or judge but rather honor their unique experience of God.

> *God is the sparkles I see on water.* (Age five)

Try to emphasize divine love rather than retribution—a God who supports us, not one who's waiting with a punishment stick. The sense of not being alone gives children the courage to stand up to peer pressure and to cope in tough situations.

When my son was seven, he went on a field trip with his class. He came out of the bathroom to find himself alone in a large park. The bus had left without him. "I was so scared," he admitted later, "but every time I started crying, I told myself that God was with me." (Mother of four)

Invite God into Your Everyday Life

Children feel cared for when they communicate with God. Help your child ask for and accept divine guidance. Encourage her to try many different ways to make contact with God. These times of communication can be as brief as a passing thought:

I don't know how to pray yet, I just talk to God in my head. (Age four)

Or as fixed as formal prayer:

**Help me to feel that you are near, O God.
Open my ears, that I may hear your voice. Enter my heart that I may know your love.**

How are you most comfortable communicating with God? Does your child know the spiritual methods that soothe your soul? Try speaking out loud to God throughout the day. "Help me get all the dishes done, God, so we can go out to play." "God, help me find the perfect parking place so we aren't late for the concert." "I know you are always with us, God, and I ask you to shine your loving light on our car as we begin this trip." "God, surround John with your healing light and help him fall asleep easily tonight."

To access God's guidance takes more than Sunday morning practice. Invite God into your everyday life. Ask your child how God was involved in the soccer game or the spelling test. Link God with things in your child's life that she loves. If she loves to dance, let her know that God gave her a strong, healthy body, and by dancing she is celebrating her spirit. Talk about God as you would a member of the family. Through your conversations you will all come to know this Divine Universal Power in a deeper way; children will realize that God does care what they do and how they act.

I get involved with God when I am reading. (Age eight)

God makes my cat Bubbles come home when she is lost. (Age six)

I want to know if God looks over everyone and if He appreciates everyone. (Age nine)

Invite your children to write letters to God. It is helpful to put feelings, fears, thoughts, and wishes into words. Maybe you can make a "God box" to store the letters. This is a private place for a child to communicate with God and should never be probed or read without permission. Light candles around the box or put it in a special place of honor. Ask your kids for ideas.

Dear God, I am confused. I thought that dinosaurs came before Adam and Eve. I want to know if you can tell me! I'd like to think the dinosaurs came first. (Age six)

Dear God, thank you for my little brother. He was a surprise, right? I think my brother wanted me, right? (Age six)

Dear God, why do you have to be a kid before you are a grown-up? (Age five)

Make Time for Meditation

Meditation is the practice of quieting our physical bodies and minds while focusing our attention inward. As you begin to practice meditation it will become easier. You might also notice that the sense of peace you experience during meditation will begin to carry over into the different parts of your day. Meditation is truly an avenue to the voice of God and God's incredible serenity.

Maybe your family can meditate together. Practice becoming still along with your child; it is a powerful spiritual experience to share. You will receive divine ideas from a tranquil, more focused state of being. Anyone can learn to experience the calming effects of purposeful silence by following a few simple steps. A good way to start is to lie side by side with your child somewhere quiet. Explain that you are going to take a few minutes to concentrate on your breath. Place your hands on your belly and ask your child to place his hands on his belly. Become aware of your stomach rising up and down with each breath. Think of your breath as bringing in energy and beautiful light and with every exhalation letting go of anything negative or stressful. Spend a few minutes explaining this idea to your child as you focus on your breathing. That's it! That's beginning breath work that can be the foundation for many other relaxation and meditation exercises.

Make time for your children to meditate on their own and connect with God in silence. Even just a few minutes a day is time well spent. Because our culture doesn't reinforce the idea of idleness, we must be bold to ensure that our children have time to explore their inner world. When there is a problem or a decision to make, this quiet "listening time" will be a source of direction. Meditation, or becoming still, gives children the gift of connecting with their inner vision—something no one can take away. Peace, tranquillity, and a closeness with God are all available during this marvelous retreat. Meditating need not be a rigid, forced activity, but rather a time when we become quiet and turn down our mind's chatter. Use some of the relaxations offered at the beginning of each Guided Journey for children included in the chapters. Or ask your child to close her eyes, sit or lie down, and focus her attention on her breath or her heartbeat. This is the simplest way to begin meditation. Try any of these additional relaxation ideas with your children:

1: Imagine you are watching a leaf flutter gracefully from a tree limb onto the ground. The leaf slowly falls closer and closer to the earth below. As the leaf weaves through the air you become more and more relaxed.

2: Pretend you are ice cream melting on a warm sidewalk. Your body sinks into the heated ground and your muscles relax. Imagine you are spreading out and slowly melting.

3: Start with the number ten and count down to zero, taking a breath for each number. Become more relaxed as you count—by zero you are very quiet and peaceful.

4: Picture a blank movie screen in your mind. Allow all your thoughts to go by this screen. The screen becomes blank after the thoughts have passed by.

Once your child is relaxed, ask him simply to be still for a few moments. As a child gets used to the sensation of a still mind and a relaxed body he will be able to meditate for longer and longer periods of time. Go slowly and don't force it. Encouraging your child to listen to God's voice within is a great gift. Through meditation and quiet, he will hear the wonderful ideas God has put there for him.

God is like a good idea. Both God and good ideas seem to pop up when I most need them. (Age nine)

Meditation is when I settle down and my thoughts get softer and softer. (Age six)

The meditation explanation we have provided below is for you to try. Meditating at sunrise is not possible for many of us—up during the night nursing a baby, calming a five-year-old's nightmares, or waiting for a teen to make curfew leaves us savoring our sleep. But if you can take some time each day or every other day to do some version of this exercise you will find greater serenity and more energy in your life. You might adapt this exercise for use with older children.

❋ ❋ ❋ ─────────────────────────

Start by getting into a comfortable position. If you choose to sit in a chair, keep your spine straight, your feet flat on the floor, and your eyes closed. Find a comfortable position for your hands, placed either in your lap with palms facing up or at your sides. Slowly take a few deep breaths and begin to relax. Inhale the air deep into your lungs, hold it for a moment, then slowly exhale. With your mind, search your body for any tension or tight muscles. Let the tension melt away by breathing deeply and sending the breath to the tense area; imagine it is relaxed and loose. Gently massage any tightness with your fingers. When you are comfortable and relaxed you are ready to move on.

Focus your mind on one, single, peaceful, calming thought. Instead of thinking about what went on in the past, what has to be done with the remainder of your day, or what the children might be up to in the other room, try to focus on a thought such as "God is love" or "I am at peace." You can use any prayer or affirmation that is meaningful to you. (Check out the Affirmations at the end of each chapter.)

Clear your mind of passing thoughts and focus on your affirmation. Think about the words. After a few moments of thinking the words, you should be able to move into feeling the meaning behind those words. For example, you can say the words "God is love." The feelings those words bring can be much more powerful than the actual words themselves. It's like the difference between thinking the words "I love my children" and experiencing the actual feeling behind those words. Once you begin to feel the meaning of the affirmation, try to hold this feeling in silent attention. Gently bring your focus back to the words of the affirmation every time your mind begins to wander. Don't become discouraged when you find yourself thinking more about distractions than the affirmation. Gently focus on one thought. Spend anywhere from three minutes to fifteen minutes trying to hold the affirmation silently. At the end of your meditation, send out prayers, good thoughts, or peaceful energy to your children. If you have been focusing on love, try to send a sense of that love to someone about whom you're concerned. Simply with a thought, you can also send out the energy of peace to your neighborhood, far-away friends, or anyone who needs healing and light.

────────────────────────── ❋ ❋ ❋

Reprogram Self-Limiting Thoughts

Clue your child to the fact that the world around him will change by his own shift in attitude. It is empowering to realize that all possibilities are open to us through the magnificent power of God, a force within us all. God has given us the power of choice, and through our choices and thoughts we are participants in what we experience—we cocreate our lives with God. Sadly, as many of us grow up we accept limitations we pick up along our way. We accept as truth false ideas we have turned into truths. The more we hang on to these personal lies, the more they will become our identities. Catch yourself if you contribute to your child's false beliefs: "I'm awful at math, it runs in our family, that's why you are having such a hard time." Squash! There goes their miracle power. When kids hear definitions that limit their potential, a little more of their souls' joy fades. Instead, let's convince our children that they have the ability to create miracles in their lives. They are equipped with everything they need and have come into this world limited only by their thoughts.

Divest yourself of old programming on parenting, mistakes your parents made, or the "shoulds" that creep into your parenting style. You are your own person, as is your child. You both have specific gifts, talents, weaknesses, and strengths. Ask for God's help to be the ideal parent for your child's divine plan. You and your children are together for a reason. Trust that God has perfectly matched you for your lessons on this earth. You have the ability to parent in a way that feels right to you and balances the needs of each of your children. When you love your kids and make decisions based on that love, coupled with your deep intuition, you are parenting in God's light.

At the moment of conception I had this deep knowing that I was being prepared to parent a special child. When I was six months pregnant five sentient beings came to me in a dream to tell me they were directly assigned by God to my mission. They told me that a little girl was being brought to me. I asked, "What's wrong with her?" They said, "No, it's what's right with her." Amanda was born with her eyes open, without a sound. The room was thick with a mystical aura. Her guides that had visited me were there. This child has severe defects in the eyes of humans. She is now almost three years old, and as my son at age four said, "She is perfect for what she's supposed to be." She can't talk, but some nights I can hear her giggling in her room and I hear bells tinkling. I know she is being comforted by God's angels. I learn from her each day and know we are meant to be together. (Mother of two)

Establish Daily Spiritual Habits and Household Rituals

Create and incorporate spiritual habits into your family's daily life. These should be routine practices that automatically reconnect you with God. Go beyond mealtime and bedtime prayer. Perhaps when your children brush their teeth they can thank God for their strong healthy bodies. Maybe each time they begin a baseball game or soccer match they can whisper a silent prayer of thanks for the weather or for the time they have to play. How about silently praying when they get off the school bus, "Thanks, God, for a safe journey home"? When children are afraid, they can say, "God surrounds me with protection," or when they yawn, they might cover their mouths and whisper, "God fills me with clean air," or "Aah—God." When children sneeze let's really bless them and teach them to do the same for others. There is nothing like a sincere "God bless you!"

You could incorporate a spiritual habit around your child's evening bath. As she finishes bathing, watch the water whirl down the drain and pretend the graceful swirl of water is a "forgiveness ballerina." She is taking with her all the hurt or anger from the day and spinning it down the drain—allowing your child to release any resentment or tension she might be holding.

Make it a habit to pray anytime you hear a siren—regardless of where you are or what you are doing. Send a blessing to everyone involved in the emergency incident.

Every time I hear an ambulance or fire siren, I whisper a special prayer in my head for whoever is in trouble. It's kinda a habit now. (Age six)

Encourage your child to create his own personal altar as a way to honor God. For some children altars will become elaborate places to demonstrate who they are, as well as how they connect with God. To others a simple bag of well-worn marbles, carried around, may be their concrete way to feel connected to spirit.

My daughter has created an altar in her bedroom. She created it two years ago when she was five and it hasn't changed much since then. A pink tablecloth covers a little table. She's put animal statues, shells, crystals, and

*bird feathers on it. She has a semicircle of pennies
around the table's edge. She says that each penny represents a worry she has and that by placing the penny on
the altar she is giving the worry away to God and to
nature.* (Mother of three)

Create a family altar. This shrine could be a creative expression of the spiritual dimension of your family, tucked into a little corner of your living room or backyard. Ask each family
member to place something on the altar as a symbol of his
identity or spiritual self. Children love to select special rocks—
perhaps they can pile them up to create an altar. Remind them
that ancient shrines were made of rock. Maybe you'd like to
plant a tree as your family's shrine—a beautiful symbol of
growth. The center of Mimi's much-used kitchen table has
evolved into an altar of sorts:

*An important rock we discovered on a family hike is
next to an angel candle that was mine as a little girl. A
clay cat made by our oldest daughter leans against a
photograph of my father, who is battling cancer. As we
sit together for breakfast and dinner we join hands and
the items in the center of our circle are empowering and
empowered. The items change and evolve. During the
holidays we light lots of candles, and for birthdays we
select objects that are meaningful or represent the
birthday person. A beautiful flower lovingly placed in a
pitcher from our youngest daughter's pitcher collection
may join an interesting stick or a small animal statue.
They appear for a few days, then are replaced by a photograph of someone we are praying for or a picture one
of the children has made.*

An entire room can become a sacred, personal space.

As I prepare for the birth of my first child I prepare the birthing room where this child will enter our physical world. I see this room as a giant altar to cradle me and the baby during our sacred birth together. I have put branches around the periphery of the room—some hanging, some in floor vases. I have pictures of my ancestors in the room along with statues of the Buddha and Jesus Christ. (Soon-to-be mother of one)

Here are some more techniques to incorporate the wonderful gift of God's caring into our lives.

• Give thanks every day. Celebrate what already exists in your life. The saying "For that which you are thankful you will never be denied" is a simple but profound truth to share with our kids. When children have a predictable forum for sharing their gratitudes they will boldly give thanks for God's blessings. Perhaps at night children can write down—in a designated book—what gifts came to them during the day. They can decorate the book with gratitudes, such as a picture of a pet or a sport they enjoy. When we write down or acknowledge in some way the gifts in our lives, we can't help but feel good—we put our attention on the bounty in our days rather than the lack.

God, thank you for my brother Joey. His head smells good after a bath. (Age seven)

Thanks for having me be born, God. I really like it down here. (Age five)

Thank you, God, for music. I love singing to Singing in the Rain; *it makes me feel so good.* (Age six)

* Offer your child tools to paint or draw pictures of God. How does God look to him? What does she see in God's world? When your child is given permission to be expressive and spiritually free, the results are illustrious and holy.

* Point out the simple signs of God in your child's life: the perfect snowflake, the lunar eclipse, the magic of spring, fall leaves, a baby's first tooth, a robin, a bird's nest. Get out in nature and feel God's presence in the trees, flowers, grass, rocks. Talk about how all this beauty was created and how you feel in the presence of God.

* Learn about our world's religions. What beliefs do other people have and how do they celebrate them? What do they call God?

* Let your child know that he can call upon God's light when he is feeling hurt, sad, or afraid. This light circles around him like an uncoiled Slinky toy, wrapping him in a sacred cocoon. He can close his eyes and imagine that he is inside this special spiral of light, his own safe place, and feel the warmth and protection of God.

* Remind your child that God has really big plans for her. This is an exciting and positive concept to give a child, not a pressure placed on her. The universe is open, her options are many, and her powerful, loving friend, God, will help her carry out the plans.

I remind my children that no one gets missed in God's plan. (Mother of two)

- Center religious holidays around God. Steer away from "things" and move toward the reason for the holiday.

When our children were small we wanted them to understand why we celebrated Christmas, not get all hooked into the presents. We placed a rustic crèche near the fireplace on the first day of Advent. Each child placed a piece of straw (we had plenty on a horse farm) into the crèche when they did something kind, to "make it soft for the baby Jesus." By Christmas morning the cradle was full and very soft for the representative doll who was lovingly placed in it. I hope it sent the message we intended. (Mother of four)

We have made an effort to enrich our children's spiritual experience by living our Jewish traditions—really living them—and embellishing what my wife and I take from our own families. For instance, Passover is a time when we open our home and invite a new neighbor or someone without family to our seder. We have adopted many customs over the years from these seder guests. Our children have created a tzedekah box that they put their change into as a daily reminder that we give good deeds throughout the year, not just on Yom Kippur. (Father of four)

- If you attend a particular church or temple, arrange to take your child to it when there is no service. In the quiet sacred space you can talk about how it feels to be there, observe the light coming through the windows, explain the symbols, light a candle.

- Suggest to your older children they gather "God data" by taking a survey of friends and neighbors, adults and kids. They might ask, "Where do you think God lives?" Children can even interview imaginary creatures or animals. A third grader we know had a ball with this idea and was certain that the lizard who lounged on her kitchen window thought God lived in each sunbeam that baked its back.

- Think about the God you knew growing up. Take some time to write about your beliefs as a young child. What fed these images? How has your image of God changed since you were a child? Is the spiritual atmosphere in which your child is growing up the same as what you knew as a child? How is it different?

PARENTS' INSIGHT-BUILDING EXERCISE

We pray for many blessings for our children; now take a moment and pray for yourself as mother or father. You were given the ultimate gift, the gift of molding a human life. God blessed you with this gift of a child. Now feel God's love for you, His dear child. Let the love of God wash over you in waves of warmth. Feel that warmth beginning in your head and warming your face, then your neck and shoulders. Let it go all through your body. You are filled with light and love and are held in God's eternal embrace. As you bask in the warmth, thank God for His constant protection. You are a beloved child of God. Know that the Almighty Father/Mother is with you always, surrounding you with love and light, support and wisdom. Your ultimate parent, God, cherishes you. He gives you all the comfort you wish your child to feel.

In what area of your life would you like God's light to shine more brightly? Think of that part of your life now. Allow the warmth of God's love to flow into this situation. Your needs are being met at this very moment as God cares for you.

When you are ready, come back to the room, thanking God for being the presence that watches over you at all times.

Parents' Check-in Questions

- How have I experienced God?

- When do I feel tuned into God's love?

- When do I see the evidence of God in my children?

- What have I done to nurture my spirit this week? What about my child's spirit?

- What is my deepest gratitude? How would I like to thank God?

- Did I fall into a habit that took me off my spiritual course? If so, what was it?

- What could I do in my home this week to link my family more closely with God?

CHILDREN'S GUIDED JOURNEY

Sit or lie down so you are very comfortable. Now take a deep breath through your nose as if you are smelling the most fragrant flower. Then exhale, blowing the air out of your mouth. Again, breathe in through your nose and out through your mouth. Breathe deeply in through your nose and slowly let it out through your mouth. Drop your hands to your sides. Rock your head gently from side to side. Quiet your mind and allow the thoughts gently to float away. Imagine a candle. What is it like? See the details of this beautiful candle. Does it have puffy, golden stars on the sides, or is it a pink candle with a yellow wick? What does the holder look like? Now I'm going to light it with magical matches that never burn or hurt us. See the sparkles when I light your candle. Keep your eyes shut, keep looking at it in your mind's eye. What does the flame look like? See the light all around your candle. Nothing can blow out the flame—nothing is strong enough to put out the light. Let the light just wash over you. This light is inside you and is always glowing. Whenever you want this beautiful light to fill your mind, just picture your candle. The light can wash over any bad dream or fear you have. It can brighten the darkest day, shine on the saddest face, and make the gloomy guy glorious. Like a piece of God, this light is always available for you. It is your Divine Spark of God—let it shine.

Children's Check-in Questions

- What does God look like to you?

- How do you know God loves you?

- When do you feel closest to God?

- If you could call God on the telephone, what would you say?

- What question would you like to ask God?

- How might we bring God into our family more often?

Affirmations

ADULT

God's light fills me, flows through me, and touches everyone I see.

I am the parent my child needs and a channel for God's light to reach him.

I live a sacred life with God as my guide.

God supplies all that my family needs.

I nurture my child's faith in God and in me.

God appreciates, understands, and loves me.

CHILD

God is showing me the way now.

I am never alone—God's love surrounds me.

I take the time to listen to God's voice.

God's energy flows through me.

God is the power within me.

There is not a spot where God is not.

I am one with my friend God.

God is perfect and is right where I am.

TRUST AND TEACH THAT ALL LIFE IS CONNECTED AND HAS A PURPOSE

My children know the importance of being kind to the earth, to people we know, and to strangers. Every Halloween, Matt, who is six, and his dad collect canned goods for the food pantry in our neighborhood, instead of trick-or-treating for candy. The minute Sallie, who is four, outgrows something, she puts it in the "too small bag" to be passed on. They have begun an Earth Day trash pickup in our neighborhood. Matt found out that a boy in his class is living in a residential motel and invited him to play at our house (he had never played at a friend's home before). (Mother of two)

As God cares for us, we care for ourselves, each other, and all living things. God has a purpose for us all in His divine plan. We are not separate from God. When a child feels this wondrous concept he perceives the sacredness of all people everywhere. He can connect to that amazing source of power and light inside himself—his own sacredness—and value it in others. He has the potential to share the God energy with us, with his friends, and with the world. This magnificent power flows through all of us and we share equally in the presence that is God. A six-year-old said it beautifully:

Each day God fills up your heart with love to give to people. (Age six)

This principle focuses on the natural world and on the connectedness and value of all living things. The idea is twofold: We trust that all life has a reason for being, and we teach our faith in that belief to our children. We help children see the connection between themselves and others as crucial to the purpose of their own lives. Certainly we cannot keep such a marvelous and vital secret to ourselves, especially when our life's purpose sometimes gets lost under the glamorous blanket of materialism. This chapter helps you look under that blanket.

On the morning of her eighth birthday Mimi's thrilled daughter announced to her family:

The universe gave me the most incredible birthday gift. I woke up in the night and from my window I saw a constellation. It was Orion. It was a perfect present.

Children seem to accept life's plan naturally and easily; just help them along a bit and allow their enthusiasm to ignite you.

I saved up all my change for months and months, then rolled it up and gave it to a lady who needed help with all the stray cats she was looking after. She had fifty-eight hungry cats with no homes. I felt happy to help those cats. (Age seven)

TRUST AND TEACH THAT ALL LIFE IS CONNECTED AND HAS A PURPOSE

It is no secret that our culture emphasizes the material. Violent disrespect for life is everywhere. We are bombarded with messages telling us how successful, beautiful, loved, respected, smart, and happy we will be if we buy this or that product. "Acquiring" and "having" are touted as the purposes of life. Yet people with all levels of financial resources are depressed, discouraged, angry, and empty. Things go very wrong when our children are brought up to live just for themselves with the belief that their main goal is to have wealth, power, and prestige. The ubiquitous materialism of our culture makes it difficult to prioritize our children's inner lives and maintain their connection to the universe. Yet that is exactly what we must do. The blueprints for discovering our purpose can be found inside, in the soul where God lives, and outside, in God's magnificent natural world.

Trusting that all life has a purpose gives our children meaning in a complex and confusing world. It grounds them when they feel tossed and battered by external events. Knowing they are part of God's plan gives them strength to move through their days with security.

Believing that all life has a purpose allows us to be open to new people and experiences—we see how well we fit together and how our lives touch. Both child and adult learn that many varieties of life are necessary for the smooth functioning of God's world. We delight in the differences and discover the commonalities among all living things. As we become conscious of a tiny creature, an unusual culture, a brilliant star, a fascinating language, a hidden meadow, we begin to value God's design.

When children trust that all life has a purpose, they respect and appreciate themselves and the people around them. Kindness, empathy, compassion, and love grow from appreciation and respect, and in turn create more of both. When you and your children incorporate this principle into your lives, a spiritual circle has begun.

> *Gray is my comforting color. It is the color of old people and I move away when I am walking near them to give them room to walk. That is my way of comforting them when I can.* (Age four)

> *A few weeks ago we when we were in a restaurant a little girl at the next table let her balloon float to the ceiling and it popped. She was sobbing and completely distraught. Her mother refused to get her another. My daughter, age seven, stood up, untied her balloon, brought it to the little girl, and said, "From me to you." The little girl stared at my daughter with her mouth making the letter "O" and began to cry a happy cry. My daughter came back to our table and said, "I like being me. I just gave her some energy to wear."* (Mother of two)

WAYS TO TEACH THAT ALL LIFE IS CONNECTED AND HAS A PURPOSE

Again, as with all parenting, we begin as the example. When the important people in the child's environment exhibit respect for the meaning and value of all living things, the child will absorb the principle "All life has a purpose." Kids explore this without any prompting. How often do you hear: "What is this?" "Why does this happen?" "Who is this bird's mommy?" "What do toads eat?" Children seem to be unconsciously aware of the need to know the purpose for everything. Feed that need!

Children seldom forget a direct experience. A marvelous and available way to educate them to the purposes of living things is to expose them to nature. They come to us already equipped with a magical connection to the environment, with their senses turned on. They explore a caterpillar by touching it, by rubbing it gently against their cheeks, by trying to find its eyes, by sniffing it to see if it has a smell. All we need to do is expose our children to more of the great outdoors and encourage their exploration and "at oneness" with living creatures. They will learn the lesson!

> *My five-year-old daughter has always loved worms. She would bring used coffee grounds outside and dump them in the soil where "a worm family could use them." She would name worms and often sneak a kiss or two. Now that she is in first grade she has been teased about "kissing worms" and pretends to squeal with the other children when a worm is around. I called her on it the other day, saying, "But, Jessie, you love worms." "I know, Mom," she whispered, "but don't let the kids know about that."* (Mother of three)

As children's days become full of plans, classes, school, and friendships, they slowly drift away from their rich relationship with nature. One way to reinforce the connection is to incorporate nature-celebrating rituals into their lives, rituals that offer children ways to coexist and honor their Mother Earth. Why not create an autumn family festival, a first snow party, a full-moon bath, a spring fling, a fall harvest feast? Friends of ours celebrate the first day of spring (usually on March 20 or 21) each year:

> *In our little family of three we all wake up early and get dressed in "spring-looking" clothes. I put my daughter's hair in an inside-out French braid with some colorful dried flowers worked in. (We save this hairdo for*

the first day of spring.) We go to work or school or wherever we have to go that day. Then when we all get home we go strawberry picking at a local farm. We make lots of shortcakes, using a recipe that's been in our family for over one hundred years. Then we feast on strawberry shortcake. (Mother of two)

Another family we know was moved to honor the earth's gifts of flowers by celebrating the "flower moon":

Tonight is the Native American flower moon (complement to the harvest moon). We are in full prep over here getting together our tools of joy: flower petals, dandelion chains, glitter, spritzer of lavender, and poems, and Missy is already wearing a dress that has moons and stars on it. We'll go out at eight and begin our celebration. (Mother of two)

Could you stir your child to investigate a traditional Native American custom? What about an "I discovered" event that honors a nature discovery made by your child? It can be a bee-hive, a bird's nest, a special constellation, a flower growing in an odd spot, a snake's home. Create a celebration around the sighting. Make it important and special.

Let's teach children to view nature as a source of strength and peace, instead of something scary. Kids feel connected and in control when they are comfortable in a natural setting. When they trust that all nature has its purpose they can release some of their fears. If a spider has a purpose maybe we don't have to be so afraid of it. Knowledge is power.

The natural world was a part of me as a child. I read a lot of nature stories and spent time outdoors. In the stories where animals were portrayed as having human qualities, the animals were familiar and safe and helped me to understand rules in the human culture. These books let me know we were equal—animals and humans. The human world was telling me we were better than animals. When I went into nature alone, I thought about the animals. I observed nature—noticed where the deer had been, where the rabbits lived, what the impact of a running dog was, where the animals' trails were, where something had been eaten. I saw how everything affected all things. The land was a story to me. I decided to believe the lessons from nature— that we are all equal. (Age thirty-nine)

Children are attracted to animals because they are unambiguous and honest; animals don't keep secrets or make fun of us. Children dream about animals, have pretend animal companions, and imagine they are animals themselves. How often do you see a young child prancing around like a horse, barking like a dog, lifting an imaginary trunk like an elephant? They love stories about animals and represent animals in their artwork. Animals have energy that children find useful in many ways. Encourage your kids to call upon the "power of an animal" for help with a particular problem or situation. There is a kind of strength that comes from the idea of unity and oneness with all beings. Explain to your child that he can communicate with the animal in a way that feels right to him. He can ask to feel the animals' energy and essence in his life as this girl did:

My daughter was having a particularly difficult day at preschool. That night as I was tucking her into bed she told me about an owl she sees when her eyes are closed who tells her wise things to help her through the next day. (Father of two)

I saw my guardian animal—it is special, it is private, no one would believe me. (Age six)

Maybe you can make a family totem. Totem poles are spiritual statements about a tribe's guardians. What animal spirits could empower your family? Or ask the universe for an animal gift to touch your life, as Mimi and her daughter did:

My daughter and I were about to take a walk on a beautiful wooded path. Before setting out we closed our eyes and asked the universe to give us a sign—to show us we were loved. What happened will live with me forever. We were a few minutes into our walk when a frisky black rabbit scurried in front of us. He zipped back across the path, inches from where we were walking. We stopped—he stopped. He came closer. We froze. He began to eat, pausing to look up at us— totally unafraid. We were simply transfixed. My daughter picked long grass and offered it to the rabbit— whom she named Yogi. The rabbit ate it, then looked deep into her eyes—they connected. She reached down and patted his back, begging me to join her. I did and it was like touching velvet. We finally left Yogi and arm-in-arm returned to our world, magically touched. We were given the sign we asked for, in a delightful way.

Celebrate special times in nature. Autumn Equinox, the last day of summer and the start of fall, is a clear transition to mark. It begins the cycle of the earth quieting to prepare for rebirth and growth in the spring. Have a mini festival and give thanks for the fun and joy of the ending summer. Maybe you can make up a song of thanks for all the fruits that you enjoyed during the summer: your sun-filled days, the swimming pond, tadpoles. The earth is planning to take a rest and will soon be covered with its own white blanket—asleep to our eyes. Let's celebrate before our Mother Earth rests.

Examine life's cycles. When we observe the cycles of nature we can illustrate for our children the idea that our world has been designed by an All-Knowing Intelligence. Sometimes life may seem out of control, but we can always count on the order of the seasons. We can believe that God is present when we observe the miracles of nature, the details of a robin's egg, the perfectly formed spider's web, the birth of an animal, the care a mother bird gives her baby, an acorn sprouting new growth, the smell of lilacs.

Have fun with this concept; learning isn't all serious. "What do you suppose is God's purpose for the flea? What about the roach, or a blizzard, or snakes, or cowlicks in our hair?" Let children answer and ask. One rule only—even if we don't know and cannot imagine the role, all life does have a purpose.

Try to get outdoors at different times of the day. Slow down and enjoy the wonder around you. A shooting star can be seen only when you look. Witness the experience one mother had when watching an eclipse with her daughter:

Today she's nine. When she's ninety will she remember that she sat on her mother's lap on the dewy grass wrapped in blankets and loving arms and watched so patiently the moon hide behind the earth's shadow? Will she remember that we talked of the stars hanging from the moon on threads spun on a fairy's loom? That the fuzzy ring was in fact an angel's halo? The moon seemed to anchor us to more earthly matters. All the while gazing at the magic unfolding before our eyes we talked of matters so important in a young girl's life. Promises that were not kept. Friendships that changed in the bat of an eye. Her world taking shape in the changing universe. Will she remember that I saw the moon reflected in her eyes? That our souls were intertwined that night? That our love for each other was as simple as a kiss on a soft moonlit cheek? (Mother of one)

It isn't necessary that you trek off to a great wilderness or nature preserve. You and your child can go outside and look at the grass in your yard or a nearby park. Take off your shoes, wiggle your toes, feel the grass, examine any tiny creatures who live there. What an interesting home the ant has. Could you make an ant farm indoors? Where do you suppose the grasshopper goes at night? What is the purpose of the gnat?

Children's true selves are often revealed when they are in the embrace of their Mother Earth. Sunlight, water, fresh air, rich soil, bird song are spiritual food. By putting his feet in a flowing stream and listening to the whisper of the wind through the trees, a child can get lost in the sensory experience of sound, touch, movement, wonder. He is a part of the water, a part of the wind, a brother of the stream. He is in harmony with God. Robert Browning said, "What I call God . . . fools call Nature."

If you have shared nature with your child you will not be surprised to learn that researchers at the University of Illinois found that Chicago public housing residents who had views of trees reported better relations with their neighbors, a stronger sense of community, and a greater sense of safety than those who did not have views of trees. They also discovered less domestic violence in the families who lived near trees. More harmony?

Programs such as Wilderness Discovery, a nature-based program for at-risk kids, have reported improved self-esteem, a stronger desire to attain goals, and improved mental well-being among the participants. Interacting with the natural world increases children's spiritual sense of belonging, and when we believe we belong to something larger than ourselves, we feel valuable.

Nature restores our sense of peace and allows us to feel life touching us. The more-than-human world soothes and nourishes our spirits and sometimes frightens us with its power. We make this gift available to our children as we teach them to respect nature, to walk with awareness, to speak softly, to listen well, to disturb nothing, and to leave no destructive record of their visit. The natural world is a magical, perpetual, ever-changing process that links us with the universe. God/nature/child are all part of the same space, connected in the powerful web of life. All parts of the web have importance and purpose. Give your children the opportunity to meet our natural world. This powerful ally in raising a spiritual child is always inviting, receptive, and available. Nature is God's altar. It is one big church or temple, free, open, and without dogma.

Nature compels children to become involved. It's often the adult's agenda, fear, and priorities that disconnect the child's exploration. A little boy was on an apple-picking field trip with his first grade class. As he was strolling with the large group of children, being told what to do, where to go, and how to get there, he noticed a flat gray rock on the ground that somehow called to him. The little boy gently picked up the rock and examined it with his fingers, his eyes, his cheek. As he continued to walk on he saw another rock that looked very much like the first. He picked it up. He put the two rocks together and realized they were a perfect match. The rocks fit each other—they were parts of one rock that had broken in half. The boy marveled at his finding. There was even a yellowish stain on the inside of both rocks, in the same spot, that proved they were once one. The child had made a delicious discovery; he had a natural treasure and was thrilled.

A large, loud teacher saw this little boy with two rocks in his hands and immediately her antenna went up: Boy + Rock = Trouble. "Drop the rock," she barked, startling the boy from his reverie. "I said drop the rock or you'll be sitting on the bus for the rest of the day." "But they aren't ordinary . . . they are—" the boy tried to explain to this large presence charging toward him. "*Now!* Do you hear me? Drop the rock." *Squash.* The boy made a lasting discovery this day—it wasn't about the difference between Cortland and Macintosh apples; it was about being closed to God's wonders. Luckily there was a sensitive mother volunteering with the group who conspired with the child to bring his superb and special rocks home—safely in her backpack.

Some simple ideas for reinforcing the idea that all life has a purpose include:

- Bring nature inside and let your family observe growth. Children love to dry or press flowers, grow herbs, have a plant in their bedroom, sprout an avocado pit.

- Arrange a fall festival for your child and let him ceremoniously tuck small bulbs, like crocus, into the dirt to sleep until spring. Let nature into your life, live with it as a partner in the world you share. Have fun and play naturally, as your children do. Find sticks or rocks and spell out your names. Stack up some rocks and run water over them like a waterfall.

- Gradually begin to use more natural materials in your home. Stumps, with the rough edges sanded, make great little tables for children. Let your child put a special, smooth rock in her pocket as a touchstone to carry. It can be her connection to the larger world, available when she needs to feel that connection. A branch from a flowering tree makes a dramatic impact when brought inside to bloom. Surround kids with the beauty of the natural world—it nourishes their senses and fosters their appreciation of the gifts of the earth.

- Even a lowly compost pile can teach your child about the purpose of everything, even garbage. Those old potato peelings and rotten fruit turn into earthworm food and then dirt. Kids find this remarkable.

- Watch for milkweed pods in the fall. These magical, lumpy pods make wonderful wands. Carefully open the pods and let your children run with them to let the milkweed fairies fly free.

- Get involved in neighborhood beautification projects. If your neighborhood doesn't have one, can you be the instigator? Buy trash bags in bulk and distribute them to neighbors for "pickup day." You can volunteer to collect the filled trash bags and take them to the local dump.

- Tell your children about Henry David Thoreau, who said, "It is vain to dream of a wildness distant from ourselves. There is none such." Indulge yourself in some of his writing. (We've listed a children's book about Thoreau in the Appendix.)

- Explore *Sharing Nature with Children* by Joseph Cornell. This beautiful book with its nature-awareness games will spark ideas for outdoor possibilities.

- Mythology tells us that gnomes are little beings who help take care of the earth—working underground during the winter months. Keep your eyes open and you might catch a glimpse of a hardworking gnome.

- Celebrate Earth Day each April. Have an Earth Day party and invite your children's friends over for a neighborhood parade. Make bicycle floats with recycled materials and sing songs to honor Mother Earth.

- Take a hike in the woods or near the water and really explore nature. Hugging trees may seem silly, but see if you don't feel the difference in energy from tree to tree— your kids surely will. Bring along a journal and spend some time writing about your feelings when you are connecting with nature. One seven-year-old spent time with her family near a riverbank and wrote:

I am here on Sachen Trail. I am here looking at the water. It is rushing and running. I feel very good when I am here. I feel very sacred. All the trees seem to give me more breath. (Age seven)

- Honor St. Francis on his feast day, October 4. St. Francis is a friend to the animals and can remind us to help our animal friends. Perhaps you could scatter birdseed to the wild birds during your celebration or put a salt lick out for deer. If you live in the city you could visit a local zoo and say a special prayer for each animal you come across. You might donate money to a cause that helps animals. Try communicating with an animal as St. Francis did, by being a silent observer. Your children may startle you with their insights into an animal's thoughts.

Since I can remember I could "think talk" with my cat. It's like we know each other's thoughts when we lie together and it is quiet. She licks my tears away when I am sad. She is my best friend. (Age eight)

- Invite all the neighborhood pets over for a pet blessing ceremony. Sing "All Things Bright and Beautiful" and make up some prayers to say together. Here are a few to get you started.

Creator God, we give you thanks for all the animals on the earth, in the sea, in the air. Help us to use our power over them wisely. May we treat your creatures with respect always. Amen.

Divine One, bless all the animals here today and those who have died. We give you great thanks for these companions who bring such joy into our lives and those who have enriched us in the past. Shine your warm, loving light on them.

- Many churches have pet blessing ceremonies. Everyone brings a special animal companion to be blessed. Check in your area and you may find such an event.

- If possible, allow your child to develop a connection with a pet. Sharing love and caring for a living thing provides comfort, teaches responsibility, and reinforces daily how important all living things are to one another. The repetitive responsibility of caring for a pet is rewarding. Celebrate your pet's birthday or the date it came to live with you. What is the purpose of a pet? Ask the child who has one!

Wally, my old dog, is my number one favorite thing in the whole wide world. (Age nine)

I didn't realize until recently that my little cat is much more than a pet in my home. He's another person, a loved four-legged friend. (Mother of three)

My favorite friend, a dog named Lucky, died a while ago. I loved that dog even though he didn't belong to me. I knew him since I was born. After he died I kept his collar right next to me in bed. One morning I was feeling so sad and missing him—just then a pretty little bird looked right at me from outside my window where she was sitting on a tree. That bird told me in silent words that she was the spirit of Lucky and he'd always be with me. (Age eight)

My cat gave me the loveliest present. She walked on my back and kneaded it just the way I adore. (Age eight)

• Put up a bird feeder, notice which birds come. Try to recognize different bird sounds and imagine their meanings. Remember, if you begin to feed the birds, when their food is gone they will depend on you, so don't stop until natural food is again available.

I bought one of those see-through birdhouses and attached it to the outside of the kitchen window. It comes with a privacy panel that you attach to the inside of the window that can be easily removed, allowing the kids to take a peek. We have a mother bird building a nest now and the children are thrilled. They check on her progress each morning when they come down for breakfast and include her in our prayers. (Mother of two)

- Plant a butterfly garden or window box. Flowering nectar bushes such as honeysuckle and clumps of flowers such as impatiens, marigolds, zinnias, and asters are favorite haunts for these colorful creatures. The butterflies suck out the nectar as food, traveling from flower to flower, carrying pollen with them. This close relationship is one of nature's finest cycles.

Each spring I visit a local nursery with my four- and six-year-old kids to select several new plants to add to our butterfly garden, which is next to their playhouse. We all get excited every time we see a butterfly, and as they get older, we can look up and identify the ones we see. (Mother of two)

Plants offer great possibilities for increasing your child's understanding of the purpose of life. Many children love to grow things, and if this appeals to your child, help him plant a small garden. What a great illustration of cooperation between humans and plants gardening can be. Steer away from something so large that it becomes *work*. A window herb garden can be enough responsibility for some. Your kids can take responsibility for nurturing the plants and credit for sharing the delicious fruits of their labor. While you are in the farming mode, investigate the many purposes of different plants. Many plants have healing qualities—for example, aloe helps heal burns. Discover other plants and herbs that have particular protective and healing functions.

Be generous with your produce, share cuttings from your garden. Maybe you could plant a cutting from a place you cherish, a childhood home or a lovely park. Most people are happy to spread beauty around when asked kindly. Let your children in on these exchanges, and talk about what happens between people and between gardens. Working with flowers and plants enriches the garden, the table, and the soul of the gardener.

> *We have lilacs in our yard that were taken from a cutting growing at my mom's house. Her lilacs came from her mother's farm and these lilacs came from her grandmother's home. I feel that these white lilacs are part of who I am.* (Mother of three)

> *Sometimes my kids will make up concoctions of different spices they find in the kitchen and create ceremonies for the garden. They'll sprinkle the "magic mixture" and ask for the garden to grow like crazy, then thank the plants for all they give us.* (Mother of two)

As you plant, nurture, and harvest your produce, or pick and enjoy your flowers, chat about the interconnectedness between humans and nature. Teach children to respect what grows and talk about the many purposes of vegetables, flowers, trees, bushes, grass, and weeds. Notice the ways in which God provides for living things to grow and blossom. How does He provide for children? As the sun shines on you and your child in the beauty of the garden, whisper a prayer of thanks to the nature spirits. Teach your child the beautiful quote from the Talmud: "Every blade of grass has an angel that bends down and whispers 'grow, grow.'"

> *I always ask the plant first before I take a flower and then I try to remember to give it something back like a drink of water.* (Age nine)

I spent hours as a child playing in a grove of pine trees in my backyard. I'm quite certain that the spirits of the trees kept me company all those long summer days among the pines. (Father of three)

Make a Difference Every Day

Develop a framework your family can use to look at things and to make choices. Come up with some agreed-upon standards for living. For instance, if God comes first, what is next? Decisions become easier when we have an applicable hierarchy of values and beliefs to use as a framework—to look after the earth instead of adding to the problem, choosing to love instead of hate, to forgive instead of holding a grudge, to reach out to someone in need instead of choosing silence. This six-year-old sees the domino effect of one small kindness:

I did a generous thing today. This little kindergarten kid couldn't find a seat on the bus and I said, "Hey, you can sit here." Then I taught him how to do the secret missing finger trick that my older sister had showed me. He said he was going to show his big brother the trick. So it felt neat that my sister was kind to me and taught me something—I taught it to a little kid—the little kid was going to show it to his big brother. (Age six)

Remind your children they can make a difference each day. They can touch other people's lives through simple efforts: a smile, a nod, a shared laugh, a kind word, a whispered prayer for someone else. Maybe they can ask someone new to play or speak to the child who is alone. These small deeds are truly important and worthy and fill the soul with grace. Making a difference doesn't imply that we have to sacrifice or change our lives in an extraordinary way. A busy mother of two told us: "I'm so busy just getting through the day, it's hard to open my heart or my calendar to helping others." There are wonderful opportunities for spreading goodness that exist right now in all our lives. Reach out to others who are put on your path in life. It is easy to ride the bus silently, but taking a risk and caring is a more expansive, exciting way to live.

> *Yesterday my five-year-old daughter and I passed a homeless woman on the street. Samantha wept when we didn't stop to give her "ten dollars," which is the magic number she thought was right. It was at the entrance to a major highway and we would have been killed stopping . . . no doubt as this woman might. What struck me was the passion of the caring. I felt that I wanted to explain homelessness in political and spiritual terms and was so frustrated. I said, "Let's send her love and light and know that she will be protected." Sam said, "She needs real money right now. Not love and light." I understood that, I really did, but I didn't know what to say.* (Mother of one)

We might not understand people's lives but we must trust that each life has a purpose and we are all part of a larger plan. We can't help everyone in the world or fix all the problems, but when a particular issue speaks to us or our children, we can come up with ways we might help. Surprisingly, our children frequently have practical solutions to problems we consider complicated. Why not ask them for their ideas? "Samantha, how do you think we could help that woman since it wasn't possible to stop there in the traffic?" You might be amazed by what you hear.

It's not easy for our kids to focus on goodness when the world around them is applauding power and possessions. We can counteract this group thinking by helping our children tune in to the subtle gratifying internal reward that comes when they reach out. A first grader befriended a fourth grader who had been shunned by many because she was overweight. The first grade girl told her mother, "Never judge anyone by their size, Mom. There is so much to like about Stephanie, she is fun to be with and I don't care what the other kids say. It feels good that I started talking to her and now I'm her friend."

It's truly the little things that make a difference. Often a small gift freely given brings light into an otherwise dark day. Develop a habit of giving gifts for no special reason. Not necessarily expensive items, but something to show you thought of the person. Maybe you could bring a small gift when you go to a friend's for dinner, or drop by, for no special reason, with some cut flowers from your garden. When you see something that is perfect for someone you know, buy it for him, even if it isn't Christmas or his birthday. Type up a resource list that includes service organizations you use—plumbers, electricians, snow removers, oil companies—and keep it handy to give new neighbors. What a help to have a personalized guide to their new town. Include directions and phone numbers for grocery stores, drugstores, baby-sitters, vegetable stands, doctors, hospitals. You will save them hours of work when you share your experience via a resource list. If you think of someone, call her, or drop her a note. One thoughtful woman we know picks up postcards wherever she goes and keeps them stamped and handy to send to long-distance pals. You can make this easy for your children by addressing and stamping some cards ahead of time so that if the mood strikes, they are equipped.

It's also fun to give anonymous gifts—to demonstrate our compassion in quiet, uncelebrated moments when no one is around to judge. Carry groceries for a stranger who has her arms full, take some toys to a family and don't tell anyone. Offer to bring food to the local soup kitchen or AIDS task force without leaving your name. Children can be "secret pals" to a brother or sister, a friend or relative. If a child's friend is home with a tummy ache, leave a rhyming note and a box of ginger tea or a small gift at the door, ring the bell, and run away. Use May Day, May 1, as an opportunity to leave spring flowers on the doorsteps of your friends and neighbors without their seeing you. These secret gifts give the spirits of both giver and receiver a glow unlike any other.

Sometimes when we are going into the city on a big highway my mom will give the person at the tollbooth extra money for someone who might not have the toll. It makes our whole family happy to think of how the people who don't have to pay the toll might feel. (Age eight)

I like to shovel sidewalks and driveways for my elderly neighbors in the winter—it's especially nice to do it in the evening when they are asleep, so that they come out and find it that way and don't know who did it! (Father of four)

The United States Congress has passed legislation proclaiming February 17 as Random Acts of Kindness Day. It seems a shame that we need legislation to remind us to reach out with kindness. This day, however, can encourage generosity. Celebrate by having a dinner party—ask each of your children to invite one friend and his family. Or better yet, a child and family they'd like to get to know.

Come up with your own list of everyday opportunities to

show kindness and share the list with your child. He may be inspired to create his own. Some ideas to get you started:

1: When you make soup, double the recipe and share with your neighbor.

2: Bring the bus driver a morning muffin.

3: Compliment a stranger.

4: Return shopping carts to the store.

5: Buy dog bones for your neighbor's dog.

6: Drive a neighbor without a car to the market.

7: Buy a subscription to your favorite magazine for a friend.

8: Hold the door of the train or bus for the person behind you.

9: Say hello to a stranger without expecting a response.

10: Pass on to someone else an article or a book that really touched you.

11: Write a note of appreciation to your mail carrier or your child's teacher.

12: Help someone find something he has lost.

13: Give up your place in line at the grocery store to the person with just one item.

14: Pass on information you receive in the mail for things or events that you think another person might be able to use, instead of throwing them away.

15: Recycle magazines to the local library.

16: Put a chocolate under someone's pillow.

17: When visiting in a hospital, spend a few minutes with someone who has no visitors.

18: Write a note of encouragement to someone who has just received sad news.

Acknowledge when your child acts in a generous and kind way. Encourage and validate compassion for others. The idea of being either winners or losers is prevalent in our society, but people commonly forget who is the real authority on winners. Remind your children that God sees winners, and purposes, where humans do not. Talk about winning and what it means. What winners do you know?

Remember that if we see God in one another we will cherish and respect one another. How can we not do so? There can be no room for prejudice, animosity, and hate in the person who is God's child. Children seem to understand this concept easily, while adults struggle with it. Maybe your child can teach you this one.

Today at school I built the most amazing structure. It was so beautiful—awesome—the best I have ever built. Then something happened and I got disappointed. I heard kids yelling my name, saying, "Look, look what happened to your building." This kid who can't talk very normal had his foot on my destroyed structure. He had stepped on it. The disappointment came all the way up to my throat. I wanted to be angry at him but his eyes were getting wide and kind of watery. I knew he felt like crying just as much as I felt disappointment, so I just gave a smile and didn't say anything. It sure was a beautiful structure. (Age six)

Of course, kids aren't always going to be this articulate. We are all learning to manage our angry, bitter, frustrated feelings. There are many ways we can help our kids when their feelings are hurt or they feel an injustice has been done. The six-year-old quoted above has the wisdom to empathize with the boy who destroyed her structure. She chose the high road and decided to be kind instead of being angry—a very mature and loving choice. We can remind our kids that like the girl, they get to choose their reactions. The source of their anger is within them, not some exterior power that comes down and grabs them by the throat—although it sure does feel that way sometimes.

Adopt a Cause—Take Action

You can incorporate routine good deeds on an individual as well as on a community level. The field of charity is large enough to offer kids a wide variety of opportunities to discover their talents, hone their skills, and explore their interests, all while making a difference. People, animals, the environment, organizations, and causes all benefit when we take action. Best of all—good comes back. Remember the old saying "Whatever goes around comes around"? Let's send good deeds on that round trip as we show our kids we care.

One Saturday each month I take my three boys to a nursing home in our town. It's tough to schedule it in with games, practices, parties, and all the millions of other things we do. I really feel strongly about it because it brings such joy to the faces of these older people. My guys complained at first about going, but now they even ask if they can bring friends along. It's a small thing, but I hope it makes a difference. (Mother of three)

I don't have a lot of extra money, but my kids and I help out by giving our time. We join the semiannual Clean Up the Beach group every year and try to do some extra picking up on our own. I'm trying to teach them the value of our beautiful ocean and how important it is to maintain it. (Mother of five)

Charity is more than giving away money. "Charity" is an ancient word that means to help others for the sake of love. The spirit of charity exists in kids naturally, but as they grow older, they get the message that they shouldn't feel so deeply for strangers or be quite so charitable with their "things." Let's allow our kids to express their empathy and get involved in causes that pull at their hearts.

Is there a local Red Cross your kids might join, or are there improvements they might make in your community? What about lending their support to environmental projects?

What cause does the family as a whole feel strongly about? Is it a religious mission, a secular fund, an organization that fights injustice, or perhaps a local charity project? If you agree with the goal, find a way to support the cause—not necessarily by writing a check, but by writing a letter of support or praying for the volunteers and the people who receive the help.

As children begin to incorporate kindness into their lives, it is important for them to see the results of their good deeds. Stuffing envelopes for a fundraising project may not be as fulfilling as cleaning up a littered neighborhood. An experience that allows a child to impact directly the lives of another human being empowers him—he has made a difference. Let your kids respond to the needs they see in their world—then help them take action. Does your child love to read? How about setting up used-book collection bins in her school and neighborhood for homeless shelters or writing to publishing companies and asking for donations of books? If he likes to write, perhaps he could write a story, then copy and laminate it for distribution among the family shelters. Does your daughter love to be a part of a club? What if she organized a club with other kids whose purpose was to respond to poverty in your community in some way? Do you have a young gardener in your family? Many families don't have access to land for gardening or even to fresh produce. Would your child like to grow a garden for a local soup kitchen? Do you have an artist in the house? Buy brown lunch bags in bulk and let him go wild decorating them for shelters to use to package lunches, or create fun, funky place mats by laminating artwork. Does one of your children really know her way around a computer? Perhaps she'd like to share her computer skills with an unemployed adult who needs computer tutoring. Do you have a new puppy? Maybe your dog lover can share the joy of his new puppy with those at the local nursing home who are interested. What about a bicycle enthusiast? Could he collect "broken" bicycles and repair them for kids who can't afford new bikes? Ask the counselor at your child's elementary school or the local clergy who might need a refurbished bike. Maybe the bike fixer has a friend who is a great writer who can compose an article on his efforts for the local paper to solicit more bikes.

> *On Christmas Eve, my fourteen-year-old and I went to a local arcade and bought ten dollars' worth of tokens. We took them to a homeless shelter to be used by children there. I remember that, when times were tough for us, the hardest things to come by were fun-filled activities. We were blessed with plenty of offers of clothing and food, but I missed being able to do fun stuff with my kids. A gift of fun may not fill the tummy, but it sure can fill the heart!* (Mother of four)

Children's efforts can be astounding, they have the ability to make a difference in big ways as well as subtle small everyday ways. A boy of eighteen wondered what it would be like to walk in a needy child's shoes, and when he found out he persuaded manufacturers to donate 10,000 new ones to kids who needed them. Everyday kids are selflessly becoming heroes.

Reach Out and Make Connections

All children have the need to attach and bond with others, with friends, family, and community. We have isolated ourselves for all sorts of reasons: safety, time, lack of interest. Slowly, carefully, we can change that for our children. Kids long for connection; let's help them assuage this longing. Go to work in your small circle. Organize a block party, visit the neighbor who is housebound, start a neighborhood newsletter, make your house a safe house for neighborhood kids—then let everyone know what that means. Buy a bench for the front of your house and encourage neighbors passing by to stop for a visit. Join your kids at the bus stop with a thermos of coffee to share with other parents who can pause a moment before rushing off to work.

You can inspire your children to find their seed of brilliant light—their higher purpose—whatever it may be, and let them know you honor that gift. When you support and encourage them to ask of themselves, "What can I give?" you help unlock their divine potential and acknowledge their honorable gifts from God. Together ask God each morning to make it clear how you might give during the day. When you come together at day's end, share the opportunities you each had to show kindness. Perhaps you could turn it into a "kindness game" and count the kind things you have done during the day, reporting back in the evening. As these two mothers discovered, helping others begins right outside your door:

One morning a friend came over for coffee. We both work full-time and try to remain active in our children's schools but we still feel we want to help the world in some way. We discussed this need all morning and together prayed for God to show us how we might help. When my friend was getting ready to leave we heard a scream and across the street we saw an older woman who had slipped on the ice. We raced over and helped her up, brushed her off, picked up her spilled purse and found out where she was headed. My friend drove her to her doctor's appointment and we got her name and number to stay in touch. We were so thrilled to have an opportunity to help someone and had to laugh at how easy God made it for us. We didn't have to join the Peace Corps or quit our jobs, we could help right in our own neighborhood.
(Mother of two)

Deep within we are all the same, we all face spiritual challenges. When children reach out to others with kindness they open to their own spiritual purpose as well as the purpose of the person to whom they have connected. We can guide our kids to opportunities that help them form these connections:

- Encourage your children to write one letter a week. Suggest they write to family members, authors, heroes, newspapers, nursing homes. Write notes of comfort, empathy, consolation, cheer. Send drawings or cut out articles of interest to the recipient. Write to the new family in town, the new teacher at school, the family in the local paper whose house burned down, the bus driver. When a child reaches out to write he touches the life of another of God's beloved family.

- Ask your kids to visualize world peace. Design a cover of *Newsweek* magazine with the title "World Lives in Peace." What would that look like? Teach peace at home and in the community. The Hebrew word for "peace" is "shalom." Why not add it to your everyday language?

- Arrange for your child to have a pen pal from a different country. As they write and read their letters, children will discover similarities. Pen pals bring the world into your child's life and make it a more personal place. There are pen pal organizations, lists on the Internet, and names given in many children's magazines. Ask your child's teacher for suggestions; perhaps the class can adopt a class from another country. Remain alert to the content of the correspondence and screen your child's pal carefully.

- Demonstrate how God acts through us. We are what God is doing. God is closer than the air we breathe. We can be

God's hands, feet, words, ears, eyes. How can we activate these parts? Maybe by caring for a smaller child or an animal. Maybe by using a talent or learning a skill. Perhaps by defending a belief or standing up for another person. God cares for us. We care for each other. We can expand our godlike qualities and radiate them outward.

Once I was snuggling with my cat and I put my hands on her and practiced giving her Reiki. (That's when my energy can help heal others.) I sent the power from my hands into her. She looked up at me and licked my nose. She has never done that before or since. (Age nine)

- Encourage your children to use manners in their everyday lives; they are a gesture of kindness and respect for others. Manners are not meant to make others approve of us; rather, they allow people to feel more comfortable with us. Basic civility is on the decline in our country, so we need to state clearly our expectations for our children's behavior. This doesn't mean putting on a false front, but rather finding a compassionate, civilized way to handle life's inevitable conflicts. Rude behavior, poor sportsmanship, and a lack of consideration for others does have consequences, and our kids need to be held accountable.

Let your children in on the value of each person's cooperation in making a group work. Point out how each individual can add something to a big project and by working together the group can do it all. Improvise, but try to strengthen your particular community. Could that be one of your special purposes?

Ask your child to picture an invisible cord attaching him to all people, or to people in his neighborhood or on his block.

Imagine the cord is made of light, attached to all of us and held by God. Maybe this can be a sacred lasso wrapping people together in glorious light. Or share this seven-year-old's concept of unity:

> *Do you know that we have a star inside of us? We are all connected to the stars and that is what makes us human. The stars keep us from doing bad things because they pull us up to heaven instead.* (Age seven)

As a society we have spent time teaching our children about differences, but have we shown them how much we have in common? Is it any wonder the Golden Rule is at the heart of most religions? Let's remind our children of our similarities and teach that all people are connected. Illustrate this idea by using beads. Kids love to create their own necklaces; find some loose beads or buttons with holes in them and a piece of string or a shoelace. Ask your child to select some beads and thread them on the string. Each bead should be different from all the others to illustrate the differences in people. Each is individual, but all are together, connected by the string. Like the string joining the beads, Divine Spirit connects us all.

Talk to your children about God's love being passed down through the generations. Arrange for grandparents to tell how they have experienced God's love. As Mimi's father, Marsha's husband, wages a long fight with cancer, he is an example to his granddaughters of how to call on God's love to face each new day with optimism: "My Poppy closes his eyes and turns his thinking to God when they poke him with needles at the hospital. He is always happy even when he's not feeling well. He uses God's love to get better but mostly he uses God's love to love us."

Look for different ways in which other people you know ask

for love and support. A third grader we know clings to God's love during a difficult time in her life:

I ask God to please help me out. I am so scared about my parents and their fighting. I'm not sure who I should pick to live with if they get a divorce. I might just pick my grandma. I ask God to help me not have this sick feeling in my tummy. At least I know wherever I end up living God will go with me. I feel God's love and I'm not as afraid. (Age nine)

Reach Out to Children and Parents Everywhere

I live in a farm town with several migrant worker camps. I noticed the children, who I saw playing in their yards and around town, seldom had shoes on, and their clothes were worn, frayed, and dirty. Now my favorite pastime is going around my neighborhood asking if people have any children's clothes or shoes they don't need or want. Then I take them to the camps. The people are so grateful and so goodhearted. They always try to fix me something to eat or give me things, which makes me feel even better since they don't have much to give! (Father of three)

Be an advocate for all children. Volunteer at a day care center, a children's hospital, a family shelter, or a classroom. Open your heart to any child placed in your life, not just your own. Apply these spiritual principles to the child next door, your child's pals, all children God puts in your life. You cross one another's paths for a reason.

Respond to the needs of children in your own community.

Become a pen pal to a homeless child and give her a new connection to an adult. Visit a sick child in the hospital and read her some of your children's favorite books. Read books on tape for children who can't see. Spend a Saturday jazzing up a day care center to create a stimulating environment for the children who spend so much time there. Do you know any latchkey kids? Maybe you could organize a call-in network so they have a local resource if problems come up while they are home alone. Are your arms aching to hold a baby again? How about offering to rock babies for an hour a week in a low-income infant day care? Have season tickets to the ballet, the symphony, or a local sports team's games? Perhaps you'd consider donating one performance or game to a child who otherwise wouldn't be able to attend.

Let's visualize peace for all children. Picture them as healthy, whole, loving, creative beings, for that is how they come into the world. Imagine them tucked into safe and cozy beds and happily going off to a school where there are kind teachers and a warm lunch. For what we see can truly come to be. Picture light surrounding our world. Imagine a globe wrapped in pink cellophane—that pink light is pure love that fills the consciousness of all who inhabit the earth. Every picture of peace and light makes a difference and can begin to transform the earth.

All children have a purpose and are treasures to value. When you witness, read, or hear about any unkind treatment to a child, *take a stand against it*. Become involved in causes that help children around the globe. We are parents of the next generation. We don't own children, we have them for a while to love and care for. Find out more about causes that benefit children, such as:

Big Brothers/Big Sisters (215-567-7000)
Boys and Girls Clubs of America (212-351-5900)

Children's Aid International (800-842-2810)
Children's Defense Fund (202-628-8787)
Kids Against Crime (909-882-1344)
Fresh Air Fund (212–221–0900)
Make a Wish Foundation (800-722-WISH)
National Center for Missing and Exploited Children
    (703-235-3900)
National Children's Cancer Society (618-667-9563)
Pediatric AIDS Foundation (310-395-9051).

We often witness children suffering in our own world. A tired parent, at the end of a stressful day, stops at the grocery store for dinner items with his cranky child. He loses patience and his child suffers. We'd like to speak up, but we hesitate. Is it our business to intervene? And if we do, will we antagonize the parent, putting the child at even greater risk? Or perhaps we are imagining what we thought we saw, and speaking up would only make us look the fool. There seems to be a common assumption in our society that intervening on behalf of a child in a public place is a dangerous thing to do. There is a way, however of offering help instead of attacking the parent with criticism and threats. "How could you treat your child like that?" would elicit a different reaction from "It looks like you're having some difficulty. Is there anything I can do to help you out?" Then follow through with specific ways you might help: Offer to find groceries, entertain the child for five minutes, give the child a small treat to keep her occupied. A friend of ours always carries colorful stickers in her purse for just this reason. The child is happier because of this unexpected gift and the parent is usually quite grateful.

   If you find yourself in a situation where a child is being compromised, take a moment and tune into your inner guidance. "How might I help here, God? Give me the courage to speak up." Then follow through on your guidance. You give as clear a message by walking past a distraught child as you do by intervening. If you ignore the situation you give the message to the child that no one cares about his suffering, and to the parents that you approve of their actions.

When I see a child being spoken to harshly, shoved, ignored, mocked, or even crying, I make eye contact with the child and send him light, directly from my heart to his. I pray to his guardian angel to step into the situation and provide the child with comfort. Then I decide how I might approach the parent or caregiver. (Mother of two)

Adults have told us they clearly recall the time a stranger stepped in on their behalf, and how much it meant that someone cared enough to recognize their situation. Many have said that this one intervention changed their lives and gave them hope—that the person who spoke up was an angel in their lives.

Support other parents in their parenting. Offer an evening of child care to an overworked friend or a single parent. Volunteer for a program that helps new parents—often a local hospital organizes such groups to provide emotional support for overwhelmed parents. Could you be a phone staffer for a parent hot line? Offer your prayers to other parents as these women do:

Oh, I chant for all moms. Especially all the single ones, for wisdom and strength and finding true happiness. All things happen for a reason, families are together to work out karma and learn. I pray for us all . . . we learn all our lessons and move this whole planet faster and further toward world peace. Peace in our lifetimes for the kids, grandkids, and all. (Grandmother of twelve)

I pray for all the foster parents, who love their foster children genuinely like their own, although for a short time. (Mother of three, foster mother of one)

Institute a "Positive Talk" Campaign

Make a supreme effort to avoid judging, labeling, complaining, and criticizing others—it dims our souls' light. All of us, child and adult, fall into this lazy and contagious mind habit.

Last night at dinner my husband was telling me a story about a conversation he had with a fellow he works with. Our six-year-old daughter said, "It feels like every time Daddy talks about his work he criticizes someone. I don't like it." Her face became red and her eyes filled with tears as she spoke her feelings. It was a huge wake-up call for my husband and myself. For years we have sort of talked over the heads of our kids—or so we thought. They get the drift of more than we can imagine and she was picking up a lot of negative feelings that shouldn't have come out at the dinner table. We will be much more attentive to how we speak about others. (Mother of two)

Put up signs or make buttons with slogans on them. "Say a Nice Word About Someone," "Be a Cheerleader for Someone Today," "Judges Wear Black Robes, We Don't." Put up a picture of the word "judgment" and run a red slash through it. Catch yourself when you slip into criticizing and judging and instead try turning toward the light as you visualize it surrounding and infusing you. Revel in the differences between people; let go of judgments.

We put a sign up on the refrigerator that says, "Label Jars, Not People." If someone starts name calling or passing judgments, it's only a matter of moments before someone else points to our big sign. (Father of three)

We met a guy in a wheelchair in the park today. He was really nice to us and let us pat his dog. He was just like regular people. (Age five)

My friends always take sides and say mean things about the kids not on our side. Sometimes I just go along because I don't know what else to do. (Age seven)

Reach out to groups or organizations that teach and promote understanding and acceptance of all people. Children's International Village is a wonderful organization that teaches understanding and appreciation of differences and similarities between people. It is funded through UNESCO, with sites throughout the free world. Each summer the participating countries select groups of four eleven-year-old children and two adults to attend one of the villages. There, for four weeks, they mix with kids from other countries, share their customs, and have fun! Language differences are quickly overcome and friendships are formed.

Look for God's Light in All People

When we teach our children that everyone has a purpose we also have to illustrate how to go beneath the surface of a person's facade to see God's light.

Look for the positive in others and encourage your children

to do the same. Point out the positive aspects of your children's friends instead of criticizing them. Make it a habit to praise the good in others each day. Teach your child to look at others with "spiritual vision." It allows us to look beyond appearances to see all people as expressions of God's love. If we look past preconceived notions we will see that we all belong to the same large family of God.

- Remain open to the ideas and energy of others. Affirm, "Today, I will be open to all who come my way." Try it in the morning with your children, then report back on who was put on your paths. It is not necessary always to agree or adopt another's idea or way of living, only to be open.

- Kids can help end discrimination of all kinds. Begin by coming up with a family list of "nots." These are things you are committed to "not" doing. Your list could look like this:

1 **Not** entering into a conversation that makes fun of someone.
2 **Not** hiding our own uniqueness.
3 **Not** telling jokes or laughing at jokes about differences.
4 **Not** picking as friends only those who look or act just as we do.
5 **Not** allowing someone to sit alone at lunch because she looks or acts different.
6 **Not** trying to fit in with a group of kids by being just like them.
7 **Not** holding back when someone is being wronged.

- One way to get children to focus on other points of view is to ask, "How would you feel if . . . "

> *Once we got caught in a horrendous traffic jam on the*
> *way to a birthday party. One of my children suggested*
> *we turn around and go back home. I asked, "How*
> *would you feel if you were having a birthday party and*
> *your best friend didn't come?"* (Mother of four)

Encourage Forgiveness

If your child is having a problem forgiving someone, suggest
he write a letter of forgiveness to that person. Or he might picture her and visualize a conversation in which he tells her she is
forgiven. It may be more comfortable for him simply to send
love to the person who needs forgiving, from his heart directly
to his friend's heart. You can do this too. Think of ways you
can move past feelings of anger and bitterness. The event happened, now how can you move beyond it? It hurt and we can't
go back and make it go away. We can, however, choose to forgive and move on. We have the power to keep the negative
experience from filling us up. As one mother said to her child,
"Don't let anyone rent space in your head."

When a child is having difficulty forgiving, ask him what he
feels. He may feel weighed down by the burden of hurt feelings
or resentment; he may feel anger, or sadness, or confusion. Let
him know that he can do something about the feelings. He can
help the hurt by forgiving. The power of forgiveness is astounding. Suggest he ask God to help him forgive by picturing God's
love flowing through him as he takes the hurt feelings and
exchanges them for forgiveness.

The weight of resentment or anger can become overwhelming. Encourage children to assess routinely if they need to forgive anyone or anything. Illustrate the importance of releasing
our hurt feelings and forgiving by using the example of a backpack heavy with stones—each stone represents a person or act

we need to forgive. The pack weighs heavy until we forgive and throw out the stone. Once all the heavy stones are out, the pack is light and comfortable on our backs.

Some more ideas to help your children find their purpose and feel a connection to all living things include:

- Help your child become clear on her own beliefs and help her discover ways to live by them.

- Use the occasion of Memorial Day to tell your children about their ancestors. If possible visit their grave sites with flowers and stories. "This is your Uncle Ted's grave, he was a tremendous outdoorsman. He loved to hike and sleep in the woods. You love to be in nature too. Here is the grave of your great-grandmother Gretchen, she loved to play board games and to knit. You have her coloring and the same eye shape. You know your way around a Scrabble board pretty well." Help your children develop a passionate respect for the lives, ideas, and contributions of the past and to feel their own connection to those lives.

- Each day find a way to assure your child that he belongs and is needed.

- Give each child a purpose in the family that meshes with her abilities—then stay open for a change in interest or talent.

My daughter has a lovely singing voice. Often she will sing our evening prayer. The other children appreciate her unique talent. (Mother of three)

- Pay attention to times you suspect your child is feeling lonely and purposeless. Try this happy visualization. Have the child pretend that he is flying over the earth looking down at all the activity below. Suggest that he can see into homes and buildings and look at all the other children in the world who are alone in their homes: children who are singing, playing, drawing, dancing, working alone. Tell him he is connected to all these people—we are all parts of the huge web of life.

- Remember to treat your child with respect. Never do something to your child that you wouldn't like done to you.

Above all, trust and teach that all life is connected and has a reason for being. Believing this, often on faith alone, makes life better for both you and your child.

PARENTS' INSIGHT-BUILDING EXERCISE

Relax your body. Relax your mind. Breathe naturally. Take a mental walk with your child, in a familiar place. Maybe it is a local neighborhood. Maybe it is in a more distant setting—in the city, in the country. Design it to your wishes. Now as you walk along, notice who or what you meet. Why do you think that person or animal appears to you on your walk? How are you and your child touched by that person or animal? How do you relate to him? How does this touch your child? What do you offer this person or animal? What does your child offer her? Continue on your walk, easily and quietly. Watch for other elements that affect your walk—the sun's light, the temperature of the air. How do they feel to you and your child? What about flowers, trees, noises, other children? All are welcome here, all belong. Pay attention to the differences and similarities in things and people you see. Focus on how important and necessary each person and thing is to the others. Focus on the purpose of your presence there. As you return from this lovely walk, bring with you insights into ways you and your child can touch other living beings. Know that all life has a purpose and you and your child have a role in that purpose. Take with you the image of who and what you met on this walk, thanking the universe for illuminating and blessing you and your child.

Parents' Check-in Questions

- Have I been focused more on the material world than on the spiritual? How do I feel when I direct my energy in this way? How do I feel when I become more spiritually oriented? How does my child respond as I change direction?

- What new people am I bringing into my life and the lives of my children? What new experiences have we had to demonstrate my belief that all life has a purpose?

- Am I critical of others? Do I often blame others to protect myself? Are my children often critical of people?

- In what ways have I recently celebrated life and its many interrelated purposes?

- Did I see my reason for being in any of the day's situations? What about my child's purpose?

- In what ways did I point out life's purpose and value to my child today? Did this view help her understand or accept some person or situation more easily?

- How can I create a sense of community for my children?

- How can I help other children?

CHILDREN'S GUIDED JOURNEY

Pay attention to your breathing. Imagine as you breathe in, you are taking in shimmering white light. Each breath is allowing this magical white light to travel through your body to soothe and calm you. Your body is now filled with this light and you feel wonderful. You are relaxed and calm, ready for an imagination journey.

Now pretend that you have a set of "inside eyes." These eyes can see things that normal human eyes on the outside can't perceive. Put these powerful inside eyes anywhere you wish. Some children like to think of them as being on their heart and others like to think of one big inside eye placed right on their forehead between their other eyes. Wherever they are, your inside eyes can see perfectly and in a very special way. They can see the purpose for every living being.

Imagine now that you and your marvelous inside eyes are climbing into a beautiful pink bubble. The bubble is perfectly safe; it cannot fall or be punctured. You are safe too; you cannot fall from the bubble, and you are warm and cozy inside. You are rising slowly and beautifully inside your bubble to just a few feet above the ground. You can look down and see people and animals in a very unusual way; you can see the reason each being is there! Look at that beautiful puppy. Why is he with that little girl? So she will have a friend? Can you imagine that? Oh, look at the lady with the baby. She is soothing the baby with a quiet song. Do you see her purpose? Maybe to calm her tired child? Imagine you are floating over a playground. Who do you see? What do you imagine is the purpose of the children and grown-ups there? What about the birds, the trees, and the flowers?

You may continue in your beautiful bubble for as long as you wish, looking at the land, the animals, and the people below you with your magic eyes. You may notice the wind, the sun, the rain, or the snow. Let your magic eyes tell you what the purpose is of all those living creations. Stay as long as you wish, and when you are ready to end this journey, quietly float down to the ground in your bubble, step out of the opening in its side, and come back to this room. You may make this magical journey anytime you would like to look again with your magic eyes.

Children's Check-in Questions

- What is your purpose in our family?

- How do you feel closest to nature and all living things?

- How do you think our family might help others?

- How are you different from other kids your age? How are you similar to them?

Affirmations

ADULT

I see the goodness and purpose in others today.

I see my own goodness and purpose.

I am a part of all things.

Today I find ways to give of my time, talent, and money. I look with eagerness for expected and unexpected ways to give and to receive God's blessings.

Today I open myself to deeper understanding of my relationship with the universe and all that it contains.

CHILD

I am kind to all I meet today—they are kind to me.

All life has a purpose.

I am surrounded by love.

All things are beautiful.

I am one with all of life.

Principle 3
LISTEN TO YOUR CHILD

I attend angel classes each night when I go to sleep. There is a schoolroom with desks like the ones here except there are computers that we use to look at and into people to see how they are doing. There are special glasses we wear to learn to see the colors around people, but now I am good enough at it that I don't need the glasses. One time an angel named Mary took me out flying to meet the really big angel that holds the earth. They made me big too and let me hold the earth for a minute and it was really heavy. (Age seven)

Our workshops and discussions with adults and children have made it clear that many of us have profound spiritual experiences during our early years. Yet, over and over again people tell us they had no one with whom to share these magic moments. How can we as parents be aware of our children's unique spiritual dimension and create an environment that encourages and supports it? How can we enable our kids to stay connected to their visionary experiences so they don't leave them behind in childhood? Indeed, what are these children encountering? The trick is to be aware and accepting—*listen*—so that our children feel free to bring their inside feelings, visions, and perspectives out. Then we will learn from them what a spiritual experience can be. This nine-year-old was delighted to share her angel experience with us:

When it rains I sit under the roof and I sing songs with my angel and she keeps me busy and makes me feel good when I am lonesome for my mom. Sometimes when my dad can't find me I am under the roof singing songs with my angel. Her name is Marie. Her hair is long and black and her dress is long all the way to her feet. (Age nine)

And a child accepts as natural something most adults would miss:

Sometimes I'll just be sitting there and a light will flash by me. It's not the sunlight but more like spirit light. (Age seven)

A child's spiritual connection need not be a profound esoteric phenomenon. It is in the humblest moments of their daily lives that God reveals His face to children's hearts. It is their sharing of these moments that offer us, as parents, a deeper understanding of our children's inner lives. The toddler examining a leaf, reveling in the delights of nature, and joyfully sharing her discovery with us, is a spiritual moment. It could be as mundane as working out sibling rivalry:

I think that God is having one big experiment. He put two people who are very different in one house to live and He wants to see what happens. (Age seven, girl talking about her five-year-old sister and herself)

My youngest child told me he didn't like his brother—not what I want to hear. I swallowed hard and told him he didn't have to like him—it wasn't required. (Mother of two)

Our society emphasizes instructing children instead of listening to them. The instinctive spirituality of children needs to be nurtured, kept alive—not stamped out in favor of some practical reality. If instead of always managing our children's lives and observing them from the outside, we create a relationship based on their intuitive wisdom—and our own—we can develop a much richer kinship. Children are innately blessed with clear perception. By hearing, understanding, and honoring this treasure we enrich our children's world and the world into which we send them.

My daughter talks a lot about her baby sister who died. I used to feel uncomfortable about that kind of talk until I let go of my old ideas about mothering. Now, by listening to her and being receptive, I feel a new closeness and she shares so much more. (Mother of two)

Have you ever thought that your nighttime dream was something that had happened to you long, long ago? (Age six)

I wonder who I am sometimes. I mean who I really am. Am I just a girl—a plain, ordinary girl—or is it something bigger inside of me? If I look in the mirror and just stare at my own face I start to go outside of my body and get unattached to the outside me. (Age five)

WHAT ARE OUR CHILDREN SAYING?

It was summer when I was born, but it was cold then, I was sooo cold. (Age four)

Our children are telling us things we once knew but have pushed aside, forgotten. We, who have lived awhile, miss a great deal of what goes on around and within us. To children everything is new—they miss very little.

In heaven it is like a sunset and sunrise combined. The colors are all around you. It smells like roses and lots of fresh air. It's like when things are really good and my parents are happy with me. (Age five)

Children are observant, receptive, and aware, and we can share some of that awareness by listening to them. They have an innate gift of inner vision that, in their innocence, has not yet been lost. A child sees things in his world that we may not be able to see. Talking to a receptive adult about what he senses gives his world a voice and gives him a vocabulary for his rich experiences and esoteric ideas. Sometimes these theories are quite involved and often profound.

I know how you get to heaven. You go into the ocean, then you go up with the water to the clouds, then you can see your ancestors and God, then you fall back down to the earth in the raindrops. (Age six)

Angels practice flying in the lower sky. The upper sky is where they live and God has a place down the road. It is a castle—a beautiful castle filled with light. (Age four)

Up in heaven a person lies very still in one position. They have their thoughts stored in their minds and they do it their own way then like in dreaming. (Age five)

Listening validates children and gives them trust in themselves—they feel special and secure in their own uniqueness when they are heard. Listening lets kids know their feelings and ideas are okay, and gives them an opportunity to express their emotions instead of stuffing them away.

I feel lonely. (Age five, in a room full of other children)

Children have to know their feelings are important and they mustn't be shamed or disciplined when they express an emotion. Early disregard of one's feelings leads to denial of emotions and lack of communication later in life. To honor a child's feeling is to honor her spirit.

I just go up in my room and put my feet on my dressing table and I kick it sort of. I stop crying for a minute, then I fake cry, then I real cry, then my crying is done and I come downstairs. Sometimes this gets the anger out. (Age four)

I don't stop the crying. I don't really do anything because it is sort of nature. Like, I get this crying in my body and it's not exactly a real cry, it just comes to me. It's like a little groan but more like a cry, and then after that comes, it seems to get better. (Age seven)

Children feel as deeply as adults do, but they haven't yet
developed the vocabulary to share their emotions. What a
relief it must be when their parents comfortably accept their
expression of feelings. "I can see you are having a sad time and
crying seems to help you."

Listening can be one of the easiest things we do. It doesn't
take any special equipment, degrees, or muscles. Hear what
your children say. See what they see. Don't miss these opportunities. A child is free to share personal thoughts and experiences only when she is in an accepting environment.

*It feels good to cry—sometimes. I'm not really that sad,
but the crying feels good somehow.* (Age five)

*My father just doesn't understand me. He doesn't see
how much I've grown. I just avoid him now.*
(Age fourteen)

When children are "heard and seen," instead of "seen and
not heard," they will naturally express their feelings. Be a parent to whom your child can trust his feelings. A trusting child
feels free enough to share.

*When my sister is mad at me, when she says she
wishes she didn't have a little sister, the love part in
my heart for her is crossed off. When she is happy and
loves me again, it is uncrossed and not hard anymore.*
(Age four)

Listening encourages children to share future thoughts and
feelings with us. When people are heard they grow stronger,
they expand their ideas, they feel able to take emotional and
verbal risks because they have felt comfortable about their past

exchanges with the listener. This six-year-old has a sense about girls who hold their anger inside:

> *I think boys show their anger more than girls. I think girls know how to keep it in. I think it makes them sick and that is why they have that chemo where your hair falls out, because they've kept it all in.* (Age six)

We learn what goes on inside the minds and hearts of the people we love when we take the time to engage in focused listening. Often we are slowed down, and in quieting become aware of our own spirit. Truly listening to your child, in the moment, is the giving and receiving of love that enables your relationship to grow—the beautiful essence of your child is available to you when you pay attention.

> *Before I came here, I was a little angel with small wings. As it got closer to the time for me to come my wings started to disappear. I think that when I go back up there—where I was before—my wings will come back, but as bigger angel wings that will last forever.* (Age five)

Listening to children does a number of other marvelous things for both child and listener:

- By taking the time to hear your child's wishes and hopes you keep their dreams alive. You allow their unbounded creativity, their open-ended approach to life to flourish when you make honest listening a priority.

> *My son and I take a writing class together. Yesterday he wrote how lucky he was to have a mother who under-*

stands his feelings and listens to him. I felt so grateful. I've tried to make listening to him a priority and it has paid off. (Mother of one)

- We encourage children's problem-solving skills as we listen to their solutions to dilemmas and ideas on how things should be done. What do you think? What are your ideas?

I guess I shortchange my kids. Maybe if I spent more time finding out about them rather than just dictating what they can do and what they can have, we would all learn something. (Mother of four)

- When we listen, we bring forth and hold the sacredness of our children.

- We are reminded to stay in the moment, give from our hearts, go beyond self-imposed limitations, and open to a more expansive universe.

- The vital decision to listen can dissolve any distance between us and our children. When we listen we accept our child's gift of ideas, stories, experiences.

WAYS WE CAN LISTEN

I am so guilty of not being "fully present" and I hate when I do that to the kids. (Father of two)

Listening to children means focusing on them completely, if only for a few moments. Give them your full attention. How about putting aside some task for just two minutes to hear about the angel dream Lia had or the tale of nighttime monsters from Ben? You don't need to "fix" the nightmare—just be a safe listener. Remain genuine and supportive and your listening will be effective. One four-year-old became frustrated with his busy mother and proclaimed, "Will you listen to me with the front of your face?"

> *When you have lots of kids, and work full-time besides, it's hard to spend separate time with each child every day. What about being together each night and special time on the weekends? Is that okay?* (Mother of four)

It is not always possible to stop our lives for a child at the exact moment she requests it. But can you establish a "listening time" every day, or every other day, when you make yourself available? "I can't stop now or I'll be late for work, but I'd love to listen tonight when we have our walk." Designate certain "listening places": a cozy chair, in bed after stories, sitting on the front steps. Establish specific times your child can count on being listened to: Saturday-morning walks, bathtime, waiting for the school bus. If you're too busy to listen when your child wants to talk you can always say, "We'll talk about it when we walk the dog," or the time you have chosen to be your listening time.

Many families find the quiet time before children fall asleep to be special listening time. You can call it "pillow talk" for your young child and something else for the child who has gone beyond this. Lights are out, things are quiet, and the parent is available. This routine gives the child the assurance that he can always talk to Mom or Dad "tonight at pillow talk." It helps if the parent bites his tongue and waits for whatever the child wishes to discuss instead of opening with "So, how was school today?"

Ever since I have been having a pillow talk with my two girls our nighttime routine is dragged out a bit, but it's definitely worth it. When I started, all I could think of was the dinner dishes waiting to be washed downstairs, the work I had brought home from the office, and if I was giving this child more time than the other. Now I relax, slip off my shoes, and breathe . . . my daughters snuggle up and even if the talk is mundane we feel reconnected after our busy days. (Mother of two)

Mommy, are you crabby tonight? When you're crabby you don't seem as cozy to me. (Age six, at pillow talk)

Daddy, when I'm all growed up and have to leave this house, can I have one last look around?

Of course, darling, you can just stay right here always.

Well, how about if I get to decide?

That's good. I love you, Beth.

What's love mean, Daddy?

It means you're special, I cherish you.

I love you, Daddy! (Age four, with her father at pillow talk)

Listen to your child as if he is a national hero. Listen as if she is a spiritual prophet. Listen as if he is your boss. Listen as if she came down from Mars. Listen as if he holds the future of the world stored in his mind. Try for one minute giving her the attention you would give the people mentioned above. Listen with respect and he will be comfortable expressing his thoughts—both good and bad. Through this listening will come conversation. Through conversation will come questions. Through questions will come understanding, philosophy, belief in and trust of spirit.

Attend to the silences, to the unspoken messages your child gives you. Listening means being attentive to behavior as well as words. Perhaps your child doesn't have the words to describe her feelings or isn't clear about what she feels. Be aware of the nonverbal ways children ask you to listen. Is David complaining of a stomachache every morning before school? Is Karen biting her fingernails again? What about Emily's thumb sucking? Is Jackie getting into trouble at school? Children, like grown-ups, channel their unspoken anxieties into their bodies. Listen to these important clues. What are the messages your children are trying to send? Don't forget to pay attention to the "throwaway" statements your child makes. Write them down to explore later if you haven't the time when they are said. A somber five-year-old shed some light on his behavior with this statement, muttered as he was apologizing for spilling a glass of milk:

> *Life's a big batch of sorries, good-byes, shaking hands, and new people.*

Respect Children's Intuition

Part of listening to our children is honoring their intuition. Children can often feel the energy, moods, and intentions of others. They don't always have the vocabulary to describe what they are sensing, but if you listen closely and take the time to understand their responses you can help them maintain their intuitive gift. Mimi and her nine-year-old daughter had an errand in a local jewelry store. When they left, Whitney gulped a big breath of fresh air and said, "It was more than stuffy in there, Mom, it felt heavy. That lady wanted you to spend more money and I felt a heavy lump in my stomach."

Honor your child's divine nature and spiritual perspective and you will be clued into a world without walls. Giving your child permission to trust his intuitive voice validates his internal wisdom and helps him to access this knowing. We should applaud our children when they follow through on their intuition with appropriate action. More than anything children need to have the confidence to rely on their gut feelings rather than give in to outside pressures. A four-year-old was playing at a friend's house when the two little girls slipped out the back door and into the woods to explore:

> *I felt all hot and prickly, even my breath, and I knew that we were getting too far away, so I used my words with Alice about going back to her house. She didn't want to and called me a fraidy cat but my body told me to go back toward the house.* (Age four)

Be prepared to support your child when he takes his vision into the "real world." Not everyone has chosen to stay open to spirit and so may not understand. Home needs to remain a safe haven for imagination, expression, and exploration. It's not always easy to affirm and support your child when she follows her intuition and acts on her inner voice, but by doing so you give her a precious gift and a powerful lifelong tool. So empower your children to trust their gut feelings and remind them to access their inner wisdom, then applaud when they follow through with appropriate action.

> *My daughter is a sensitive and bright eight-year-old. She doesn't like to watch television or movies, as the suspense and violence cause her anxiety. Her class was planning to watch an adventure video when they were*

*studying panda bears. It was a PG movie and suppos-
edly revolved around the adventures of a panda bear.
My daughter worried about being required to watch
such a film. When the day arrived she spoke to her
teacher, a hard thing for this shy girl, and asked if she
could be excused from the movie and read her book in
the hall. The teacher, wouldn't allow it, and my daughter had to watch an hour of the film. She came home in
tears and told of a father being shot and mistreatment
of the panda. "Please," she begged, "talk to my teacher
so I don't have to watch the final hour tomorrow." I
called the teacher, and when I explained that my husband and I supported our daughter's choice she belit-
tled me and my daughter, saying, "I can't believe she
can't handle a little adventure." She did finally allow
my daughter to be excused from the ending of the
video.* (Mother of two)

This mother is doing her daughter a great service by backing
up her feelings. This positive parental response will enable the
child to continue to be bold and speak up when another
uncomfortable situation arises. She knows what her comfort
zone is, and when her spirit is being compromised. Listen,
empower, validate, no matter how you anticipate *you* will be
regarded. After all, what's more important, what people think
of you or how your child's spirit is affected?

*My daughter wrote a beautiful story about her angel.
She brought it into school—beaming with pride. That
afternoon she came home and burst into tears. Her
teacher had told the class that Sherry's story was a perfect example of what is not real. She's in first grade and
they happen to be talking about what is real and what*

is fantasy. Sherry's angel is very real to her. We have created an angel book for Sherry to write about her angel free from the probing eyes of a teacher or doubting adult. (Mother of four)

Our children can often become our teachers. They offer simple, clear intuition about people and situations. When they have strong feelings we often assume it is a power issue. Instead we can honor the child's feelings, and in so doing reinforce their intuitive trust. "It just doesn't feel right, Mama," is a signal to go deeper and help your child determine why.

It took my husband and me about six years before we recognized our son as a very old soul who had come to awaken us on our journey. He is now nine and teases us about how long it took us to wake up. (Mother of one)

Make it a habit to listen to your own intuition. One mother of four grown children says the only mistake she made in raising her children was following the advice of someone else and not trusting her gut feelings. It's great to explore resources from experts and friends and to gather parenting techniques and advice, but remember to modify and filter these ideas through your own inner guidance. You must be true to your intuition when you parent.

I began to see subtle changes in my kids as they spent more time in public school—changes I didn't like. They were bored, cranky, competitive, and materialistic—not the children I knew them to be. My friends told me all kids are like this at these ages. My gut told me, "No, there is something else here." I started to read more about home schooling. It sounded right to me. I tried it

for a year, even though my parents did not support me.
They didn't think it was the right thing to do. It was a
wonderful choice. I got my real children back. I've been
home schooling for six years now and my four children
are happy, socially adjusted, and scored very well in all
the state achievement tests. I followed my intuition
even when others thought I was crazy. (Mother of four)

You can listen to your child when you share secrets and
really keep them. Play imaginary games of What If? "What if I
were very little and you were very big?" "What if we could
fly?" "What if we lived closer to Grandpa?" "What if you
were in charge of the world?" This is great for children of all
ages, just adjust the questions to fit the age. (Use the Check-In
Questions at the end of each chapter as a start.) Listen without
the worry that you have to supply all the answers—and
remember, don't interrupt.

It seems like grown-ups do all the talking and even when
it's my turn they still talk . . . talk . . . talk . . . (Age four)

Grown-ups always talk to each other and never talk to
me. (Age five)

Make sure you have someone to talk to—someone who listens to you. It's too much to expect our children to become our
confidants on deeply personal issues or worries that may be
frightening to them. We need a friend, a parent, a sister, a minister, a therapist, a journal, a tape recorder, a healer to play
that integral role. To be good listeners we need someone to listen to us—it supports our spirit. It's okay for you to take time
to nourish your soul; in fact it's essential. Listen to yourself,
your body, your aches and pains, your need for quiet.

Remember that spirituality is in each moment—each day. Spirit lives in the mortgage and the meals, the ins and outs of our days, the worries and celebrations. This is it! Take the opportunity each day to listen respectfully to yourself and your children. Weave listening time into the routine of your family life.

Mealtime Conversations

Mealtimes provide an opportunity for adults and children to talk about the day. The experience of sitting around a table with family is a soulful memory for many of us. Think about kitchen or dining room tables you have known. Recall the conversations that took place there. Where does your family eat meals now? Take the time to create a sense of peace at mealtimes. Light candles if you really want some soulful talks, especially from teenagers. Try making mealtimes sacred times— even if you can do so only once a week. Some busy families can't arrange to eat the evening meal together, so celebrate with a Sunday morning breakfast that no one misses. It's not so important what foods are prepared, but rather what attitudes are brought to the table and how much listening goes on.

We try to have dinner together at least three times a week. It's tough to do, but we encourage conversation between the children. I try not to be critical of manners and instead let the children direct the conversation. (Father of three)

Each Sunday we drag out the linen tablecloth and eat in the dining room. The kids take turns saying grace. I'm always moved at their sincere words of prayer. (Mother of three)

Listen to Your Child's Unique Prayers

Ask your child to write some prayers that the whole family can use. These are prayers in her own words from her own soul. Some suggestions to get her started are: "Write a prayer for our Mother Earth." "If you could write a magic chant to help our family, what would it be?" "Write a prayer for the animals of the world." "What about a special prayer or magical saying to protect you when you are scared or lonely?" Respect her personal prayers, and if she is comfortable having you incorporate them into your family's prayer time, do so.

Angel be with me today.
Help me in all I do and say.
Please guide me on my way.
Take my worries away. (Age six)

Dear Mary,
Please let it be a better world for me. Some days I wish
I could just sleep all day. (Age five)

Thank you for the world, God. Thank you for the fall
leaves to jump in. (Age nine)

Dear God,
Thank you for this day. Help us to help one another
and to love and respect one another. Help us to be
open and caring and let the angels sing to us. God help
us to do what is right. Amen! (Age nine)

Sometimes listening prayers can be the best tonic—when your child gets quiet and listens to the thoughts God delivers directly to him.

*I don't always pray at night. I mean, not like real pray.
Instead I get quiet and ask God to talk to me. That is
when I get the best ideas and stuff. It is kinda like God
shares these good plans with me on how to sort things
out.* (Age eleven)

Some other techniques for how we can listen:

- Make dates for one-on-one time with your children. This
  should be time for talking and listening, not a movie or a
  soccer game. Set aside your calendar so you are truly free
  to listen. Of course it won't always be spiritual gems
  rolling off his lips—but without some junk you won't get
  the jewels.

*We had chicken nuggets for lunch today. They were
burnt. Mawmaw said she really liked heaven.* (Age five,
reporting on kindergarten lunch and her recently deceased
grandmother's words to her)

- Teach less—listen more!

- Set up specific discussion themes and times. For example,
  on Sunday evenings you could discuss your child's feelings
  about the upcoming week. Does he have worries? Is she
  anxious? Is there an exciting event coming up? What are
  her expectations? One night a week could be family prayer
  group when you talk together to God.

- Talk about your inside thoughts—when appropriate. If you
  are comfortable and free with yourself your children will
  feel safe to be open. When you are angry, sad, lonely,
  excited, thrilled, proud, ashamed, embarrassed, frightened,

or worried, it's all right to say so. When you have a spiritual experience, share it with your child. This sharing of your humanness and spirituality gives him permission to be human and spiritual as well, and to share himself with you.

• Pay attention to the people around your children, such as caregivers, friends, and teachers. Talk to your kids about these people, then listen carefully to what they say.

Keep a journal with children who are old enough to write. You might call it the "family journal." You can write about your feelings, your day, your thoughts, then pass it along to your children so they may add their words. It is a safe sharing place. One eight-year-old passed the family journal back to her father with the following notation:

I am happy and a little sad. It is my first time at Anna's house for a sleep-over. I had a boring day at school. I wish Midnight [child's cat] was here. I miss my house a bit. It is a pretty good day. (Age eight)

Dad was able to listen to his daughter's first sleep-over experience in her own words at the time of the experience. He was privy to inside information that helped him better understand his daughter and made her feel as if she were sharing this special time with her dad.

Another child shared her deepest dislike in her family's journal.

Please don't use a harsh voice with Elizabeth. It hurts her. From Elizabeth to my family. (Age six)

The family journal can help when there are things that are difficult to talk about. The reader can listen to worries, struggles, or problems. The journal is a safe place, with no limits, where the truth can be told. You may find that each child wants her own journal to correspond with Mom or Dad privately, or that the journal isn't written in for weeks on end. Use it for your family in a way that facilitates honest and open communication.

- Car trips are wonderful opportunities to listen to your children. You can overhear them talking with their friends, often very differently from their family conversations. Many parents choose to drive their children to school just to have the alone time in the car to communicate.

I want so much for my daughter to talk to me about her life and it seems like the only time we're together is in the car. I'm trying to make better use of that time by turning off the radio and listening to her. (Mother of one)

- Read books with your child. In the Appendix we have listed some books that have lovely spiritual messages. Ask your child what he thinks about the story. How would he like it to end? What would he change? How does she feel about the people in the story? Read, then listen to the child's response.

- Family meetings are a great way for each member of the family to be heard. Set aside a specific time each week, or month, and use this forum to talk about family issues. Members can discuss what affects the family, such as upcoming vacations, chores, rules, or even what movie to see on Saturday night. In these meetings everyone needs to be free to talk about his feelings and to know what's said will remain within the family.

Family meetings help me tell my family what's bothering me or what felt good. It really helps me learn how to talk to my parents other times, not just during family meetings. Before we did family meetings I wasn't able to talk it out. Now I am able to get my words out about worries or things that are good. (Age eight)

• Family meetings, no matter how frequently you can arrange to have them, are worth the effort. Children have a structured forum in which to be heard. Begin with a prayer or a moment of silence. Many families begin their meetings by having each person thank other family members for one kindness that they have shown over the course of the past week or by giving each member a compliment. Powerful stuff to hear your sibling say:

Thanks for sitting with me on the bus Monday, Mark. I felt a lot better about going to school. (Age seven)

Tim, thanks for knocking before you came in my room. (Age eleven)

Or to hear your mother thanking you in front of everyone else for setting the table without being reminded.

If we had such a thing as family meetings when I was little, maybe I would have been able to get closer to my

siblings. There were five of us and it was always chaos around our house. We never talked about anything. How I would have loved to be in on things like planning trips or even what kind of food I would like from the grocery store. It would have been great to have had an opportunity to talk with my family about our life as we were living it! I am trying to do things differently with my kids. They are definitely part of the process.
(Mother of two)

- Play with your child and notice the stories he tells. Play without trying to teach your child something. Play on her terms. Draw and paint and observe the messages of the pictures your child creates.

My five-year-old drew a picture of her family. It was incredible. She drew her sister much taller than she actually is; they are the same size. She also colored her sister in vivid colors with a red shirt, pink hat, and bright pants. They were holding hands. My wife and I were stick figures on the other side of the page in black crayon. I'm not an art therapist, but I sure know who is the strong influence in her life. (Father of two)

- Wish upon a star with your child. Listen to his wish.

- Ask your child to make a list of all the things he wants to know more about. You may be very surprised. Follow through on this information and provide her with materials, books, teachers if appropriate, opportunities to explore her interests. Encouraging your child's natural inquisitiveness about all things nourishes her soul.

There is so much I want to learn this summer. How to do handstands, how to swim across the pool, all about Atlantis, the Titanic, *colonial times, St. Francis's life, how to whistle and blow bubbles with my gum.* (Age six)

• Long or short walks together give families a gentle relaxing time for talking and listening. Walks are so simple and yet so overlooked. We can be all "ears" on walks—no phones, faxes, pagers, or visitors to interrupt us. Walking can help us sort things out, thoughts and ideas seem to flow. Allow the rhythm of the walking to lull you into synch with your child. Don't resist a walk—slow down and head out. Stretch your legs and your spirits.

• If you sense there is something going on in your child's life that is making her unhappy or worried, ask her about it. Select the time and the tone, but make it a priority. Then perhaps you can help her strategize a resolution. Come up with three specific things that can be done to make the situation better. As a result of this discussion she might be able to visualize, or picture, a solution. Maybe you decide to compose a prayer together for insight into the problem or lead her in a Guided Journey where insight is gained from a wishing well full of answers. She can dip her cup in and read the sage words she has pulled out.

• Often your child will talk to a neighbor or friend instead of directly to you. Are there enough of these removed "listeners" in your child's life? Can you be a receiving adult for a child other than your own?

• Perhaps you are open and available to listen to your child but feel there is more that you need to know. Try talking directly to your child's soul, guardian angel, or spirit. Get quiet and mentally ask if there is something you need to be aware of. You can ask for a picture or message that will help you parent in a deeper way. Listen to the thoughts that come.

Children are wise! You may want to post the following words to remind you of the importance of listening:

Out of the mouths of infants and children your majesty is praised above the heavens. —Psalm 8:2

PARENTS' INSIGHT-BUILDING EXERCISE

Think of a time when you were heard as a child. Who listened? How did it feel to be heard? What did you say that was acknowledged? How does that experience live with you today? Now think back to a time when you were there to listen to your child. What was that like? Why were you available to listen, had you made the time, was your child demanding you stop and listen? What did you hear? How did your child react when you listened?

Ask for guidance this week on how best to hear your children's needs. Ask for divine insight into ways you can help give your child's feelings a voice. Now let go and remain open to receiving insight and guidance. Listen to the subtle ways your inner wisdom is revealed. Trust your ideas and insights; *you* are wise.

Parents' Check-in Questions

• Did I set up a specific time to be with my child this week? Did I listen during that time?

- What were my feelings when I listened? Was I anxious about the many things on my mind, or did I let go and focus only on my child in the moment?

- If my child could remember one thing I said to her today, what would it be?

- What would I like it to be?

- Who listens to me?

CHILDREN'S GUIDED JOURNEY

Sit or lie down with your spine straight and long. Close your eyes. Take a nice deep breath and relax your body. Another deep breath and let go—relax. Breathe deeply and let your thoughts just float away. Allow your busy mind to slow down and become quiet and peaceful. Think about your breath moving slowly in and out of your body. Breathe in, and as you breathe out imagine all the tension and worry is flowing out of your body with the breath.

Now picture a beautiful light shining down on your head. This light feels warm and comfortable. What color is the light? Feel the light entering your body through the top of your head. Imagine this soft light flowing through your body. It warms your head, your face, and now your neck and your shoulders. The light travels down your arms into your fingers. It stops in your stomach. Feel this soothing light warming your tummy. Imagine that this is where you have a connection to the entire universe, to your deeper wisdom, to God. Any time you relax your body and your mind and come to this deep, quiet place, you are in touch with your intuition. You can ask for guidance or for information. You can ask about a problem or a worry you are having. Ask for a feeling of what you should do or what you should know. What do you want to say to God? Ask it now. Then get quiet and listen. *Listen!* Hear the subtle answer or notion as an idea or an image going gently through your mind. You may not get an answer right away, but one will come to you in the near future. Just trust this *gut* feeling is being sent to you from a deep safe place. If you aren't sure what you've heard, ask again. This is a wonderful place to come when you aren't sure about a situation, need help solving a problem, or just want to connect with your intuition.

Take another deep breath in—and out. When you feel ready, come back to the room.

Children's Check-in Questions

- When do you feel the happiest?

- What do you like best that we do together?

- What do you want to say to me right now?

- When is your favorite time to talk to me? What do you like to talk about?

- Is there anything you would like to know about or want to ask me?

- Do you trust God? Do you trust me?

Affirmations

ADULT

I listen to and honor my child's feelings and experiences.

I make time each day to be available to my child.

I pay attention to my child's silences.

I listen to God's voice.

CHILD

I use my words to say how I'm feeling.

I trust my intuition, my inside voice.

I speak up and put my inside voice into action.

I listen to God's voice.

WORDS ARE IMPORTANT, USE THEM WITH CARE

When my mom says, "Good job, you really tried," I feel so nice because I did try! (Age five)

The last chapter was about listening, the act of receiving words. Now we focus on the art of sending words. The differences are subtle but important. Words have marvelous powers—they can cast wonderful spells. Once a young child fully absorbs the meaning of a word he is under its magic. Say the word "mother" to a child and all kinds of associations and meanings will come pouring out. What happens to you when you hear the word "cozy"? How about "failure"? Words have the power to make a child feel worthy or wrong, complete or lacking, delighted or dejected. "Yes" and "no," spoken by her parent, can influence the course of a child's day, week, life. Just as words have the power to limit, so too do they have the power to lift the child beyond the ordinary and into the flow of God's miracles. Words offered in prayer, affirmation, and celebration are always heard and supported by a loving God.

Words, as well as deeds, are a big part of the message you

give a child. When you speak positively, your child hears a positive message about the world. What the child hears and repeats about herself will help determine her self-worth.

Thoughts also fall under this principle, because thoughts are words we say to ourselves. You can help turn your child's thoughts into constructive "self-talk."

One reason we are given the gift of words is to communicate our feelings to those we love. When we look at words as blessings we will be more careful how we dole them out. The old saying "Think before you speak" has great value. Be accountable for your words—they are under your control.

USING WORDS WITH CARE

Kind words are the music of the world. They have a power which seems to be beyond natural causes, as if they were some angel's song which had lost its way and come to earth. (Frederick William Faber)

Affirming words nourish a child's soul—he hears and believes. Positive words can give hope and open possibilities for both the speaker and the receiver.

The singing child hears her mother say, "When you sing in the mornings it starts my day so beautifully. Your voice makes me happy." The child's spirit soars and she sings again.

Words—round musical notes that bolster the spirit. Words—winged thoughts that fly out of the mouth and wedge themselves firmly in the mind of the receiver. Words can clobber the spirit—the spontaneity—the joy—the soul. "Stop making that awful noise" puts a lid on a child's musical moment.

Our words can inspire or cut our children to the quick. Do your words and tone tell your child that he is a burden and a chore, or do they build him up and assure him of his sacredness?

My dad always tells me that his life got better after I was born, that I am his lucky charm. That makes me feel so special, like he really wanted a girl like me. (Age six)

Words are a window to the soul. Through your child's words you can glance at her inner world. Pay attention. What is she saying? Is that what she really means? She may need you to help her put her feelings into words.

I have these feelings sometimes. My mom says, "What are you feeling?" but I'm not sure. I don't know how to say what I am feeling. There are many of those times. (Age five)

- Ideas come to life when they are put into words. Someone else knows what you are thinking, feeling, exploring, understanding when you communicate. Questions can be answered, inventions can begin, games can start, friendships can grow, wisdom can be shared, spirits can be enriched when children express their ideas.

- We illustrate our individuality with our words. Children see the world differently from adults, and by their words they share their unique view.

In heaven, trash smells like a skunk. (Age five)

- Positive words are contagious. Never underestimate the power of a kind word and a little recognition.

A few days ago, I took my three children to a fast-food restaurant in the middle of chores and errands. We said our silent prayers at the table before eating, and were talking, as usual, during our meal. A woman stopped at our table and said, "Your children are so well-behaved, and I couldn't help but notice their bowed heads before they ate. I know it's hard work, but I wish every parent knew that the most important thing they can do for the future is to raise their children well." Later in the day my kids commented on how happy I was, and I realized it was because of the lady. It must be contagious, because I found myself complimenting the grocery packer for doing a good job of bagging my food, and I think he stood a little taller. (Mother of three)

Children can be reminded to use their words with care. Language is one of the incredible aspects of being human, and it is important that kids treat this tool with reverence. Words can help and hinder, can be used to communicate important thoughts, and can shake us off balance. Children become more thoughtful about communicating when they are shown how to say what they mean, take responsibility for their words, and learn the difference between their wants and needs.

All words start with a picture or a feeling of what we want to say. Help your children to pause before they speak to become clear on what it is they wish to communicate. It takes a lot of wisdom to know what to say and when to say it. Words are gifts and we all need gentle reminders to give them with thought.

WAYS TO USE WORDS WITH CARE

Pay attention to the power words have on your children. It's always a boost for kids to know what you—almighty parent— are thinking about them. Assess your child's positive qualities, then let him know what you think. Why shouldn't your three-year-old know that she is beautiful with apple-red cheeks or your ten-year-old hear that he is a quick learner? Let kids "overhear" you use positive statements about them. Somehow it is much more powerful to hear, "Let me ask Lynn about decorating the living room, she is so good with color," than "Lynn, what color do you think we should paint the living room?" The same goes when we pass along words of praise or compliments. Kids need to hear how great they are directly from you, but they also need the message indirectly, from other people, through you. It seems to stick better. When you relay a positive remark that someone else has made, it lodges in a child's mind and adds a glimmer to her heart. You might even write the positive words on index cards and keep them in a "compliment box." Your child can pull out nourishing words when he needs a boost.

Ted sure knows how to climb a rope ladder. He has great balance. (Mr. Mac, gym teacher, January 9)

The written word has a tremendous impact on us. It is empowering for a child to put feelings or ideas into writing. Encourage your child to keep a journal. Children of all ages can use their words to express feelings and thoughts in a private and confidential diary; they can practice communication free from judgment, ridicule, or failure. Children can relax with their journals and get their feelings out on paper without having to analyze or edit the work. Writing without the anxiety of external scrutiny can open up the child's innate intuition and creativity. Kids are free to explore their personal values, preferences, desires, spiritual connections, and talents in their own journals. If your child doesn't know how to begin, here are some ideas:

Write about all the things that make you feel happy.

Write a poem that starts with "Joy is . . . "

Write about something that makes you frightened.

Write what you do when you feel scared.

Write a poem that starts with "Fear is . . . "

Write about quiet.

How do you feel when you have quiet in your life?

When is it quiet?

Draw the first thing that comes to your mind. Don't worry about making pretty pictures—just let your marker or pencil free to draw whatever comes.

Write about your drawing.

Write about what you dislike at school.

Write about what you value most in life: courage, honesty, independence, respect for the earth, freedom, equality. Then write your ideas for standing up for these beliefs.

Write about what you need in life to feel good.

Write about the most wonderful experience or experiences of your life.

Write a poem about your pets.

Write a poem about your fantasy pets.

Write about what makes you angry.

Write about what makes you cry.

Write about our earth.

Write a poem that begins with "God is . . . "

Write a letter to someone you love who has died.

Write a poem about an angel who watches over you.

Write a letter to your mom or dad. You can choose to send it or not.

Write about your greatest blessings.

Write about your greatest sadness.

Write a poem that begins or ends with "I am grateful for . . . "

Write about your wishes.

Create a cartoon character that represents you.

Encourage your child to write or tell her stories. No matter how awkward the words, they reveal the child's inner life. Stories can become a road map to the soul. Write your young child's narrative as he speaks. Ask your older child to compose the story of her life. Let her know it's okay to "waste" tons and tons of paper when she is writing. It's also okay to make mistakes and to stare off into space and let the images and ideas float into her head. Don't judge your child's writing, but if she asks, help her discover new words and new ways of telling her tale. Sometimes stories are a way for kids to deliver the words they might otherwise leave unsaid. Often, deep spiritual themes expressed in unique and individual ways show up in children's stories. Mimi's daughter explored another time and another aspect of herself through her writing.

My daughter began writing about a tribe of people she calls the Savapes when she was seven years old. She wrote as if it were a diary entry from a Savape girl. The format and the content were her own idea. She continues to write about this imaginary tribe of people who heal each other with ordinary stones and rocks, who ask permission of the plants and animals before using them for food or medicine, and who live on the shore of a bountiful ocean. The young Savape girl has become her alter ego, and the ongoing diary entries have become rich, detailed accounts of a time and place full of spiritual meaning.

Give your child enticing topics to get him started. Ask him to write about how the world began. Together you can explore the many creation stories in various cultures. According to Hopi legend, Spider Woman sang the world into existence a word at a time. Ethiopians believe God created both the world and Himself by saying His own name. According to the New Testament, "In the beginning there was the word." What story can your child write—from her divine creativity—about the beginning of the world? Maybe he could write about a wise being who knows all of life's answers, a particular saint, a problem and how to resolve it, a unicorn who speaks magical words. Perhaps she could invent words that cast spells or words that change the world, or he might write about a third grader who had a bad day. See if you don't see a little of the hurt from your third grader's life leak into the story.

It can be fun to use "story starters" if your child needs a spark to get her writing going. Mimi gave the following story starter to a class of first graders: "Flower moon on Seven Star Lane . . ." One seven-year-old wrote: "She fancied herself a shepherdess of the stars, born from angels, brought to earth by the clouds." This young writer created a rich beginning to what became a radiant story.

Create a story box from a basket or shoe box and fill it with words such as "God," "angel," "love," "helping," "moon," "scary," "dark," "compassion," "eternity," "freedom," "forbidden," "caring," "order," "harmony," "surprise." Your child can select a few words and create his own story.

Sometimes the horse angel flies over to the moon and gives the grasshoppers holding it with their legs a rest. He holds up the moon on his wings, but sometimes he is so busy he flies away with the moon and forgets it's there. That's why we can't see it sometimes. It's called a blue moon. (Age four)

Write a story with your child. Create a quiet time and special place where you can explore writing cooperatively. Often bathtime is the perfect opportunity to write the stories your young, relaxed child narrates. As children grow older the roles might switch:

My daughter always wants to work on stories together. I love the idea but I work all day and come home beat. We have found something that works well for us. After dinner I soak in a bubble bath while she reads me what we have written so far. I can focus on the story because I am her captive and I'm finally relaxing after a crazy day. It's great for her to practice her printing, and we really work collaboratively. Inevitably the stories have a moral or a spiritual thread to them, and that comes from her. I just follow her lead. We are always proud of the end result and read it to our family. (Mother of three)

If your busy week doesn't allow writing with your child, perhaps you can post ongoing stories somewhere convenient.

You each may add to the story when you wish. Writing together empowers a child. It blurs the line between expert and amateur and unites you in a creative merging of words. Write about topics that interest your both. Exploring together through writing can become a spiritual adventure.

How about creating a "family story night"? Begin by telling a story from your own childhood experiences: "When I was a little girl I loved to . . ." Children relish these family stories; it gives them a sense of belonging and history. Maybe a themed story night would be fun. You select the theme—sharing, courage, the nighttime sky, nature sprites—and encourage everyone to come up with a story line to share that incorporates that theme. Young children might like to be given a specific character to get them started with their tale—Willie the Worried Whale, Gammy the Greedy Gazelle, Zelda the Zipper-Lipped Zebra.

Stage a play your child writes or read it aloud as a family. Family play readings can be memorable, soulful times, especially when the words are written by your child. Remember not to judge the play or try to act as the director. Enjoy being together to bring your child's words to life.

Poetry

Play with luscious words that resonate with your spirit. Don't forget how much kids love to read and write poems. Write poetry together. When children are too young to write, you can become the scribe for their words. One five-year-old dictated her first poem:

My angel makes me feel so dear.
I know that she is always near.
She keeps me warm with all her love.

She cradles me from up above.
I wish that I could see her face.
I trust in her forever grace. (Age five)

The child's father couldn't believe his daughter had written this with no prompting. "I had no idea she knew what grace is!" he remarked. Another young child wrote:

When I see across the sea
I always see about me. (Age five)

Using Poem Magnets is a wonderful way for children to express themselves. These magnetic words are sold in many toy stores and mail-order catalogs. A nine-year-old boy created this poem with magnets on the side of his refrigerator:

I love and shine
through light moments
and play in power. (Age nine)

Other magnet poems created by kids:

Peace goes around
One butterfly upon the sun. (Age six)

Silent moon
Flower sun
Music rain
Boy am I fun. (Age five)

Make a book of your family's poetry or start a collection of published favorites. Read poetry that wasn't necessarily written for kids. You will be surprised how many "grown-up" words kids understand. Teach your child this poem:

> If I thought that a word of mine
> Perhaps unkind and untrue,
> Would leave its trace on a loved one's face,
> I'd never speak it—
> Would you?
> If I thought that a smile of mine
> Might linger the whole day through
> And lighten some heart with a heavier part,
> I'd not withhold it—
> Would you? (Anonymous)

Discuss what words would look like splattered on someone's face. Quite an image.

Try writing a nature haiku with your child. These seventeen-syllable poems are arranged in three lines of five, seven, and five syllables and are meant to be a simple reflection on one event happening *now*—the curl of the shell, the bird's soaring flight, the wavering blade of grass. Pack up a notebook and pencil and set out to sketch nature through this simple word structure. Children's pure, in-the-moment awareness lends itself perfectly to the way of haiku.

> brown dirt all around
> green grass grows among the ground
> blue sky up up high. (Age six)

> soft light reflection
> dances around the stone walk
> goes through the green trees. (Age seven)

Words Can Help Your Child Recognize His Own Potential

A fun way for your child to use words to bolster his sense of self is to make a word collage. Ask him to go through the dictionary and pick out words he would like to describe himself—brave, caring, helpful, strong, giving, kind, peaceful, loving, fun, clever, protecting. He can then glue the words on a poster to hang on his wall, or write them on colored squares of paper and glue the squares onto a picture frame that holds a photograph of him. Or he might make a mobile and allow these empowering words to dangle from the ceiling, with his photograph hanging in the middle of the mobile.

Ask your children what words might describe their lives ten years from now. This is an interesting exercise for all of us. Close your eyes and picture yourself in ten years. What are you doing, what have you achieved, what words describe how you are feeling? Jot down the images that come to you. A six-year-old tried this exercise and happily opened her eyes to report, "I am sixteen and love me and life." She drew a picture of the word "yes."

Sit down with your child, with paper, pencils, and some free time. Brainstorm ideas of how to feel close to God. List the ideas as they come to you and ask your child to do the same. Don't edit or stop the flow, just write what comes naturally—then write ten more ideas. Think of it as dumping ideas into a list form. Try this when you need ideas or inspiration about anything. Somehow we tap into our creativity by forcing ourselves to get the words out. When your child needs to come up with ideas for a report or a story, she can use this list technique. Words, jotted down as they come to mind, can reveal some wonderful solutions and unlock our divine creative flow.

Words are powerful parenting tools. Don't forget to use

them to show children how much they are cherished. Write poems, stories, letters, and songs to tell them how much they are treasured.

My mom sings me a special song each night before I go to sleep. It is all about me, and she told me she sang it to me even before I was born. (Age six)

Capture Her Childhood with Words

Grab your journal before you go to sleep at night and jot down five images of your child from the day. When you go back and read these simple, short entries years from now, your memory will be stimulated and deliver simple snapshots of your child. A few words can evoke powerful images. After all, spiritual parenting takes place in our everyday lives, so capture the moments in words and chronicle your journey together by writing down five things you remember about your child at the end of each day. Here are some examples of this kind of short entry from a mother's journal—ordinary occurrences that bring back vivid memories when she rereads them:

BETH TODAY
_____

1. Going off to preschool wearing a huge blue bow in her hair, off to the side. Proud of her selection as it is picture day.

2. Playing dress-up in a tennis skirt, plastic jewels, drenched in my perfume—dancing around the living room.

3. Creating Valentine cards for her friends at school. Taking an excruciating long time to make each one.

4. Eating vanilla ice cream with rainbow sprinkles to cele-brate school picture day. Sprinkles all around her smile.

5. Playing with a dog at the ice cream place. Open, loving, no fear.

KATY TODAY

1. Modern dancing in front of the fire—hair down—Martha Graham poses.

2. Ice skating—a bit timid—not happy with sweat—doesn't want to go again.

3. Putting on a show in her room—the stage is the top of her dresser—she climbs up.

4. Eating plate after plate of salad for dinner.

5. Trying to be very dramatic with everything that doesn't go her way.

Use a journal any way that works for you; carry a blank book in your purse, briefcase, diaper bag, car, or any conve-nient spot where you can put down thoughts as they come. A friend of ours jots down simple statements on her kitchen wall calendar. Because the allotted squares are so small she is forced to consolidate her thoughts. She saves the calendars and has quick images of her three children going through ordinary days. "Adam—singing to his brother." "Nicole—sledding, red cheeks." "Christopher dragging his blankie through the snow." She squeezes the essence out of her days—captures sim-ple moments and in so doing makes them sacred.

Journaling is so important to me that I have many. I have one that has just four chapters: 1. goals, 2. kindness shown by others, 3. accomplishments, 4. grateful list. This journal really makes a difference, it keeps the focus more on appreciation in my life than on what is wrong. I also have one that has just sayings, and I write a comment if it touches me. I have a monthly feelings journal—this is very important in helping me to understand how I am feeling in relation to my baby and to my life. (Mother of two)

You wore your hair in braids today—a schoolgirl with her first braids. Your golden brown hair twisted and shiny—your smile so bright—your pert face so alert and pleased with the feel of two perfect little braids tucked behind your ears. (Mother of one, journal entry)

Write the story of your child's birth, or if she is adopted, write about how you felt as you drove or flew to pick her up. What did you think when you first laid eyes on her? What were your first few weeks together like? How did you get to know each other? Use the words that come to you—don't try to edit for a child to understand. Write so your child hears your wonder at the miracle of her birth.

When I was pregnant I asked my family and special friends to write letters to my unborn child. I couldn't believe the responses. People were delighted and honored to share their input and to be a part of the anxiously awaited child's life. These letters are filled with advice, aspirations, feelings about the upcoming birth, and words of wisdom. Some letters included pictures of the author at the time of writing. I sealed the letters and saved them in an ornate box until my daughter turns sixteen, a time when guidance and family involvement can make a real impact. (Mother of one)

Perhaps you can write her a letter each year on her birthday. Seal the letter and put it in a safe place for her to read in her later years. Or give her the letter each year as a birthday gift. Let your child know about his unique place in your heart. Write of his accomplishments and how you felt as he achieved them. Be free with your words and share them with your precious child.

Children love to find secret notes from Mom and Dad and will joyfully join in this exchange. Leave notes in unexpected places, under her pillow, in his lunch box, in a shoe, or in a pocket. Write notes for no reason, notes to say thank you, notes on silly paper, notes to slow down or speed up, or to say, "I made this just for you." Notes are a marvelous way to communicate!

To Mom. I hope you had a good meeting tonight. I love you. (Age six, note left on her mother's pillow)

This loving habit can become a family custom. Children are quick to join in the fun of note decorating, writing, and hiding. Notes have many applications; they can be a nice, no-nag way to remind kids about chores or obligations or can lead to prizes in a treasure hunt. Messages from home can be a big energy boost during the day at school or on an overnight. Notes are a generous gift of your spirit—scatter them around your child's world.

My mom travels a lot for her work. I always look around my room like crazy after she leaves because she hides little notes for me to find. I have one in my underwear drawer that is funny. I just left it there even though she wrote it about six trips ago. (Age nine)

Note writing has become quite a family thing. My mom always left notes on my bureau that had to do with chores or unmade beds. When I went off to school I could count on finding a note or two in my bags. Now when she comes to visit me we leave notes in each other's suitcase or desk drawer. I've started leaving notes for my husband. When we were dating I would leave notes on the outside of his car—tucked under the wipers. I treasure all the notes from my mom, my husband, and now from my young son. His notes are incredible nuggets of love. (Mother of one)

My daughter writes me notes from school when she is having a bad day. She puts them in her backpack to set the problem away from her for the time being and we open it all up, note and discussion, when she gets home. (Mother of two)

You may have to be subtle with your notes for some children:

I put a note in my son's (age twelve) lunch bag, and he said he was so embarrassed he opened his lunch under the table! (Mother of one)

Prayerful Words

When children create their own prayers they are free to offer words of thanks or forgiveness—they can customize their prayers to fit their needs. If you say only formal or set prayers, make sure your child understands the words. If he does not, go over each idea to explain the meaning in words he can understand. "Thee" and "thou" can be confusing.

I thought it was "Our father who loves art in heaven— hollow bees around his name . . . " (Age six)

I try to pray in church, but people are talking and my clothes aren't comfortable and I feel all itchy and it doesn't ever work. Prayer works the best right before I fall asleep and my prayer gets worked on through the night. When I wake up my prayer has made it all the way through to God. (Age eight)

When I am at school and something bothers me, I just rush to my desk, get real quiet, and say a prayer. (Age seven)

Sometimes when I see a fire engine, I get worried that they're going to my house, so I say a fierce prayer. (Age seven)

Write your own parenting prayer and proclaim yourself all you desire to be. Use this prayer as a chant, an affirmation, a mantra. Write it down and decorate the paper. Frame these sacred words to display as a beautiful piece of art. A parent's prayer may look like this:

God supplies all that I need and all that my family needs—I thank you.
God blesses me with abundant opportunities to share the divine spark of Spirit with my child—I thank you.

God centers me, grounds me, and guides me as I center,
ground, and guide my child—I thank you.
God is at work in my life and forgives me when I am
controlling or afraid.
I let go and forgive my child—I thank you.
God is the peace that fills my life and the life of my child.
Alleluia—I thank you.
Amen.

A mother we know composed this prayer that she says regularly:

*God, help me to be a happy voice in my daughter's life
today. It's a privilege to have this time with her. I don't
want to hurry my way through these precious years; I
want to savor every minute and have fun with our
child. Help me take this responsibility seriously, but not
too seriously. Help me to remember to laugh more.
And give me the strength I need to be patient when I
feel I have no patience left, to listen when my ears are
full, and to forgive myself when I blow it. Her very life
is a miracle to be treasured and respected. Thanks for
giving me the opportunity to help this child grow.*
(Mother of one)

Pray together as a family and experience the energy of the
universe. When we unite in a focused prayer we create a powerful
force for healing and love. It's never to late to add prayer
to your family life. Begin in any way that feels comfortable.
Sing your prayers or memorize meaningful traditional prayers,
poems, and verses. Compile a family prayer book that includes
both traditional prayers and prayers your family writes
together. You can take turns reading aloud from your family's

book. Perhaps it will have sections that include morning prayers, evening prayers, meal prayers, prayers of praise and thanksgiving, prayers for others, prayers for pets, prayers for understanding, prayers for health, prayers for forgiveness. Every prayer that comes from the divine spirit within you and your children is magnificent.

> *My children and I often pray by standing in a circle and holding hands. We take turns beginning, usually with a short prayer like "God, we have come to glorify your name. As we offer our prayers to you, please help us to live within your will." Then everyone is welcome to say whatever prayers they would like. Each prayer is followed by "God, hear these words." When we start the kids are a little apprehensive, but once they start praying the things they say are amazing. My kids are teaching me how to pray rather than the other way around. When I explained that prayer is simply talking to God and saying what is on our minds as well as giving thanks for all we have and asking for help, they "got it." (Mother of four)*

Maybe now is the time to teach your children St. Francis's beautiful prayer:

Lord,
Make me an instrument of thy peace;
Where there is hatred, let me sow love;
Where there is injury, pardon;
Where there is doubt, faith;
Where there is despair, hope;
Where there is darkness, light;
And where there is sadness, joy.

O Divine Master,
Grant that I may not so much seek
To be consoled, as to console;
To be understood, as to understand;
To be loved, as to love.
For it is in giving that we receive.
It is in pardoning that we are pardoned.
And it is in dying that we are born to eternal light.
Amen.

Refrigerator prayers are lots of fun. For most families refrigerators are the heart of the home—cover yours with words that bolster the soul. Post prayer requests on the fridge. Start a prayer list by jotting down names of those you are praying for and stick it up with a magnet. Leave a magnetized notepad on your fridge as a prayer request spot—anyone can leave his prayer need there. "Pray for Nina's lost hat." "Send energy to Sam for my upcoming soccer tournament." "Pray for Mom's friend Gina." You can designate special prayer time and tune in together to pray for your refrigerator requests. Soon you'll find that friends, neighbors, and even repair people are asking for a place on your fridge.

Is there a place you can record "God moments" with your family? How about an empty notebook that awaits notations of beauty, harmony, kindness, joy? Anytime someone experiences a "God moment"—when daffodils bloom, a rainbow is spotted, a perfect note is played on the recorder, the deli man gives you a slice of cheese—he can jot it down in this notebook. Celebrating these moments helps us acknowledge the miracles God lavishes on us. Sure, unpleasant things happen to us, but when we are on the lookout for good we cultivate more "God moments" in our lives.

Take Responsibility for Your Words

Are you accountable for your words? How do you word important messages? Does your child understand what you mean? One mother told her young son that his grandfather had gone to sleep for a long time, when actually he had died. This mother wondered why her child had tantrums every night at bedtime. Be clear with your words. Say what you mean. Express yourself with precision and double-check to make sure that your child grasps what you mean.

Remember to be honest when you talk with your child. When he asks you a question and you are tempted to appease him with a tiny white lie, don't. Never tell her it won't hurt when you know it will or that she'll have fun in a situation when you know she'll be bored. Don't tell your children you won't be long on the phone, for example, when you know it is going to be a lengthy conversation.

Be understanding when you listen to your child. Don't jump to conclusions without becoming clear on what he is telling you. Take the time to understand his words, just as you take the time to make sure he understands yours.

Try to use questions in place of dogmatic demands. Controlling, scolding, threatening words create frightened children. Turn things around with gentle questions, and you allow children to maintain their dignity. Instead of instructing your child to "Do this" or "Do that," try asking him the best way to resolve the situation. "Why do you think I ask you to wash your hands before dinner?" "How do you think Max would feel if he wasn't included in the party?" "Why do you think we are going to have a quiet time today?" "What are ways our family can be together without fighting and hurt feelings?"

Change your speech habits. If you use negative words, catch

yourself. Count how many times you say "don't" to your children. One study estimates that the average child hears the word "no" or "don't" over 148,000 times while growing up, compared with just a few thousand "yes" messages. Say "no" and "don't" out loud to yourself and experience the feeling. These words can push the spirit out of any situation. Of course we need to use firm words at times and alert our children to emergencies and dangers, but the habitual "no's" begin to eat away at a child's spirit.

Say "yes" as much as possible, without compromising your limits. How often we snap a "no" out of habit. "Mom, can I have a snack?" "No, sweetie, it is almost dinnertime." "Mom, can I make an experiment in the kitchen?" "No, honey, it's too messy." So what? We can clean when they are gone. What does it take to make it okay for you to exist without the "no's"? Do you need to know that each evening before going to bed the dishes are done? Then it is not okay to say "yes" to a trip to the park between dinner and bed if the anxiety of dirty dishes spoils your time together. Be flexible. Find a compromise. "Let's all pitch in and get those gross dishes done and then, yes, we will go to the park before the sun goes down." Everybody wins.

My daughter left for school this morning with two different-colored socks, party shoes, polka-dotted pajama bottoms, and her brother's turtleneck. She thought she looked grand. I started to fuss, then took a breath and decided to pick my battles. Her preschool teacher knows that I didn't dress her, so why should I care? (Mother of two)

This mother could create a little button to wear that reads "I didn't dress her." Her child could freely express herself—Mom could say "yes" to daughter's choices and let herself off the hook. A little humor goes a long way.

Eliminate the following phrases from your vocabulary: "It's not logical." "It's not possible." "You can't do that." Instead, include more of these phrases: "Of course." "Anything's possible." "You can do it." "I believe in you." Try to respond "You're right" at least once a day to your child.

> *We teach our three kids that we don't use the word "can't." Instead we teach them to say, "I need help." This is our reason: "You can have/accomplish whatever you think about." That also means that if a child (or anyone) is always saying, "I can't," pretty soon, they won't even try. But if you say, "I need help," then there's always hope.* (Father of three)

Play the Everything Is Going Right game with your kids. Think of all the events happening today. Now picture everything going exactly the way you would like it to happen. "I have a calm bus ride to school and get to sit with my friend Ricky. In gym class we play on the obstacle course outside; I don't trip or fall once. My day at school goes well; I get all my spelling words right." When you face a decision, employ this game. Think of everything that could go right with each choice. This really helps children let go of obstacles, release negative thinking, and open themselves to the possible. Remember to use descriptive words when you discuss the "rights." For example, in what ways is your day going to be great?

Stop using words that reflect what you don't want to be: "I'm so controlling." "I'm not patient enough to be good with children." If you call yourself limited, you block the possibility that you can be anything but limited. If you want fearfulness to expand, keep talking about how afraid you are. If, instead, you want a dose of courage, speak of yourself being courageous. To create happier events in your life, think and speak positively. Take the high road with your words and remind your kids to do so as well.

Take stock of old childhood messages you were given about happiness and success. Did you hear "You can't have it all," or "Don't be too happy" or "You're asking for trouble"? Were you led to believe that if things were too good something terrible would happen? Did you hear, "It's too good to be true"? What messages are you giving your children? Do they believe they deserve to be happy? Do you become anxious when their joy bubbles over and intrudes upon your calm? Are your words and actions limiting your kids? Reword some old negative messages. "It's so good and it's so true." "You're asking for blessings." "You can have it all." "Let's be happy—and make the happy last all day."

Be conscious of your tone of voice, facial expressions, and body language when you speak. Pretend with each word you send out you also send waves of harmony and joy. Your energy is sent out with your words—make the energy positive ripples. Assess your use of words and speech habits. Come from the heart when you speak to your children. Don't make threats. Pause before you speak and count to one hundred if you need the time to calm down. Try the one-minute exercise for clear speech: Pause at least one minute before you answer a question or issue a request. When you reflect and select your words carefully, the likelihood is that you will use your words wisely.

Your words today become your child's script later in her life. The words you utter, even casually, about your children will often come true—think about what they hear: "She's so messy, clumsy, picky, loud, friendly, helpful, courageous, slow, cautious, ugly, talented, sickly." Words are potent, and offhand remarks can become painful burdens a child carries all her life.

> *I was never allowed to wear my hair behind my ears because my mother told me my ears were too big. I'm forty-eight and only now have the courage for a short, short haircut, ears showing and all.* (Mother of one)

Never give your word if you can't follow through. Children remember promises. Don't say "yes" if you really mean, "I'm not sure." Don't make a commitment if you aren't ready. It is okay to say, "I can't make that commitment at this time." Be a person who values words—respect the power of the spoken word. Your child will learn to trust what you say. This trust supposes that your words tell the truth. Honesty with our children is of utmost importance. We can use the one-minute exercise when faced with a dilemma concerning truthfulness. Pause, reflect, and ask for guidance with your words.

Making corrections with our children calls for careful word consideration. Are our admonitions timely, truthful, useful, kind, delicate, workable, understandable? When we are cautious with our corrections, our children can use the words without feeling ostracized or diminished. If you need to correct or remind your children, do it with the intention to love and help them. Think of the words as coming from your heart and ask your Higher Self to help you present the information in a way that will best serve the receiver.

How do you say "good morning" or "good night"? How else could you say it? Speak loving words first thing in the morning to your child and to yourself—words set the tone for the day. Compliment her as she leaves for school or day care. Give her positive, affirming words to take with her. What are the first words out of your mouth when you greet your child at the end of the day? Do you focus on the positives? Does he tell you all the bad things that happened to him? Be aware of the feelings words create. Try to share a positive experience from the day rather than a full-blown negative account, and your child will follow suit.

Help children with their "self-talk." Remind them that their mind is a powerful tool over which they have control. Here are some ways to present this idea: The hammer is a tool used to pound nails—not to pound your finger. So too with the brain. It is a tool to help you, not to hurt you. Take charge of the words that swirl around your head. If you get an answer wrong don't berate yourself with "I'm so stupid." What is the purpose in that? You become what you believe. Focus on the positive and use the magnificent brainpower God gives you to do your best. When your mind focuses on negative messages, cross them out. Slash the contrary message with a bold red slash mark like the "No Smoking" signs that picture a cigarette with a slash across it. Try saying, "Delete" when you think of debilitating messages, and move on to more affirming words. Say, "I am strong, caring, abundant, light, happy, fun." When you are feeling bad, saying loving, positive words can begin to make you feel better by changing your thoughts. Remind kids to use this powerful idea. Tell them they send off vibrations. When their inner dialogue is negative, so too are their vibrations. Children have fun discussing and describing the idea of personal vibrations. You might try these techniques yourself.

Teach your children they have the ability to cancel out negative messages they hear from others. They can choose if they want the message to enter their consciousness. It is the old saying "Sticks and stones may break my bones but words will never hurt me," with a new twist. Words can and do hurt, but children are able to use their minds to replace the negative words they hear. If someone says, "The world is so frightening today," and a child doesn't want that to be his reality, he can substitute different words: "The world is so beautiful today." If someone calls her a name—"You are such a shrimp"—she can reformat the words in her mind and accept it as "You are such a great girl, a perfect size." This empowers kids. They are in control of how they choose to prioritize messages. They are in control of *their* thoughts.

Words are important—please use them with care. Try some of the following ideas to do so:

- Create a "Word for the Day" or a "Word for the Week." Type or write words such as "forgive," "health," "order," "light," "prayer," "strength," "freedom," "hope," "peace," "bliss," "unity," "service," "wisdom," and "silence" on index cards or square pieces of paper—one word on each card. Children can pick a Word for the Day each morning to discuss, think about, and embrace for that day. Post a Word for the Week on your family bulletin board and discuss it throughout the week. Perhaps children could watch for instances of the word and report them at dinner. If the word is "prayer," you have a great opportunity to talk about the power of prayer. You can discuss how you each like to pray and remember to pray throughout the day. If your child picks "health," you can give thanks for how great you feel and remember that God is the source of health and vitality that constantly nourishes us all. Maybe the "health" card is a reminder to send energy and light to someone you know who is feeling under the weather. Open your hearts to the words that come your way and have fun with this spiritual word play.

Another way to create a Word for the Day is to write a word for each day of the week on your family's calendar in bold print. For example:

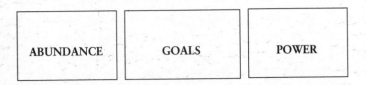

ABUNDANCE   GOALS   POWER

Encourage your kids to be sleuths and recognize these traits in their own actions and in the behavior of people around them. Use your calendar words as wonderful spiritual prompts. Customize this idea and create a word calendar for each child.

- Attend to the words your child hears from television, radio, the Internet, music, and other chatter. News programming can be extremely frightening to a young child. Children take the information into their consciousness and the vivid details can throw their sense of security off balance. The negative messages that bombard our kids via various electronic media can damage the spirit. Don't get accustomed to constant noise in your home. Check out the words to some of the songs your child hears. Do they take the listener to a dark place? Be aware of what is going into the precious mind of your child—it affects the soul. Talk about it with him.

- Play I Spy What God Has Made. Use words to point out all of God's blessings in your world. Young children are eager to participate in this word game and might surprise you with their observations.

- Another version of this game is the "God's Blessings" word game. A long car trip is ideal for this activity. Take turns naming things you are grateful for, using each letter of the alphabet. Then after each letter say, "I thank you, God." For example:

    A.   Apples I love to bite into. I thank you, God.
    B.   Books I enjoy reading. I thank you, God.

- Post your child's weekly spelling list, or any information she needs to memorize, on the refrigerator with words like "yes" and "I can," written in the margins. Word magnets work well for this. Create a positive tableau.

- Play word games that focus on how words make your child feel. Ask, "What happens in your body when someone calls you 'dummy' or 'idiot'? How does it feel to be called 'stupid'? Where does the hurt lodge in your body? How do you feel when you hear that you are beautiful or bright or holy?"

- Act, sing, dance, draw the meanings of words. What does "grace" look like? What's the color of "God"? How does the "Holy Spirit" move? What if "hate" and "love" got into a conversation? What would it sound like? Kids can explore esoteric words with their bodies, voices, and paintbrushes. "Let's paint a picture of bliss." "Bliss" might look very different for your ten-year-old than it does for you. Have fun.

- Come up with symbols for words so the message is delivered in a fun or humorous way. If family members are prone to harsh tones and sharp words, the message could be "snappy," and a plastic turtle could be handed off to the offending speaker. Perhaps all she needs is to be reminded in a funny way that her tone of voice is hurtful— "snappy" could be the one-word reminder. The turtle could remind her to ease up on brusque messages.

- Create a positive, loving, inspirational message on your answering machine so those who call receive a zap of goodness.

- Ask your child to write his personal "code of honor" or "rules to live by." You might be surprised.

- Affirmations are more than just nice words—use them daily. Type your favorites and post them on the front door, bulletin board, computer screen, refrigerator. Put them in your child's lunch box or backpack. Use a bar of dry soap and scrawl some positive words on the bathroom mirror for your child to discover in the morning. How about "I let my light shine"?

    Daily affirmations help us to use our thoughts constructively to align with our souls. Close your eyes, meditate deeply on the meaning of the words, and let them become a part of you. It is important to say affirmations in the present tense. Rather than saying, "I will be peaceful," which puts it off somewhere in the future, say, "I am now peaceful." Your subconscious does not know the difference between what is true and what you think is true. As you say these positive statements you allow your subconscious mind to accept the thoughts as your truth. Your child will join you in the use of affirmations when they become a part of the daily routine. Continuous realization of the Divine Presence is the pivotal element in experiencing the kind of life we desire for our families. When we consistently envelop ourselves in a spiritual atmosphere, we create fulfillment, joy, peace, and abundance.

- Make up a word that means something special just for your family. Perhaps it is a nonsense word that signals, "We are not judging, we are in line with God." Maybe it is a word that means, "I want to get out of here." Whatever the meaning and whatever the secret word, it will last a lifetime and can get you out of uncomfortable jams.

- Include your children in conversations instead of talking over their heads. Often we assume children don't understand what we are discussing with other adults and talk as if they are invisible. Respect your children and when appropriate bring them up to speed in conversations.

- Use inclusive language: "Let's all go to the grocery store," instead of "I'm going to the grocery store—come on."

- Introduce your child to the idea that he can send words as thoughts directly to another person. This can be explained as "telepathic messages," which adds to the mystery and excitement. When there is something a child has a hard time expressing to someone, he can send mental messages first. Have him pretend he is talking to the person he would like to receive the information. Let's say it's a teacher that he wants to ask for some special help, but he's shy and the teacher is unapproachable. If the child pretends to say, "I really need you to help me on my math," and he sends this thought to the teacher, it will pave the way for his actual conversation and make the encounter easier.

Remember that these "silent words" apply to you too. Every time you focus on a negative aspect of your child, you send that denying picture out to him. Instead, bless that part of him and send it light.

My son has a real problem with focus—he's been diagnosed with attention deficit disorder. I am so upset about it I worry all day. (Father of two)

This parent could erase the picture he carries of his son engaged in problematic behavior, now validated by a "test" and a label of "ADD." Instead he can center on and visualize his child as focused and attentive. He can send his thoughts to the positives in his child, instead of sending so much energy to the negative behavior. The idea is not to deny the reality of individual needs, but to focus on the whole child.

• Does your child have difficulty falling asleep? How about sending him off with peaceful words piped directly into his ears? Cassette players are great tools. Your child can listen to soothing tapes with calming songs or stories. Maybe you can make him a personal tape with stories or affirmations—in your own words—spoken to relaxing music. Record some of the stories listed in the Appendix. Ask a favorite relative to record a story, either their own or your child's favorite.

I always fell asleep, as a boy, with earphones on listening to a baseball game or sports radio. It continues to be my way to relax at the end of the day. (Father of two)

To this young boy peaceful words came from a sports announcer.

- A mantra is a secret word or part of a sacred text that can lift us up no matter our age. Does your child have a mantra? Can you help him select one, such as "God," "light," "harmony," "peace"?

- Even as your child sleeps your words can have an impact. Stand or kneel next to her crib or bed and quietly affirm your slumbering child. Say the words you would like to swirl around her consciousness, express your love for her, say anything you have left unsaid. This sweet, simple time can be quite lovely. Don't be surprised to see a soft smile appear on even the deepest sleeper's face.

- Use magical words to describe what could otherwise be seen as ordinary events. "Look at the magical mist that surrounds our house this morning." "That's Sam the spider and he sings in September. Let's scurry him south and send him on his way home." "Jack Frost paid us a visit last night. Look at the frosting he put on our windows."

- Use welcoming, loving words with your child's friends, and yours will be the house where everyone wants to hang out. Send these children light and love. Tell them what's right about them. Say words that are expansive and loving. Not only will the friends feel terrific, but your child will imitate your way of spreading the light.

- The most helpful words encourage, rather than label or praise. "You're a natural artist" may set up an expectation that he must strive to fill. It might be better to say, "Let's hang that picture here in the kitchen for everyone to enjoy—you worked really hard on it." These words honor the process he went through and bring his art into the bosom of the home.

Be cautious that your words don't set up comparisons between children. Our society does enough labeling and ranking. "You have the best voice in the choir" says "You are better than anyone else." "You have a magnificent voice and it blends with the others to create a great sound" honors the child's gift without setting up a ranking situation that he will never be able to maintain. "If my voice is the best in the choir today, will it be the best tomorrow?" "If I have the best voice in the choir, then Jen's voice is inferior."

- Tape-record your daily conversations. Leave a tape recorder on for a few hours in an inconspicuous place in your home. When you listen to it, do you like what you hear? Would you change anything? If "yes," do so. Notice how your voice changes when you speak to a particular child, or at a certain time of day. Be a gentle critic of yourself.

  Tape another day with the idea of incorporating the lessons you learned from the first tape. How did you do? Have your children's sounds changed as well?

- Look over old family home videos. How does your voice sound when you speak to your children? You might be shocked at the rushed quality of your words or the controlling tone of your voice. You may be touched to see yourself patiently reading a book or calmly opening birthday presents.

- Think up new greetings. Use "Namaste"—a phrase from India that means, "I honor the God in you." Try "Go with God" as a parting, or maybe "Live in the light."

- Be careful not to disengage children from their first expressive forms of communication—words are magical to them. They create singsong verses, chant words, and talk with trees, pets, toys, dolls, blankets, and many other nonhuman objects. We adults insist kids give up their "silly" talk and speak as we do. We use words in a linear, logical way that reflects our ordinary reality. But is our way the "right" way to use words? Tribal people use language as young children do; they speak to the mountains and the wind and understand animals and birds.

- Instigate a rule of "no put-downs" in your family. Outlaw hurtful, negative words in your house. Words like "shut up" and "hate" do dangerous things to children's souls. You might create some specific consequence for saying these words. Marsha's word rule was:

Our young children were not allowed to say "hate," so "dislike very much" became their alternative phrase. I notice now that they are grown they still use the substitute words, and I smile.

My dad makes us pay him a quarter if we ever say, "Shut up." He really thinks it's unkind to shut someone up. I guess I do too. (Age eight)

- Do not tolerate teasing words from your children or anyone who comes into your home. Teasing is a surefire way to squelch the spirit. How many of us still carry the doubt and pain from childhood taunts? When you hear children engaging in hurtful teasing, say, "How do you think it feels for Molly to hear those words?" "What do you think is happening inside her body when those words come barging in?" There is a difference between gentle humor and words that are at the expense of another—you can tell the difference. Make sure your child can.

When my sister teases me she makes me feel bad. It feels like I never get to do anything she doesn't tease. She always does tricks on me and I don't like it. She calls me lots of bad names like "freckle face" and "curly pancake." I can hardly stand my sister when she does that. My mom and dad don't pay attention to me when I say I don't like it. (Age five)

My brothers and sister always teased me about my teeth. They called me "rabbit teeth." To this day I don't smile in photographs, I'm so self-conscious about my teeth. (Age thirty-three)

• Remember that whatever you praise you increase.

• Children love to play with sound. They make wild mouth noises and create secret languages. Give them the powerful sound of "aah" to experiment with. Wayne Dyer, the well-known author and speaker, points out that "aah" is an ancient and revered sound. Most of the words for God have the "aah" sound: "Allah," "Buddha," "All That Is," "God," "Almighty." The sound "aah" is in "alleluia" and "amen." The sound of true bliss is "aah." When children take a lick of delicious ice cream they are apt to let out an "aah—good."

When you sink into a relaxing bath you release the stress of the day with a drawn-out "aah." Next time your kids need an energy boost or need to realign their thinking, have them breathe in through their noses, then let their breath out with an "aah." How does it sound when you all "aah" together? Feel the energy rise. Breathe in the sacred strength of God.

- Choose to be around people who use words that build you up. Don't pay attention to negative words of doom and gloom. Withdraw from idle gossip and energy-draining conversations. Negative words block the healthy flow of energy; constructive words open the channels for good. When someone begins engaging you in negative words, stop—shift the focus to more positive ideas. Words create our reality! Remember that kids follow your example. Give them a positive one.

- It is important for children to learn how to use their words to ask for what they want instead of whining, manipulating, going without, or fighting. Our world tends to discourage straightforward communication. Being honest with their words comes naturally to children—let's help them continue this sincere way of being. When we say what we don't mean, our spirits dim. Ask your child to think of a time when he said "yes" and really meant "no." What happened? Discuss the importance of responding honestly. Asking for what we want doesn't mean we will automatically get it, but taking the risk to say what we mean is a more honest way of living. Be sure to give your children permission to say a polite "no" when they are asked to do something they choose not to do. Help children to come up with alternatives when another child responds "no" to a request.

- Casual conversations have a big impact on our reality. How do you talk about your children? What do you point out when talking to others: "She is right in the middle of the terrible twos" or "We are entering the difficult teenage years"? If that's what you say, that's probably what you'll get.

- Pretend for a day that you have the gift of prophecy. The word "prophecy" means "an oral utterance." If there is an area of your life you are not satisfied with, use your gift of prophecy to change it. As you change your words you can change your life. So, for a day, utter only words that boldly state how you want your life to be: "My home is filled with beauty and comfort" instead of "Well, maybe someday we can move into a comfortable home." Encourage your children to use their words to paint their futures.

PARENTS' INSIGHT-BUILDING EXERCISE

Set aside some quiet time when you can relax and not be disturbed—make sure you have a pen or pencil and some paper. Focus on your child for a moment. Picture her in your mind's eye. Now make a list of all the positive qualities you see in her: disciplined, kind, even-tempered, artistic, spatial, precise. Now turn these traits into positive statements to affirm and share with her. "You are thoughtful." "You really know how to fix things." "You make me smile." The child hears, repeats, believes, and incorporates these positive statements into her identity.

Make a list of the qualities you wish your child will have as an adult: kindness, assertiveness, courage, faith, trust. Take a quiet moment to let your intuition guide you in ways to reinforce and enhance these qualities. By taking the time to ask, then paying attention to the ideas that come, you receive insight on ways you might encourage these positive qualities in your growing child. Do you get the idea to give your child more responsibility, to ease up on making all the decisions for her? Trust your intuition and follow through on the information you receive.

How can you become a pure channel to deliver just the right words to your children? Put aside your paper and again relax and get quiet. Picture warm golden light shining on your throat and lips, blessing the part of you where words are spoken. Feel this healing light surrounding your neck area—it soaks through right down to the cells. Your face and neck are aglow with divine light. You can call on this light any time you need assistance in speaking the highest and the best words.

Parents' Check-in Questions

- What ten words describe me? What ten words would I like to describe me?

- What word would I like to focus on today—"patience," "trust," "abundance," "honor," "energy"?

- What words do I remember being said to me as a child? How can I reformat those words if they weren't loving?

CHILDREN'S GUIDED JOURNEY

Sit or lie down, making yourself very comfortable. Close your eyes and let your hands drop down to your sides with the palms facing up. The upward-facing hands are open to receiving all that your spirit has in store for you.

Take a nice deep breath in through your nose as if you are smelling the most fragrant flower on earth. Now exhale out through your mouth. And again. Deep inhale and let the breath out, taking with it all your worries or busy thoughts of the day. Gently shake your legs, shaking off all tension and tightness. Now your arms. Shake your arms and hands and wiggle your fingers. Don't forget to continue slow, deep breathing.

Imagine that you are in a lovely meadow. You are very safe and it is quiet here. Beautiful trees and lovely flowers surround you. The sky is pure blue and a gentle breeze touches your cheek. You see someone coming toward you in this meadow. It is a very wise, loving being who is slowly walking down a path that leads to you. What does this being look like? Is it a person, an animal, or just a light? This being stops moving and waits for you to motion him or her to come closer. You feel so peaceful and so safe, and you can see the light all around this wise, special guardian. When and if you are ready, you motion for your companion to come closer. As the being moves closer you see more colors and light. If you like, ask for your guardian's name. Now as you face this loving friend you can ask any question you would like information on or help with. Pay attention to the words your guardian says. How do they feel to you? Does your guardian sing, whisper, talk, think, or laugh the words to you? Take some time to let these words into your mind. Your guardian is always available. When you feel ready you can thank your friend for coming. Then slowly open your eyes and bring your attention back to your surroundings.

Children's Check-In Questions

- What is the first line in the story or poem titled "I am . . . "?

- What words make you feel happy? What words make you sad?

- What does it mean to you when I say, "I promise"?

- What words would you use to describe me?

- What words would you use to describe yourself?

- What do you like best about yourself?

Affirmations

ADULT

I pay attention to what I say and send out positive light and positive intent with my words.

My words reflect a higher reality and create optimism and hope.

I choose my words with care and speak from my heart.

I communicate my needs.

I empower my children with my words.

As I speak my words with conviction and believe them in my heart, my prayer is heard and acted upon.

As I change my words I change my world.

CHILD

I'm a great kid.

I say "yes" to life.

I am careful about what I say because I know my words come true.

I point out the positives in others.

I am lovable—I am lovable at all times—I am lovable.

I clearly express my wants and needs.

Principle 5

ALLOW AND ENCOURAGE DREAMS, WISHES, HOPES

When I grow up I'm gonna go to all these beautiful places with these beautiful colors. I know I am! (Age five, drawing pictures of her dream places)

Childhood is filled with dreams, wishes, and hopes. If it were not, nothing would happen! For children, dreaming and hoping is as natural as breathing. We must allow these parts of children to continue to develop. We can do even more than that when we encourage them to dream. Dreams and hopes are the doorways to discovering our soul's purpose, our reason for being alive on this earth. It is our privilege as spiritual parents to help our children uncover their purpose within a spiritual context—to understand their power as part of a divine energy. When we encourage our children's dreams we experience joy and enthusiasm along with them; life becomes an exciting exploration.

My dream is to live on a farm and have lots of animals. If I keep the picture of that farm in my mind, when I grow up it will happen. (Age eight)

When children begin exploring their dreams they begin their upward journey to fulfillment. When dreams are shattered the child's world topples. Maya Angelou says, "We are all creative, but by the time we are three or four years old, someone has knocked creativity out of us. Some people shut up the kids who start to tell stories. Kids dance in their cribs, but someone will insist they sit still." When we enable our children to move freely through their childhood, we keep their hearts and souls open and their exploration unfettered. They are then as they were created to be.

My angel is a special friend that I can tell absolutely anything and she won't laugh at me. I tell her about my ideas for the future or what I want to be and she tells me I can do it. My angel will never get mad at me no matter what I say or do. (Age ten)

ALLOW AND ENCOURAGE DREAMS, WISHES, AND HOPES

Dreams are the child's seeds of desire—we want to nourish those seeds. If children's dreams, wishes, and hopes are accepted and encouraged they will share them and eventually believe in the possibility of achieving them. Those children who are supported in their dreaming will shine at whatever they choose to do. They will have goals and hopes and places to go.

When we remind our children that they have unique talents and unique ways of expressing them, we validate and respect their desires. Within those dreams lies their divine potential. Encourage your child's ideas, let her inspirations be free-ranging and fluid, instead of constricted by your own, perhaps limited, beliefs. Allow him to discover who he is through his dreaming, and create an authentic life from those dreams—true to his soul's mission.

A child's natural impulse is to believe in her own greatness. Her expansive soul is already "self-actualized." By respecting this boundless dimension we sustain children's inner freedom and creativity. Sadly, children's unlimited sense of potential is at risk in our perfectionist culture, where less than perfect is often equated with failure. Of course, everyone will experience defeat—it's a part of learning. We can help our kids handle rejection, disappointment, and doubt when we remind them of their dreams and reinforce their talents—when we are non-judgmental listeners. It's difficult not to judge our children by what others think or get caught up in our society's ideas of greatness. But when we step beyond popular opinion and help kids remain connected to their authentic selves, to their dreams and wishes, we give them hope. The mother of a five-year-old expressed what so many of us feel: "I never want my son to lose his childhood sense of the possible." When you fan the flame of your child's dreams you help bring the possible into his field of vision.

e. e. cummings wrote, "It takes courage to grow up and turn out to be who you really are." When we nourish our children's dreams we help strengthen their courage to stay true to who they really are—we allow them to weave their spirits into everything they do. A bright six-year-old we know is fascinated by music. Even though her parents aren't musical and don't include music in their home life, they have supported their daughter's interest. The moment this child gets home from school she rushes to the living room to play her piano. She told us:

I want to be a pianist—I've already started practicing for it. I already did one recital. I'm not that good yet but I think I will be. I begged my mommy for a piano when I was little. She got it for me and I couldn't do it at first. But I keep practicing. (Age six)

Just getting through life is not enough, we must reach higher and expect the same from our children. Supporting your child's wishes gives her permission to reach for her star and find her unique place in the universe. It allows her to follow her joy and fosters her innate pursuit of happiness. Living her dreams begins with knowing, without doubt or question, that her life has some meaning to it.

Our children can achieve whatever they set out to accomplish when they turn to God for inspiration and direction. By affirming their dreams we affirm their link with spirit. We are all spiritual beings living in a physical world that is our playground for learning. When we channel the creative energy of spirit into physical form we create something. Kids do this easily and naturally—they paint pictures, make clay sculptures, build fantastic Lego contraptions, dance freely, construct towns out of snow, write plays, dress up their dolls using bits of fabric and scarves, cook by experimenting with ingredients, sing "alleluia" at the top of their lungs. Let's remind ourselves not to disengage them from this power or their lives may become a struggle to find meaning and satisfaction—dreams can be lost.

Affirming children's hopes helps them create an optimistic approach to life. It makes life worth living. Showing belief in our children's dreams builds their self-confidence and gives them courage to try and try and try—until finally they succeed. Our encouragement helps give kids the assurance they need to remain persistent and get through the setbacks.

My parents never made me take a summer job as a waitress or a baby-sitter just for the money. They encouraged me to find a job that was in the same area as my interests, medicine and animals. I worked at a vet's clinic cleaning up. I didn't make any tips but I

*found out a lot about being a veterinarian. I'll be going
to college in the fall and hope to follow through on my
dream.* (Age eighteen)

WAYS TO ALLOW AND ENCOURAGE DREAMS, WISHES, AND HOPES

*My dream is, I'm at the beach and nobody's there. I
have all that quiet and all that sand and all that water
and I'm alone with the beach, the water, and God to
talk to. Aah—I love that dream.* (Age ten)

Supporting our children's various dreams and hopes doesn't
mean giving them whatever they wish. If we are available to
hear and respect their desires we give them what they need. We
can brainstorm ways in which they might achieve their
dreams. We can supply materials, space, and companionship
to nurture their interests. We can help define goals and offer
ways for children to reach the objectives themselves, celebrating along the way.

It's crucial that we offer our children more than mere flat-
tery. Kids can tell when praise is insincere. Many schools and
adults try to help children feel good about themselves—so
much so that the youngsters begin to tune it out. Smiley faces
and "Awesome Work" stickers appear on every piece of
schoolwork, regardless of the quality of the effort. Teachers
don't correct errors for fear children will develop low self-
esteem. These constant cheerful stamps of approval tend to
make children disbelieve all praise. We all need more than kind
words and stickers to turn a dream into reality. ·Offering a
child attention and loving interest backed by high standards

and coupled with an emphasis on hard work is a better formula for soulful growth. We feel good about ourselves when we accomplish something, complete a task, achieve a goal, learn a new skill, get out of a tough situation, please another, withstand a misfortune. It is then that we are in tune with our divine potential and our self-esteem grows.

Catch yourself when you are about to deliver glib positive talk to your child. Instead, help him work hard and encourage persistence. Join him in calling on God for guidance and insight. Praise, sincerely, a job well done.

Children will often share their desires as they think of them—and they may be different every day. We encourage you to accept this openness without pressuring your kids to perform. Hold on to a vision of the *possible* for your children without setting up disappointing expectations. Look at the process of your child's pursuit of a goal instead of focusing only on the outcome. Many kids struggle with the need to succeed at all costs, and crave constant parental approval. To steer away from locking our kids into this kind of early thinking we need to release total control and allow some unpredictability into our lives. Try to picture your child doing his best instead of pressuring him to succeed.

We can see our children's talents, hear their dreams, hopes, and wishes, but we aren't privy to the future. The flying dreams of a four-year-old may become the reality of the thirty-year-old. Somewhere within the spirit of the child the adult is forming. Not only is she developing her vocation, but she is solidifying her character and behavior. Be careful to accept and enrich the dream of the moment.

I'm going to be a famous actress, Mom, really, really I am! (Age four)

I'm going to be a very kind man like Mr. Pearson. He always helps kids do stuff. (Age five)

I'm going to ski at least thirty-five days this winter. (Age nine)

Encourage Imagination

Children begin all hopes and dreams through their imaginations. Encourage imagination by supporting and facilitating your child's play. Remember that within each child is a spiritual treasure, and she can express this gift by using her imagination. It is much more enriching to express our spirit than to be passively entertained. When your child writes a poem about sunlight in the morning and you encourage him to dance out the words, his spirit is engaged, his imagination is in action. This connection is far different from the inert response most television elicits. Children become passive as they submit to the action being played out in front of them—their imagination means nothing. Create a home atmosphere where your child's imagination is allowed to flourish.

Does your child have what you think of as "pretend pals"? If so, follow her lead and meet them; they are around for only a short while, so don't miss the magic. One mother, at her daughter's request, always set a place at the table for Kiki, her daughter's constant companion. This mother was shocked when she was summarily chastised by her four-year-old daughter one evening: "Don't you remember, Kiki left to live with Grandpa?" Another four-year-old had a whole family of imaginary friends called the Tumbling Weintraubs. This huge and talented imagined family entertained the boy with their somersaults and jumps. They traveled with him on family vacations and always dressed appropriately.

Many adults tell us their childhood visions were as real to them as humans but their parents insisted on denying their existence. Of course, these visionary experiences soon disappeared. What's the difference between imaginary friends and spirit guides, angels, little people, elves? A very pragmatic and concrete five-year-old told her parents about a beautiful angel who came to her room at night. This angel was a comfort to the child and an inspiration to her parents, who believed the angel to be the child's guardian. A three-year-old told stories of a Native American man who showed up on the nights when she was having trouble falling asleep and escorted her into dreamland. She called him One Who Runs. Are these images pretend, fantasy, imagination, or real visions? Does it matter? What matters is the latitude you give your child in her relationship with this aspect of her inner life. Black Elk, in John G. Neihardt's book *Black Elk Speaks,* advised that we "learn from very little children, for the hearts of little children are pure, and therefore, the Great Spirit may show to them many things which older people miss."

One little girl Marsha was seeing was shy and passive in school. Her teacher described her as "too sad for a four-year-old." The time Marsha spent with this child was comfortable and cooperative, but Jamie showed little spark. There was indeed a sadness about her, unexplained by known circumstances. One day while the two were playing outside, the wind stirred up "seed kites" all around them. Jamie's face lit up. Her eyes sparkled and she ran among the fluffy seeds, catching them lightly on her fingers. "Oh, my fairies are back, my fairies are back! They were gone so long and nobody missed them but me."

Did you have an imaginary friend? Close your eyes and call back to that invisible spirit. A friend of ours is a respectable grandfather of twelve. His grandchildren have inspired him to reconnect with an elf of long ago:

*My childhood elf appeared when I needed him. I had a
favorite spot where I'd go in the backyard, and sure
enough, he'd appear. My relationship with this elf was
complicated, when I look back on it, but wonderful for
me. I learned a lot about nature from this little guy.*
(Grandfather of twelve)

Another woman we know helps her children make "fairy
huts" out of twigs and leaves for a family of fairies that live in
their backyard. They often slip something shiny inside the hut
to delight the fairies; nickels and foil-wrapped candies are their
favorite treats.

Imagination and fantasy are aspects of our spiritual lives
and important prerequisites for determining our hopes and
dreams. They help children feel powerful and offer them ways
to describe who they are, to try out different personas until
they find one that fits. Too quickly we demand they settle
down and tend to practical intellectual foundations. Help your
child find a balance between his imagination and the details of
our world.

*In our house the Trickster family comes alive whenever
something is missing, or out of place. My children
invented this family of tricksters and I help keep the
spark going by looking for them in a dusty corner or
encouraging the kids to write a mystery about the
Tricksters, or going on Trickster hunts to see what they
might have left us. The children's friends come over
nonbelievers, but the bit of chocolate tucked into their
coat pocket or a leaf discovered on the otherwise clear
carpet sets their imaginations free.* (Mother of two)

Let Art and Music Help Summon Ideas

Use artwork as a vehicle for concrete expression of dreams and ideas. Encourage your child to draw his greatest wish. Provide lots of paper, colors, and freedom to create. When he finishes, ask him to tell you about the picture and the wish. Listen carefully, watch his expressions. Do you see his spirit shining as he speaks of a treasured wish? How lucky you are to share it. You might like to collect the work in a scrapbook—make one using colored ribbons and brightly colored paper. Keep the bound book of dreams on your child's bookshelf so she can indulge in it often.

Ideas and dreams can be brought to life in dance and music. Join your children in creating and performing a dance that expresses their dreams, or a song that tells their story. Make the child's dream come to life as you become the audience. Applaud or accompany her as she expresses, in song or dance, her plan for fulfilling her dream. Record her "dream song" to hear again or to send to a loving grandparent.

Set up areas at home for free expression. Encourage and support interests by providing materials and space in your home. Make sure to have equipment on hand that encourages creativity—clothes to dress up in, scarves to wave, music for dancing, broken appliances to take apart. Try keeping an empty box in a convenient area and instead of throwing everything away, toss junk into the box. Empty cartons, old magazines, bent paper clips, used tape dispensers, ripped neckties, oatmeal containers, plastic meat trays can all become something grand with a child's imagination. An eleven-year-old neighbor of Mimi's likes to check out the "junk box" she keeps stocked in the garage. He is always bubbling with excitement about some wonderful find he has come upon as he picks through the varied objects:

I found this old brass knob in the trash at a Boy Scout meeting. Isn't it awesome? I could do anything with this thing. Do you think it is valuable? I might make a race car and use it for the steering wheel. My dad always yells at me to "get out of the trash," but I find the coolest things there. (Age eleven)

Respecting children's interests enough to supply them with the necessary equipment will resonate in their souls for years.

My father gave my sister and me real tools to use when we were very little. We had real wood, our own tool-boxes, space in the basement to work, and time with Dad to teach us. We built wonderful things together. He never hesitated to include us in a household project. I know how to put up Sheetrock and fix a toilet. Now, as an adult, I love to have the time to tinker with fix-up projects around the house. (Mother of one)

Role-Playing to Nurture the Dreams

Spend time role-playing a dream. "So you want to be a painter. Let's pretend just for today that you are a real, professional painter. How would a typical day go for you, Ms. Painter? Okay, you want to wear your black beret and my cooking apron. You need a palette and rock music playing. You'd paint all day in the garden and follow the light. Great, try it. For today you will not be responsible for feeding the dog or making your bed. Today you must think of nothing but your painting. You are a painter."

After seeing the Ice Follies when I was about ten, I wanted to be an ice skater. I wished for a black velvet skating dress with a twirling skirt and a white lining. I had to have that, I reasoned, in order to be an ice skater. This was pretty unrealistic for skating on a frozen Minnesota lake, but my parents heard my dream and gave me a black skating dress. I still remember the joy of spinning and twirling in that glorious velvet dress. I don't remember being cold! (Mother of four)

Encourage your child's potential without setting unrealistic expectations. It's one thing for your child to tell you she wants to be an astronaut and quite another to nag her each day to read the NASA bulletins over the Internet. Playing with images and dreams is a natural part of childhood, but taking these ideas into the real world with demanding expectations is a sure way to kill them. Go with your child's flow and don't push. Some children do require a bit more prompting to take risks and follow dreams with action; others are in a huge hurry. Each child is different and each dream is unique; adjust your level of involvement with the situation and the child. Trust your gut feelings about when to push and when to back down. Ask God for help.

Encourage dreams even when they aren't the same as your own. So stock car racing is not your idea of a perfect occupation—look at the essence of your child's dreams. Go a little deeper and discover what about that dream appeals to her. Perhaps it's the speed of the race car or the image of a crowd cheering her on. Don't squelch a child's exploration and excitement. We don't mean to imply that you will hand over the car keys for her to try racing, but perhaps spending a Saturday night at the local stock car track isn't out of the question. Or how about putting an old key on a funky key ring and placing it next to her dinner plate one evening as a surprise token of her dreams?

Can you believe I'm at a wrestling match? Ugh! But my son is competing and I want to be here for him. (Mother of four)

If your child expresses what to you sounds like a wild idea—"I want to climb Mount Everest"—try to control your horror and fear. Instead accept this present dream and offer ways he can build the fundamentals of it. Is there a safe environment where he might climb: a climbing wall, a playground? The child's dream may fade, but not his memory of your support. You haven't squashed his spirit. When another dream takes its place he has learned ways to prepare himself to fulfill it.

A child is naturally open and on the path to fulfillment. You can assist him when you honor and explore his hopes. Hear him and he will feel empowered. You might reawaken your own dreams.

Don't Let Go of Your Own Dreams

There is no greater blessing for us as adults than to know and live our soul's purpose; it brings joy and inner peace. Examine your life. Do you feel alive, joyful, and at peace? If not, take the time to reconnect with what brings you bliss. When are you happy? Where have you made compromises? Refamiliarize yourself with your hopes and ideals. What excited you as a child? Is any of that passion in your life now? How can you reconnect to it? Your dreams about your ideal life are showing you your potential. Clarify your desires. What do you want to manifest more fully? Imagine success in every area of your life. Go beyond any previous limits, and allow yourself to have your dreams. What are the steps to get you there? There is room in your life for all your desires—just because you are a parent, your dreams don't have to wither.

Don't discard your dreams and fantasies as merely wishful thinking but honor them as messages from your soul about your life's plan and what you came here to do. Anything is possible. That's what you want your child to believe and that's what you can embrace. Remember, you have much more energy for your child's purpose when you are living yours. Look into your soul for guidance, link it with your vision, and soar.

> *It's so important to have more than one dream. I fulfilled my dream at age twenty-two and suddenly panicked because I faced the fact that I had not made another.* (Mother of two)

Nighttime Dreams

Create a dream book with your child. Nighttime dreams have many functions. They help to process and integrate the day's events and can provide clues to help solve the problems of everyday life. Buy an inexpensive notebook and decorate the cover with fabric, wallpaper, your child's artwork, pictures from magazines, old greeting cards. Ask your child if she wants to have her own dream book or share one with you. Many kids, as they get older, prefer to keep their own dream books and share only selected dreams. Keep the dream book next to your bed. Write about your dreams in the morning immediately after you awaken, and encourage your child to do the same. It's fascinating to learn about your child's dreams, and he is usually quite interested in your evening excursions into dreamland. By recording dreams you can begin to see some interesting patterns and often uncover hopes or ideas that life's busy routines keep submerged. One mother we know sprinkles imaginary dream dust on her children's pillows to help them remember their dreams. In the morning she prompts them into recalling by asking, "Now how did the dream start out? Did you see any of it in color? Did you fly?" Maybe you can concoct a special dream spray to spritz around the room before your children fall asleep. "It helps you to have lovely dreams and lets you remember them in the morning." Mimi's daughter at age four woke up early one morning and said, "My dreams are fairy's songs and it was just song time, Mama."

Don't forget to ask for specific help in your dreams before you go to sleep—an answer to a question or information on an area in which you'd like direction. Perhaps your child has to make a choice between two activities to take part in, soccer or softball, and she can't come to a decision. Before sleep she can ask for her dream to give her some guidance with her dilemma. You might ask for an animal to appear in your dream and tell you something you need to know. Kids love doing this and will probably join in with gusto.

It's a picture of my dream I had last night. There were these purple sharks trying to get me and this angel helped me get away. (Age three, describing a vivid picture he drew of his dream)

I talk to God when I think I'm going to have bad dreams. I pray and ask for only good dreams to come. (Age seven)

I made a dream-catcher from a kit. It is like the Native Americans made to make sure only good dreams would come through. I have hung my dream-catcher from a hook in the middle of my ceiling. I haven't had a night-

mare since I put it there. It's like all those bad dreams get caught in the web and can't play out in my mind. (Age ten)

Here are some more of our ideas on how you might encourage your child's dreams, wishes, and hopes:

• Find examples of situations and people who have made dreams come true for themselves. Cut articles out of the paper and post them on a special "Dreams Happen" bulletin board. Ask your neighbors and friends to describe the biggest obstacles they have conquered, then type up the interviews and keep them in an "Overcoming Obstacles" folder for your family to read. This is especially important during those frustrating down times when kids need to be reminded to keep trying. Examples of others who have defeated the odds can bolster the spirit and reignite hope.

  We know a nine-year-old who dreams of rescuing animals from harm and hopes to open an animal shelter someday. She collects articles about animals who have done heroic deeds and hangs them on a designated wall in her bedroom along with animal posters and pictures. This is her dream wall and is the first thing she sees in the morning and the last image she sees at night.

• Point out examples of good luck throughout the day. Interpret experiences with a positive spin. Become a luck hunter and cultivate lucky interpretations.

We decided that Friday the thirteenth is always good luck in our family. I have a big star on each Friday the thirteenth on my calendar. (Age ten)

- Make an image book or a hope book to record both your own dreams and your child's wishes for the future. This book can be full of pictures of things or situations you hope to have in your life. Cut words and pictures out of magazines and glue them in your book. Leave some blank pages to write affirmations or to describe perfect scenarios.

I bought two big pieces of poster board—one for my seven-year-old daughter and one for me. My daughter and I sat on the living room floor with a big stack of magazines and catalogs, scissors, and glue sticks. We cut and pasted for a few hours. It was such fun. We put these boards up in the kitchen to remind us of all we want to come true in our lives. My daughter had pictures of dogs all over the place and horses and girls in comfortable-looking clothes and a big house. She told me she wished she could dress more like these girls. I never knew she didn't feel comfortable in her clothes. I made an effort to buy her more sweat pants. My board surprised me. It was full of pink bedrooms and flowers. I realized I need more beauty in my life. I also had a lot of pictures of successful-looking career women, which gives me an image to hold on to for myself. (Mother of two)

- Help your child to take healthy risks and push past limitations. If a child is to take risks he must feel safe and trust that his environment, and the people in it, accept and support him even if he doesn't always succeed. Create that environment for your child and then encourage him to explore and expand it. Let her handle a disagreement with a sibling, build a camp, try out for the team, say "no" to an invitation, take a class, pat a horse, or climb a tree.

Allow him freedom and support to look into the engine, bake a cake, jump off a hay bale, take dancing lessons, talk on the radio, explore the woods, learn to swim, disagree, repair the fence. If he accomplishes his goal, "Hooray!" If she is not perfect, "Who cares, you tried."

While observing a preschool class return to their seats after a storytelling circle, I watched a small child struggle to stand up. I knew this child had great difficulty walking because of cerebral palsy and I was amazed that no one helped him. He slowly manipulated himself up, walked to his chair, and began his paperwork. Later the teacher told me, "We all treat Jerry like everyone else unless he asks for help. He rarely does and will try most anything." (Mother of four)

- Use an ink pad and make fingerprint marks with your child. Point out that no two people have identical fingerprints. No two blades of grass are alike, nor are two leaves on a tree. We are created as unique individuals—filled with our own gifts. We can bring our unique selves completely into our lives and explore new aspects of ourselves as we do.

- Encourage team activities, sports, and interest groups. Organized sports can allow a child to play out a dream, build a skill, and experience teamwork. Find appropriate team activities in which your child can participate. Children can gain enormous personal strength from being a part of a team or performing a special skill. It gives them positive self-esteem, a tool for later in their lives when the struggles are harder. Team involvement gives kids a sense of belonging. They feel they can contribute; they have value. Be attentive to elements of competition that creep into these activities. If there is a big focus on comparisons among the children, you need to intervene. Too soon our kids are taught to measure their self-worth against others; let's discourage that practice! Let's also remain attentive to the individuality of each child. Team sports don't work for everyone. Balance the team sport with open-ended time for children to come up with their own games and rules.

From the time he was five years old, my son spent hours drop-kicking a football in our front yard. He liked to wear his brother's shirt with a number on it, and I know he was pretending to be a famous pro football kicker during those hours. He did play high school football and he did kick well. He hasn't gone on to play ball professionally, but those youthful times of dreaming helped form who he is today. (Mother of five)

Dear God, Why can't I play pro baseball? (Age five)

I'm so happy when I'm hanging out with the guys after practice. They really think I'm a good player. (Age twelve)

Be careful to take time to separate your own past dreams from those of your child. Just because your parents didn't give you ballet lessons, your child isn't necessarily longing for them. Support her dreams, and encourage her interests in her own activities. Be flexible when the young child wants to move on to another interest. Don't force him to "stick it out." Anyone who has observed a Montessori classroom can see the organic way a child naturally moves from activity to activity.

My son is not at all athletic. He is really interested in creating and inventing. Our school has Odyssey of the Mind groups that work together for months as a team, solving a specific problem. Last year he was involved and just loved it. He finally felt like part of a team and his group went on to compete at the state level. (Father of three)

- Ask your child to turn on the television inside herself to glimpse the wondrous possibilities of what she would like to become. Remind her to stay tuned for yet another image of who she would like to be.

- Introduce children to new ideas and role models. It's hard to imagine worlds to which you've never been exposed. Books, computers, plays, dances, healthy television programming, mentors, businesses in your town creating unusual products or services can open up undreamed-of areas.

Watching the Olympics has been so exciting. My eight-year-old daughter decided she wants to win a gold medal in swimming. She now happily goes off to her swimming lesson and really pushes herself. It's the first thing she's gotten excited about in so long. I don't know if she will sustain this drive, but if it gets her to enjoy the pool I'm happy. (Father of two)

- Choose people to be in your child's life who enrich his imagination and creativity. If it is feasible, consider having an exchange student for the summer or ask an artist friend to allow your child to watch him work some afternoon.

Check the local newspaper for stories on people who are doing interesting things and call them. Children may learn how someone else sets his spirit free. People are flattered to be asked to mentor a child, and if they say no, nothing is lost.

Mom, is Margery a big lady or a little girl? I'd like to be just like her. (Age five, as her artist aunt helps her paint)

I read about a local man who makes flutes. I called and he was quite willing to let me bring my children to his studio. He allowed them to observe him working and they were transfixed. When it was time to leave he walked us outside playing a flute he had made. The kids danced behind him like he was the Pied Piper. We've gone back a number of times. (Mother of two)

- Come up with a "Family Dream Grant." When someone has an idea he wants to explore, the family can offer him practical support. Maybe a sibling will take over an assigned chore during the exploration time, or a schedule can be rearranged a bit. One family supported their eight-year-old's fascination with floor plans and architecture by giving her a Family Dream Grant. The child drew plans for building a barn out of a cardboard box and asked for her family's help to complete it. Her sister set the table, and her mom walked the dog. A beautiful barn was completed. The next time her sister had a big idea, the whole family pitched in to help her actualize the dream.

- Include your kids in parties or other activities with adults when appropriate. Children will often rise to the occasion with delightful behavior, and adult conversations can enrich their souls.

My parents had these wonderful dinner parties. They didn't have much money, but their friends all brought food to share. My brothers and I were often included in the evenings. I remember hearing about grown-up things and smelling the ladies' perfumes and feeling so included. I especially remember the music. One of their friends played show tunes on the piano and everyone sang along. I dreamed of being an actress and perform-ing in those shows someday. About nine we would say our good-nights to the adults and go up to bed. The sounds of laughter and adult voices would lull me to sleep. (Mother of two)

- Write down ten things you dream for your child. Be spe-cific. Do you want him to have a close relationship with God, good health, contentment, intellectual curiosity, opti-mism? You'll get nowhere being vague—be clear and defi-nite. Then imagine your child having these qualities. Hold a high vision of your child emerging into her full potential.

- Think big for your child. Many of us are ashamed of pray-ing for success or talking about our dreams. It's not only okay to encourage successful thinking—it's the only way to become successful. There is nothing wrong in pointing out your child's strengths. Why should he keep his light under a bushel?

- Ask each family member to draw or write his goals or dreams inside circles. Cut out the circles and glue them onto one big circle, and hang it up or create a mobile.

- Write down your child's ideas and dreams. Writing things down validates their importance for your child.

I hope first grade is full of reading, a bathroom nearby, and a teacher who isn't too strict. (Age five)

My biggest hope is for a dog. I really want one so badly. (Age ten)

Once a dream is written down or said out loud you can discuss it with your child. Maybe you didn't know how much a dog would mean to your ten-year-old. You can't envision the responsibility of a dog in your life right now, but perhaps you could arrange for him to walk the neighbors' dog while they are at work.

Setting Goals and Visualizing Our Dreams

Talk about goal-setting with your child. Make sure she clearly understands what a goal is. Ask her. Once she grasps the idea she can begin creating her own goals.

A goal is when you want something really badly and you figure out the ways to get it. (Age six)

Remind your child of his goals and help him persevere. When children have dedication they have a great tool. It's always a balance between nagging and reminders. Trust your intuition on when to pull back. Teach your kids the wonderful words of Johann Wolfgang von Goethe, written over two hundred years ago:

Whatever you can do, or dream you can, begin it.
Boldness has genius, power, and magic in it.

Just checking in from time to time to hear his latest hope can give new life to the desire, or remind your child that he is beginning to realize his goal. Ask him if he needs your help and what role he sees you taking in fulfilling his desires.

Visualizing ourselves accomplishing our goals is a good way of finding the inspiration to try. Seeing a picture of a desired outcome, with the mind's eye first, establishes the credibility for us to accept the vision as our reality. Children have fun with this concept. They can visualize themselves scoring a goal in the soccer game, sleeping through the night, riding a two-wheeler, performing calmly in the dance concert, speaking up in class, writing a book on bird calls, doing their best on the spelling test. Encourage your child to open up to his short- and long-term goals and to picture himself achieving them. Have fun with this yourself. What kind of parent do you want to be? Try to be as specific as possible and visualize yourself parenting this way.

Help Your Child Focus Her Thoughts

Teach your child to develop focus in her thinking. Use the example of a flashlight beam cutting through the darkness. Her thoughts are like this beam, piercing through the universe—pulling together and illuminating her desires. Perhaps the idea of a "laser thought" would appeal to your child, the notion that focused attention can create outcomes. An invisible laser beam is strong and makes a big impact—so too do our thoughts. When we focus them, like the laser beam, we can create big changes. Invite your child to fill his thoughts with what he wants to create. Anything his imagination can create he can achieve. But he must be persistent and, like that flashlight, gather his energy and focus on his goal.

Another way for children to focus their thoughts and get in

touch with their inner guidance is to imagine they have a spark of light inside them. This spark is the core of their being and will always give them guidance. Ask your child to close his eyes, take three deep breaths, and picture his little spark of light. What makes that spark happy, what gives it joy? Your child can draw a picture of that joy or tell you about it. Pay attention to his response—that's the seed of what makes him happy.

> *My spark likes to sing and dance.* (Age six)

Remind him that whenever he needs guidance he can close his eyes and connect with his spark of light. He can ask and listen to the answers that come.

When we make our to-do lists, let's put "Tuning into God" first on that list. Remind your child to start his day and approach his goals with time for God at the top of the agenda, and at day's end, to thank God for the blessings that came along to help move him forward.

Other ideas for allowing and encouraging your child's dreams and hopes include:

- Find outlets for your child's gifts and talents. Recognition from the outside world is important to any child. "Mom and Dad think I'm great, but the toy store actually displayed my Lego structure in the window. I must be a good builder." There are many, many opportunities to share work these days for every interest from cooking to frog jumping. How about Pony Club or 4-H? Can your child exhibit at the county fair or work toward a badge in Cub Scouts? Is there a recorder club at school? Could you phone the music teacher and help start one? What about the local YMCA or YWCA or Girls Incorporated? Seek out some of these unique opportunities for your child's light to shine without putting too much emphasis on the prize. The Internet is full of neat imagination-stretching opportunities for children. Type in "kids contests" under any search engine and you'll find hundreds of events for kids from brain teasers to poetry contests.

A bookstore in my town had a poetry contest and I entered about five poems I wrote. They called to tell me I had won second place for grade two. My mom drove me right down to the bookstore to see my poem displayed in the store window. I felt so happy to see my poem there. Mom and I were jumping up and down right there on the sidewalk. I don't play sports, so my name is never in our town's paper, but it was sure there for this poetry contest. The best thing about it was I got to read my poem at a little celebration at our library. Lots of people in my class said they saw my poem in the window. I love to write. (Age eight)

- Don't panic when your child's wishes are consumed with "things" such as the latest toy fad, cool sneakers, or the newest video game. Instead, go a little deeper with her and find out what the essence of having these "things" would be. Would she feel included, or cool? Would he feel connected to his favorite sports star whose name is on the item? Play with the idea of what the object would bring to her without judging her desires. Then look at other ways your child might create this essence in his life. Could he write a letter to the sports star or invite a friend over to feel included in a group? You might also throw out catalogs or toy store circulars that arrive in your mailbox. We are all barraged with colorful pleas for our attention in the form of seductive advertising. Let your child become an informed buyer and make conscious spending decisions instead of highly emotional ones.

- Have your child write a list of what he hopes for the world. What does he hope the world will be like when he grows up? Ask him to draw a picture of that world or write about it. We can replace the negative images of war, death, crime, and hatred we see in magazines, newspapers, and television pictures. Substitute those images with your child's positive visions of a peaceful world. Hold on to that vision.

- Does your family have time and energy for dreaming? Take a look at the "shoulds" and "have-to's" in your lives. Is there room for dreaming, for moving forward toward your goals, for rewarding yourselves along the way? Or are you overcommitted to obligations or just getting through the day? Do you or your child often feel bored or tired? These may be signals that you need to rekindle your dreams. Take stock of your life and your child's life. Set aside time on your calendar *now* for open-ended time devoted to igniting your family's interests. See a play, build a model airplane, sketch a tree, visit an animal shelter, take an acting class, make a torte, name the stars, play the harmonica, sing together. Instead of saying, "Five minutes to clean up your rooms," try, "Five minutes to write about your dreams." Won't they be surprised?

- Make a wish basket. Fill it with your family's written wishes and place it on your altar, kitchen table, wherever you can meditate or focus on it, and send those wishes energy and prayer.

- Remind your child that to succeed at something might take time—and he might be very bad at it for a while too. We all have to be willing to make a lot of mistakes. Show him pictures of himself as a baby. He was a great crawler—never afraid to try—a great toddler—not afraid to fall down when he was learning to walk—so too will he someday learn to ride a two-wheeler—just keep at it. The same goes with all his dreams. He can prevail if he isn't ashamed or intimidated by the frustrations of failing when he is learning.

- Showing a sense of self-worth is a positive step for a child—this is how she will develop a feeling of confidence. Sometimes we mistake a child's feelings of self-worth as displaying a "big ego." Of course we don't want to encourage children to become narcissistic little braggarts, listing their accomplishments at the drop of a hat. But let's also be careful about our lessons in being "humble." Being self-assured is not the same thing as having an overinflated ego. Being confident means believing in yourself. When we are allowed to be proud of our accomplishments and share our victories we deepen our self-worth and nourish our souls—we feel worthy.

- Kids are full of enthusiasm—allow them to express it. Better yet, join in and rekindle your own delight. Joy is infectious—catch it from your child and mirror it back. Joy is the fire of dreams and brings hope. Hope then brings us joy. Emily Dickinson said it well:

Hope is the thing with feathers
That perches in the soul
And sings the tune without the words
And never stops, at all.

Help your child to discover what he was put here on the earth to do—what he was created to give to the universe. Parenting with this focus is an exciting adventure. Children's temperaments and talents are often apparent early on in their lives. The quiet child who loves to be with animals nourishes his soul from this union. The active girl who needs to climb, run, and swing from the bars at the playground is freeing her spirit by movement. These inclinations are peeks into the child's approach to the world. By understanding and accepting our children's preferred ways to embrace life, we can offer soulful activities and help uncover their talents. What gives a child joy may become her passion, and by pursuing her passion she will fill her soul's purpose. By filling her soul's purpose she will oftentimes be making the world a better place. When we look at truly successful people who are happy in their lives, we will see people who have followed their passion and who are usually giving back to the world in some way.

PARENTS' INSIGHT-BUILDING EXERCISE

Relax in a comfortable position. Breathe deeply and slow your mind. Let go of your thoughts and worries. When you are feeling calm and relaxed, picture yourself as a child. Take some time with this image. What age first comes to mind? Look at that child and see what her childhood dreams are. Identify them. What are they about? Did you share these dreams, wishes, and hopes with anyone? Who? How did it feel? Do you still have a place for dreams in your life? How can you make time for these dreams?

Now bring your thoughts to your child. Has he shared his dreams with you? What are they? How have you responded to them? What happened to his face when you acknowledged his dream? Was your response what you wished it had been?

Turn your thoughts ahead and visualize how you will respond to the next shared wish, hope, or dream from your child. Create the scene. Visualize the words, the touches, the joy, the pride, the smiles. As you see it, it will be.

Parents' Check-in Questions

- What are three qualities I admire in my child?

- What is my hope for my child's future?

- Have I told or shown my child I have faith in her—that I believe in her potential and her goals? How have I done this or how can I do it in the future?

- What is my wish for my family?

- What are the desires and dreams of my soul? What brings me the most joy? What do I love to do? What calls to my heart? These activities all contain a seed of my life's purpose. Am I living this purpose?

- What are three things I might do if I knew I couldn't fail?

- Where have I made compromises in my dreams? How can I get back on track?

CHILDREN'S GUIDED JOURNEY

Get in a comfortable position, either sitting or lying down, and relax. Start with your toes and move all the way up to your head, thinking of relaxing each part of your body. Wiggle your toes and then let them relax. Now move up to your legs and feel them getting heavy. Let your body sink into the floor or chair as you move up to your stomach and arms, relaxing and letting go. Now your chest and neck and then finally your face and scalp. You are deeply relaxed and calm. Take a nice deep breath in through your nose and out your mouth. Put a sound to the breath. Breathe in and let it out, saying "aah." And again. Breathe in, then out, saying "aah."

Now that you are deeply relaxed, start to imagine or picture something you would like to have happen or a goal you would like to reach. Imagine this goal exactly as you would like it. Paint in all of the details. How does it feel? What is being said? Really picture the events in living color. This feels like a great daydream, so enjoy it.

When you have finished creating your mental picture say, "This or something better is coming true for me now. I believe that with God all things are possible." Then slowly come back to the room. You feel great.

Children's Check-in Questions

- What do you most love to do?

- What do you think your unique gift is?

- How can this gift help the world?

- What's your greatest dream?

- What are three things you can do to make this dream a reality?

- When do you feel really good about yourself?

Affirmations

ADULT

I see the divine potential in my child.

I take time today to dream.

I live in a limitless world where anything is possible.

My dreams are not limited by dollars.

CHILD

I am filled with wonderful ideas.

I have a special gift only I can share.

I focus on what I love and draw it to me.

I honor myself today.

Through dedication I unfold to my highest potential.

Principle 6

ADD MAGIC TO THE ORDINARY

Mom, it looks like God covered the world with crystals today and his friend Mr. Sun has come along to soften the picture up. (Age five)

When we're young we see the world as our spirit directs—with all our senses—and it is magic. The soul is enriched by this ordinary grace—magic is the spirit. Many adults have lost this enchantment and search everywhere for happiness, peace, or fulfillment. Countless hours are spent in therapists' offices in an attempt to find that magic, the spirituality that was lost somewhere in the past. But magic exists right now within your child. By inviting her to see magic in the ordinary, you strengthen her spirituality so that it lives forever in her life. When she reaches adulthood, your child will have no need to search outside herself for something to make her happy.

The extraordinary is in the ordinary for a child. He doesn't need a circus, an action-packed movie, or a 3-D software package. We shortchange kids by assuming they must have strong colors and fancy toys, when even the simplest time or activity can be magical. A materially indulged little girl sought her bliss not from the "stuff" she had but rather:

I like to lie on my bed and hold my blanket and think I'm up in the sky with my cat. (Age eight)

It's magic when my mom sings to me at night, my big sister reads to me, and when I'm alone in my room. (Age seven)

Our society, with its emphasis on the material, deadens the natural enthusiasm our children have for the ordinary. High-tech toys, computers, and other devices can dull imagination and creativity. The thirty-second sound and stimulation bites on television, with fast-moving pictures and bright colors, seduce our children and us. When we overwhelm our kids with plastic battery-operated devices, video games, and inappropriate television programming, we squelch their natural creative spirit. Try to keep things simple and allow your children to be in charge of the magic in their own way.

A flying rabbit, a flying lion, and a deer are coming to help me fall asleep. They are always there to help me. (Age six)

We can "catch" some of the magic from our children and reignite our own souls. Parenting becomes a magical journey when we allow enchantment to infuse us. Remember to give yourself sacred times and seek uplifting spiritual food in the form of books, friends, ceremony, ritual, nature, private time, prayer, and song. Use whatever fills your heart with harmony, for it's hard to "make" magic for others when we don't experience it ourselves. Ask the universe to supply you with a little zest today and remain alert to the amazing wonder in your life.

Children share their joy effortlessly, and it infuses all those open to accepting the magic.

> *Tonight at dinner, a baby in a high chair at the next table seemed fascinated by my husband's voice. She stared at him every time he spoke. As we left, she threw us great big sloppy open-mouth kisses. It lifted us up beyond belief and filled us with joy. Children have to learn to be self-conscious about sharing their love and kindness.* (Age fifty-five)

> *You are in a hustle, kids are screaming, there is one more messy diaper, and at that moment the baby walks her little wobbly prance up to you and gives you one of those wonderful, arms-wrapped-around-you hugs— that is a magical moment. It's one of those magic moments you wish wouldn't end, but you let go, knowing that it won't be long before another one of those hugs will again be needed. You then continue with your hustle and bustle with a smile on your face, still warm from that one magic moment that children are so good at dishing out.* (Mother of four)

MAKE MAGIC OUT OF THE ORDINARY

When we celebrate the wonder each day, life becomes exciting and rich, and our children remember. Ordinary, everyday memories are the ones they carry with them all their lives. Adults have told us again and again that it is often the unplanned events that leave the richest childhood recollections. Every day, ordinary happenings are magical memories that will be part of your children's history, their foundation, and their lives. A woman we know savors childhood memories of her father in the kitchen:

> *When my father was cooking I would find a place where I was unnoticed and be very still, hardly breathing. I loved hearing him sing, smelling the good smells of garlic and onions and basking in the comfort of his being there, so close, so accessible. Recently I told him about my fond memories and he was astounded. He claimed he never cooked.* (Mother of two)

> *I don't remember one Christmas gift I received as a child. I do, however, remember clearly the way the day went, the magic rituals my family had come up with.* (Father of three)

When we embrace our child's magical outlook we create our own happy memories.

> *Every first of the month I remember what my four-year-old son used to say to me—"Happy Oneth of the Month, Mom!" To this day I tell that to myself on the first of the month.* (Mother of two and grandmother of five)

> *I was taking a walk with my five-year-old daughter the other day. It was a cold, windy New England day. "Look, Mom," she cried, "look at that beautiful leaf moving like a crab walks." I hadn't noticed the dried-up, brown leaf, but to her it was moving in a magical way. Her words are like poetry, her view of the world so fresh. I don't think I'll ever look at a winter leaf in the same way again.* (Mother of one)

Make magic out of the ordinary because it's fun, because it's the instinctive and joyful way a child lives. Meet your child's natural wonder. Don't assume that a lot of gadgets or a fancy playroom equals joy. Observe what interests your child and you will find that it isn't necessarily what you may think of as "toys." A child will play with branches, bedsheets, pots, boxes, blocks, yarn, books, rocks, paper, cast-off adult clothing, broken appliances, and other ordinary things. These objects, combined with the parent's reinforcing, joyful attitude, give the child open-ended opportunities for play. Exploring in this way enhances his creativity and uniqueness. The everyday becomes magical when the child can respond to his environment in whatever way he decides. He is then an active participant in life, instead of a passive recipient of what some grown-up toy designer or TV producer has determined he should enjoy. When children are in charge of their own play, it is filled with magic of their own making.

A flying tiger is my animal friend. He has big wings and flies faster than a space shuttle. He can breathe fire and has sharp claws and teeth that are fangs. He's with me in my dreams and gives me rides on his back, fast like a roller-coaster. We wrestle and play fight. He's just there for me. (Age five)

Make magic out of the ordinary because our society works to educate the wonder out of children. We teach children facts and specifics without allowing them time to experience the excitement and wonder of life as they see it. A two-year-old seeing a train up close is awed by the bellowing whistle and the shuddering ground. How quick we are to jump in and explain to her how it all works instead of allowing her the room to marvel at its magic. Children recognize the magic in what we see as ordinary—don't steal that from them. When we recognize the magic that surrounds us in our seemingly ordinary world, spirituality will pour into us without effort on our part.

> *There are diamonds in the bottom of the water—that's why it sparkles.* (Age six)

Celia, a four-year-old preschooler, was referred to Marsha for counseling because she couldn't seem to get along well with the other children in her class. They teased her about her shabby clothes, her tangled hair, her coloring, her dreaminess, and just about anything else they could think of. Celia withdrew further and further into herself, and the teacher was worried. Not long into the first session Celia began to demonstrate her unusual and magical imagination and view of the world. She colored with great creativity, danced with abandon and joy in the fields outside the school, and talked about "who she would be" when she was a "lady." Therapist and child began an imagination game in which Celia chose to be "the beautiful and just queen." A spark was ignited—Celia lit up with her role. Marsha made her a crown of cardboard, Celia colored it with her distinctive flair, and they added sparkles and placed it on her head. After receiving permission from the teacher the child reentered the classroom wearing a brilliant smile, a sense of great personal value, and a handmade queen's crown. She began to join with some of the other children at playtime, and while therapy and the crown continued to be important, Celia actually became the "just queen," because in living her magic she found herself.

Turning the accustomed into a magical experience does many wonderful things for both adults and children.

- Magic opens a child's heart to dreams, hopes, and wishes.

Every year when I blew out my birthday cake candles I'd wish for the same thing—long hair. My wish came true! (Age twelve)

- Enchantment stimulates the imagination and relieves boredom. It ignites mind and spirit. When the orange leaf flutters gracefully to the ground, brushing your nose on its way, stop and pick it up. Observe its magnificent beauty with your child. Revel in this gift the universe has dropped from heaven. Give in to the gentle probings of everyday magic. Fly in the face of convention and live with *joy*. Make magic out of the ordinary because it's a lot more fun than the alternative.

- Magical moments can provide delightful distraction from fear, worry, envy, and anxiety. Marsha turned a two-hour traffic jam into a rich memory for her grandchildren:

On a trip with our grandchildren we ran into terrible traffic and it appeared we would have slow going. We suggested to the children that we pick out cars and use our imaginations to tell a story about the people in them. Soon two tired little girls joined happily in the game. What fun we all had. The stories were funny and we learned a lot about these dear children in the two hours of giggling and imaginative storytelling. They still talk about certain cars they remember describing.

- Home can become a soulful place, full of spirit and joy, a rich haven, when we sprinkle a little enchantment around.

It was magic when my mom would gather us all together to pray the rosary in front of the fireplace. It wasn't about the rosary, but all being together in such a reverent way. (Age forty-four)

Enhance your child's joy, support it, and catch it yourself. Remain open and inspiration will come. Make magic out of the ordinary when you are struck with an idea. If the thought crosses your mind to light candles in the bathroom when you are preparing your young child's bath—do it! Chances are she'll relax and delight in the flickering lights. Don't make this one more thing to add to the to-do list, but rather be ready for surprises and opportunities in your life and take action when you are inspired. You will provide a deeper connection with your child, memories for both of you, and maybe a tradition or two.

I wish we did things as a family more often. My dad travels a lot and is always busy. It would be neat if we even just took a walk together. (Age eight)

WAYS OF MAKING MAGIC OUT OF THE ORDINARY

Children are open and absorb the energy around them like a sponge. We, as parents, can do something about this element of our children's worlds, their environment. We craft and create the tone of our homes. Our ordinary surroundings become magical with a little thought. Everyday tasks become mini-festivals with some imagination; think small and simple, not elaborate or expensive. Some ideas:

- Take charge of your television set. The research is in and it is overwhelming. TV deadens the spirit. TV creates passive, unimaginative, sometimes even violent people who are fed gender and racial stereotypes to emulate. Put the TV in a place that takes some effort to reach instead of allowing it to take center stage in your home. Carefully choose the programming you wish your child to view and even tape those shows to watch with your child at a convenient time. Programs that speak to the inner life of children are slowly becoming available on home videos. Do some research, talk to friends, refer to the listing in the Appendix, and use television as a positive learning tool instead of a time-stealing culprit. Monitor the images of violence that enter your home for as long as you possibly can.

I am very concerned about all the outside influences on my children. I decided to do something about the elements I can control. One thing we did is put our television in the attic for a week-long test. That was three months ago. The first few days were pure hell. Now we don't even miss it. It was a habit that I'm so glad we've broken. (Mother of four)

It's very difficult to enhance a child's spirituality in a world where Beavis and Butt-head are role models. (Father of two)

• Look for the fairy in the soap bubbles when you wash dishes. Maybe she has a name. Maybe she appears only once a night in the largest bubble. Look closely and you will see her. She could even look like you.

• Music is a great way to touch the spirit. Don't be afraid to try different kinds. Maybe country or jazz or classical music will resonate with your child. Soon he will know what frees his soul. Gospel music can stir the spirit and move the soul. Teach your child the song "Amazing Grace," then talk about what grace might be.

When I hear music I make my hands dance. (Age four)

My six-year-old has discovered Duke Ellington. I got some of his CDs from the library and am enjoying the music myself. My son finds the humor in his music and he's taking our whole family with him on his exploration. He named his new puppy Ellington. (Mother of two)

- Walk in the rain. Tell your child how soft the rainwater makes his hair.

- Taste the rain. Jump in the puddles. Do a rain dance. Sing in the rain. Freedom in a rainstorm is exhilarating to a nine-year-old whose life is filled with obligations.

My mom let me go outside last night in my nightgown and run through the rain. I felt so free. I had to take a warm bath afterward, but it didn't even matter. (Age nine)

- Talk about where the rain comes from. Are raindrops, as one child said, "angels' tears"?

- Say "yes" when you child asks you to help her build a tree fort, a lean-to, a snow fort, or an inside fort with blankets. A handmade, private, secret place for kids is pure joy. We all need a sanctuary where we can recharge.

When I was a boy I awoke each morning so excited I could barely wait to get going. What freedom we had then. I was always building fabulous tree houses or forts with my friends. It was an unencumbered time in my life that really helped form who I am today. (Father of three)

I have a bat cave I made in my room. I made it out of paper bags. There is white paper hanging inside that looks like crystals. I get inside and I am alone and quiet. I even turn the radio in there off and the lights off and I am just real quiet and no one can see me or talk to me and I am soooooooooo relaxed. But it's over too fast. (Age six)

- Arrange the bedsheets into a tent and turn an ordinary night into an enchanted imaginary camp-out adventure. Better yet, turn the living room into a camping site and the whole family can create tents and forts. Call it "Fort Night" and make it a yearly tradition. Remember, there is no electricity at your camping site. Flashlights are permitted—television is not. Light a fire in the fireplace if you need to cook something.

- Blow bubbles when your child is in the bathtub or make big bubbles outdoors and run through them. Keep a bottle of bubbles in your car, and when you are in a traffic jam, *blow bubbles,* or better yet just stick the wand out the window and let the wind blow them for you. Make a bubble fort by filling a pup tent with bubbles. Take some time to observe the wonderful colors in the bubbles; they are magical, moving, round bits of magic.

The bubbles are all rainbows and shrink when my hands pop them. (Age five)

- Let your children design and paint their own flowerpots, choose their own seeds, plant the seeds, and watch their creations grow. The pot can stay in their bedroom or be given as a gift from the heart. Perhaps as he plants each seed, your child can endow it with a prayer or a quality he'd like to see grow in his life or the life of the recipient.

- Sit on the porch and watch a rainstorm approach. The excitement of the change in weather can displace any fear. Join in the exclamations over the lightning. Nature's fireworks are on display just for your family. Dance to the music of the thunder.

I remember pulling chairs up to a large window to watch the storm clouds build up over the lake. My son and I would sit for ages and enjoy nature's beauty and power. It was an enchanting time for us both. (Mother of four)

- Stay up and watch the moon come out. Look for the first star. Guess where it will appear.

- Whoever sets the table could have the opportunity to make another family member feel special by placing a lit candle in front of his plate. That special person is recognized for something positive he did that day.

- Have picnic night indoors. Spread a blanket on the floor and have a wonderful, simple dinner while pretending to be al fresco.

- Use natural objects as decorations and toys. Dry meadow grass makes neat stick figures. Use an acorn for the head and a bright leaf for the dress. Create characters out of pine cones or fashion wreaths out of pine needles or pussy willows. Make sand paintings using a glue stick and a piece of shirt cardboard. Mimi still cherishes the necklace made from shells she created with her grandfather when she was ten years old. Create a terrarium with any size glass container, some moss, and little plants your child selects. Cover it with Saran wrap and observe the growth. The simplest object from nature can bring the outdoors in. Playing and working with these natural elements can be very grounding.

• Crystals are very appealing for many of us. Learn about the special qualities believed to be contained in various crystals and explore the idea with your child. He can make a special pouch to put crystals in and wear it around his neck, or place crystals on his windowsill for a restful sleep. Next time you or your child has a headache, try placing a crystal on your head to soothe the pain. Hang a crystal so it catches the sunlight and makes rainbows dance in the room. Be open to the possibilities and play with some beautiful stones. You might be amazed at your child's natural connection with crystals, as Mimi was:

We went into a bookstore that also sold crystals. My daughter was five at the time. She walked over to the display of crystals and waved her little hand slowly over them. She would pause over one, then go on to another. Finally she picked up a little pink quartz and announced that this was the stone that was calling to her. The shop owner was riveted by this display. Of course I bought her the crystal. Later in the week my husband was complaining of a painful ankle after going for a run. My daughter ran to her room and brought down her crystal. She placed it gently on her dad's ankle and told him to feel the energy from the stone.

- Make a jug of herbal sun tea together and talk about the magic energy the sun puts into the drink. Put clean, fresh herbs of your choice into a lidded gallon jar, adding water and, if desired, honey or sugar and two or three bags of decaffeinated tea. Set it in the sun for the day, strain, chill, and serve with minted ice cubes and slices of lemon. A garnish of edible flowers would also be fun. (Flowers of mint, violets, sweet cicely, or sweet woodruff are nice.)

- Try waking your child with a song. Maybe he has a favorite you could play or simply make one up. Adapt it to your child's temperament. Does she awaken eagerly or is she a slow-moving morning girl? One child may want upbeat and loud mornings, the other soft and gentle beginnings.

My mom always sings, "Good morning, good morning, you've slept the whole night through, good morning, good morning to you." It makes me smile. (Age eleven)

- Play in the snow with your child. Let snow become magic dust turning you into clowns, horses, puppies, kittens, or kings. Make a snow angel family and give them names. Add food coloring to some water and put it in a squeeze bottle. Color your angels or write colorful words in the snow. Pretend that every snowflake is a kiss from God. Follow footprints in the snow—who or what made them and where do they lead?

- Read to your child. Don't forget the classics, myths, and fairy tales. The love of books is a gift that lasts a lifetime. (See some of our recommended books in the Appendix.) Designate a certain evening as "Family Book Club" and read together. Take turns reading out loud. Read books with spiritual messages, then discuss them. Perhaps you would like to include other families in your monthly or bimonthly book club meetings. What a great way to ignite conversation between children and their parents. Magic is created when we are lost in the enchantment of a book; magic is shared when we read the book together.

Every Saturday we go to the town library and load up our library bag with books for the week. The children delight in this event. My love for books has definitely passed to them. When we get home they rush to sort out the books and there is this magical time when they are all quiet in the middle of the kitchen, each kid with his nose in a book. (Mother of four)

My eight-year-old announced the other day, "Every book is a new book until I read it!" (Mother of two)

My mother always said, "You're never bored when you have a book to read." She was right. (Grandfather of two)

- Let your child paint an inexpensive pair of sneakers with permanent markers. Don't help or design the shoes, leave it to your child. Ask her to imagine that her shoes are magical wheels that will take her anywhere. What would those fantastic modes of transportation look like?

- Turn ordinary hand-me-downs into unique apparel—designed by your child. Maybe an ordinary backpack could become a statement, an expression of what your child loves. Let him choose an appliqué at a fabric store and glue it onto the backpack or decorate it with fabric paint or even slap a bumper sticker across it.

I got a beautiful yellow star and half moon appliqué for my backpack. It was my sister's pack last year and I wanted to make it neat for me. Mom glued the star and moon on and I feel so happy taking it to kindergarten. It's kinda my sister and kinda me now. (Age five)

- Put a flower on the breakfast plate. If there isn't one growing nearby, make one out of tissue paper or draw one on a napkin.

- Try clapping when you say "amen." Why can't prayers be fun? Or how about ending "out loud" prayers with "alleluia" or your child's made-up ending. One child got the word "amen" confused and said "aah-yes." It soon became the family's version of "amen."

- Ask your children to come up with a family logo or a family slogan. When Mimi asked her two children to decorate the cover of a family journal with a slogan, she was moved by the result:

I asked my kids to draw a symbol or design to represent our family. My eight-year-old drew a circle with a peace sign and a Tao symbol inside. She wrote under-

neath: *"Our family believes in miracles—believes in*
prayer—believes in peace—believes in GOD!!!"

- Let household chores become fun family occurrences—
  sing songs, turn on music, wear a costume, pretend you're
  someone else. Act childlike yourself and the dishwashing
  or laundry-folding turns into a party.

- Help your child make a secret box—a shoe box works fine.
  Let it be a special place where he can store his treasures. Find
  old jewelry at yard sales or plastic jewels at a craft store to
  glue on the box. Make your own treasure box where you
  store cherished letters or favorite drawings your child creates. Keep a special rock or sea glass in your box or write
  your wishes on slips of colored paper and keep them safe.

Find the Beauty in Every Day

Beauty is a heavenly part of our everyday world and nurtures your child's soul. A child's individual sense of beauty is
important; find out what is beautiful to each of your children.
One child picks from the flower garden according to how the
flower smells, while her brother chooses with an eye for color.
Beauty is an abundant part of God's world and is as individual
as each person. Children can find beauty everywhere: in color,
movement, form, music, words, and rituals. Their senses
respond to beauty in individual and particular ways; fra-
grances, sounds, textures, and actions satisfy each soul's need
for beauty a little differently. Get to know your kids and discover what is beautiful for each of them.

I think it's beautiful when it rains in a certain way and
the drops go split-splat. (Age five)

*Well, the whole wide world, except mud, is beautiful.
All the living creatures have their own special kind of
beauty.* (Age seven)

*I think cars are the most beautiful things I see—especially
the fast ones that have really bright wheels.* (Age ten)

How do you find out what is beautiful for your child? Ask!

*Fresh flowers in my room is what makes me feel good,
they smell sweet just for me.* (Age seven)

Also, you can observe what colors she uses in her artwork
and what style of art appeals to her in books, exhibits, posters,
postcards, and paintings. Offer her paper and paints, crayons
and markers to use freely. Large, inexpensive rolls of shelf
paper or recycled computer paper make great canvases. The
beauty of color is a powerful source of energy, so honor your
child's choices.

*My daughter loves a rich purple color. She says it
makes her feel good. It's tough to find purple pants, but
it's worth the effort.* (Father of two)

Color has the power to soothe or to excite. Extensive studies
have been done to explore people's emotional responses to
color. Some of these responses seem to be powerful and fairly
universal. Pink, for example, is a healing color, while yellow
gives us an upbeat, optimistic feeling. What color is your child's
bedroom? A red room might make it difficult for your child to
calm down for sleep—red evokes aggressive, energetic feelings.
Green, however, suggests nature, stability, and restfulness.

A four-year-old girl surprised Marsha with her sophisticated color sense. As they played and colored together Tania used every crayon and marker in the box. Her combinations of colors were unusual and beautiful. When Marsha commented on the exquisite beauty she saw in the drawings, Tania told her she saw these colors everywhere and didn't Dr. Marsha see them too? What magic from a child who had little of what society measures as necessary: pretty clothes, nice surroundings, new toys, computer games. Tania was deprived of material things, but her environment was open to her magical vision and creativity. She used colors in a way few adults dare, and how fortunate she had not yet been told that "trees are not blue, the sky is not red, and you must stay within the lines."

One of the most magical sparks to any day is to pause and meditate on a memory of beauty, harmony, or wholeness. Pause with your child before he begins his homework some evening, or take five minutes when it feels like chaos is enveloping your home. Ask your child to close his eyes and think of when he experienced great beauty. Was it a starry night, a particular painting, an idea, a song, the sight of his new dog? Ask him to recall this experience and re-feel the feelings very slowly. Now ask him to make these feelings even stronger—as if he is turning up the volume on his radio. Remind him that even when the memory of the beautiful thing fades from his mind he can call back the feeling it created in his body. Ask him to keep the feeling with him as he enters back into his normal activity. Don't forget to allow yourself a beauty meditation every now and then. It enables you to create your own magic regardless of the circumstances.

Magic Through Your Senses

Help your child make beauty out of the ordinary. Children have such a short time to be children. Let them fully explore their world using all their senses during these early years. It is often through their senses that children connect with Spirit—the hem of a skirt rubbed between two fingers, rain making music on a rooftop, the colors of a first rainbow, the scent of bread baking in Grandma's oven.

Smell has the power to evoke powerful emotions and memories from deep within our souls. Try going on a sniffing walk. Go into the yard, or stay indoors, and stroll around smelling interesting things. Outside, note the wind, sniff, sniff. How does the air smell? Find a flower, a newly mowed lawn, a fire burning. What is the smell? Pick some clover, smell the aromas from the bakery or perfume counter. Does your child like the smells? Let her close her eyes and guess what the smell is. Then you do the same. Stretch your child's limits. If you are indoors, smell the dog or the cat. Nice? Yucky? How about coffee, cinnamon, wet clothes, shampoo, clean clothes, toothpaste? Spray a bit of cologne on your child's pillow, a sachet in his drawer, or scented drawer paper in her bureau. Drop a bit of peppermint essential oil in a bowl of warm water. Watch how children's behavior changes after smelling this energizing oil. The scent of lavender has been documented as a helpful sleep aid. Try a drop or two in your child's evening bath or on a cool lightbulb in his room. When you turn the lamp on, the warmth will release the smell into the atmosphere. Sew a dream pillow with your child, using old nightgown scraps, an outgrown blankie, or other soft fabric. Stitch it together on three sides and add some fresh dried herbs or spices and some essential oils (chamomile and rose are nice). Let your child make her own room spray by putting warm water and four or five drops of essential oil in a new plant sprayer. Shake it well before spraying. Mimi's daughters have created their own special blend and call it "Angel Spray." They decorated the bottle with curled ribbons and created a fancy label using a white envelope label. They spray the air and dance in the mist that draws angels near.

What do you love to smell? Pamper yourself and your senses and nourish your own soul. What smells bring back memories for you—Grandmother's perfume, pipe tobacco, new plastic toys, sharpened pencils, cinnamon, leaves burning?

I am a smelling kind of girl. I love to put on powder. I even put powder on my stuffed animals so they smell like me. I rub it into their fur, then snuggle my nose on them. (Age four)

I don't like it when my mom and dad wash my blankie. It takes away the blankie's smell. (Age three)

When I leave my three-month-old at day care, I always leave a scarf of mine with him. It sounds kind of odd, but I sleep with the scarf, so my smell is on it and when I am away from him I think it comforts him to have the smell of me on the scarf. (Mother of one)

Touch is another gateway to your child's inner magic, her spirit. How does his blanket feel? Ask him. Mud pies are delightful when you are young. Try them yourself and rediscover their messy joy. Play a guessing game of touch like the smelling game. Let him touch objects that are round, square, fat, thin, soft, hard, furry, prickly, warm, cold. Don't forget to touch your child, feel the warmth from his body reach your heart. Hug her, kiss her, pat him, cuddle him, stroke him, rub her back, massage his feet, hold her hand, brush his hair, tickle her arm, write letters on her back with your finger. It is not only the spirit that can die from lack of use, but also the body. Loving touch reaches the soul. Don't forget this healing

essence in your own life. Children love to give back rubs—
enjoy their loving touch.

For many children beauty is found in action. The sensation
of their bodies moving freely, running, swimming, jumping,
climbing, leaping is pure joy. Sporting events can nourish the
soul just as much as a quiet walk in the woods.

> *I like it best when I have a game or practice to go to. It
> feels great to play hard.* (Age ten)

> *My children participate in kung fu with a Chinese mas-
> ter. They are learning about energy and focus and they
> are loving the intense use of their bodies.* (Father of two)

Some other ideas for adding magic to the ordinary include:

- Help your child act out a story or an idea. Try carrying out
  certain activities without using words. Save tickets from
  the theater. Your child will love to hand them out when he
  puts on his next show. Remember that he is playing with
  the inner whispers of his soul. She is trying out different
  character types and ways of expressing her own voice.

- Make puppets or simple stick figures from pipe cleaners,
  Popsicle sticks, or twigs. These can be great vehicles for a
  child's free expression to tell inner life stories. Ordinary
  items—magical results!

- Dance is beautiful and releases the spirit. Put on some
  music and dance with your child. Encourage and support
  his natural movements. Maybe she can dance in the yard
  on a lovely spring day. Find a few scarves and suggest an
  angel dance. Put an inexpensive mirror on a door or some-

where at your child's level so he can see himself move. Act out a family story through dance movement.

When my daughter was five she created this incredible dance one night after dinner. She called it "Eagle of the West" and it was very powerful. She dimmed the lights to perform in semidarkness. Her movements were prayerful, hands together, then arms outstretched to indicate wings. She used stillness dramatically. The whole thing was about an eagle and the sun and it was so sad and sophisticated. I never knew she had this kind of thing inside her. (Mother of three)

- Make some drums with old coffee cans and stretched plastic, buy some inexpensive toy drums, or drum on the table with your hands. Let your child move to your rhythm. Then switch places and you dance to your child's drumbeat.

- Hang wind chimes on a porch or near a window so you can enjoy the delicate music the wind creates.

- Point out the holiness and beauty in the religious rituals, music, buildings, paintings, statues, and stories in your church, synagogue, or spiritual meeting place.

There was a stained glass window in the church I went to as a child that captivated me. To this day I seek out the rich jewel tones of that window to use in my artwork. (Father of one)

Create Family Rituals, Celebrations, Ceremonies

Try to recall the celebrations and rituals you may have had as a child. Are there some you'd like to resurrect with your child—new ones you'd like to introduce? You don't need a special occasion. Create lots of little celebrations. Celebrate a sunny day, a rainy day, a cold day, baby's first word, a butterfly, a fly ball, a field goal, a part in a play, something found, being with a special person, being with a special animal friend, a new haircut, picture day at school. It doesn't take much to mark an accomplishment or to celebrate an event. You could clap your hands, smile together, light a candle, go out for dinner, put up homemade banners, use special dishes, make up a song, toot the car's horn, call Grandma on the phone, write it down in the family book. An ordinary moment becomes memorable with a little enthusiasm. Remember, in the uncluttered life of a child these are truly noteworthy events. Join in their excitement. A celebration often becomes a tradition.

Whenever we say the same thing at the same time we hook our pinkie fingers together and one person says, "Pins," the other guy says, "Needles," then the first person says, "What goes up the chimney?" and the other guy says, "Smoke." Then together we say, "And may your wish and my wish never be broke." (Age eight)

Dad always waits for the bus to turn the corner so he can wave at me as we come past my house on the way to school. I love to see him standing there waving. (Age six)

My grandfather has a special family whistle he does. Now I know it too. It really helps when you are in a store and want to find each other. (Age eight)

My sister and I always make a wish if the digital clock has all the same numbers, like 11:11. We make a wish, clap hands, kiss our palms, then blow on our palms, sending the wish out into the world. It's super special if we ever catch the clock at 4:44 because that's when we know an angel is near. (Age seven)

Turn ordinary days into personalized events. Declare the first Friday of each month a good-luck day in your family, or maybe a ladybug in the house means magic is on the way from the universe. Perhaps fall is a time to put lucky bittersweet berries on your front door, to be replaced by mistletoe for the winter months. With very young children days of the week can have enchanting names—"Magic Monday," "Totally Terrific Tuesday," "Wondrous Wednesday"—you get the idea. Create "Sibling Day." Pick a Saturday during the year and make it about brothers and sisters. The children can make gifts for one another and celebrate what's special about their sisters or brothers.

The most beautiful and effective rituals cost little or nothing. Yes, they take some time, and love is naturally required, but passion and consistency are the critical ingredients. It's easy to weave small ordinary rituals into your family. A toddler we know cherishes the ritual of turning on the vacuum cleaner for his mom, then pushing the button that magically eats the cord when she is done. You and your six-year-old might hide a little felt doll for each other to find. This doll could show up in an overnight bag, backpack, briefcase, or shoe. Maybe you can buy a unique glass for each child to drink from—check out yard sales or thrift shops. Make or buy napkin holders for each family member. Pour yourself sparkling water and grape juice in a beautiful crystal glass when you come home from work, before starting dinner or reading the mail.

Take a day off from work and let your child stay home from school or set aside a Saturday. Call it "Our Day" and mark it on your calendar to repeat each year. Do whatever the two of you decide would be special. Keep the activity simple and let the magic of being together have prominence. Pick a special day in your family's life—your family's saint's day, the day you moved into your home, your cat's birthday, whatever is special for your family. Then celebrate it annually. A family we know takes their children out of school each year on the day they were engaged to mark the special event. They do something together such as hike up a mountain or go to the beach and give thanks for Mom and Dad's beautiful relationship.

Established Traditions As Your Own

Rework traditional celebrations and make them your own—add your family's touch. How do you approach conventional holidays? Is yours a routine as solid as Great-Grandma's bent tin star on the top of a fat blue spruce? Is Thanksgiving all about the food? If so, how can you tweak things a little so the emphasis is on the sharing of gratitudes? Could you start a tradition of writing notes to people you want to thank? Maybe cooking is a family affair—lots of good cheer can be created and you aren't exhausted whipping up potatoes alone. What is the meaning of the holiday and how can you make that meaning have spiritual resonance with your family?

Christmas and Passover are filled with family traditions. Take a look at how you approach these holidays. Here are some ideas from other parents:

Tradition is the focus of Passover, and I take great pleasure in preparing many of the same dishes for my family that have been passed down through the genera-

tions. Life has changed, however. Little did my mother dream, when she began making seder meals sixty years ago, that her granddaughter would be a vegetarian by choice. So I have tweaked the traditional dishes to make them low-fat and to include more vegetarian choices. I like to keep the meaning of Passover alive in more ways than just the food. Our celebration at home is a mixture now of traditional and contemporary elements. (Mother of one)

I try to tone down the commercial messages about Christmas that seep into my daughter's consciousness. We have come up with our own rituals, which include a Christmas Eve gathering of friends with candles, simple foods, and lots of singing. We make a gingerbread house for the party, and on Christmas Day my daughter and I take it to the woods and leave it under a tree for the fairies to play in and enjoy. (Mother of one)

My husband built a large manger from wood; our nine-year-old helped. Then I began collecting the people and animals, not in the traditional way, but included family origin in the choosing. For example, Mary is an Indian (I have American Indian blood) and Joseph is a Viking (spouse has Norwegian blood), Jesus is in a papoose, there is a quartz donkey, and angels made of brass, wood, and straw. The Wise Men came from thrift shops and yard sales, for their uniqueness and beauty, not newness and brand name. Nothing matches, and that is the beauty of it all. The very large manger makes it easy for the children to get inside to arrange and rearrange the manger scene whenever they feel like it. It's been fun for us, and we

*talk about our family history during the holiday sea-
son.* (Mother of two)

Don't forget to incorporate your children's ideas into traditional celebrations.

*My mom asked me what I'd like to give this year for
Christmas. I came up with the idea to give things to
animals. I went around the neighborhood and gathered
up old towels for the animal shelter to use as bedding
for homeless dogs and cats. I also went out into the
woods with my dad and cleared snow from an area so
the deer, bunnies, and other animals will have a place
to play.* (Age nine)

Celebrate other occasions that appeal to your family.
Traditional religious holidays could take on a new meaning
when you interpret them together. What about All Saints'
Day? Take this opportunity to read about the lives of saints
and discuss what a saint is. Do you know any saints? Maybe
you could designate a particular saint as your family's
guardian. St. Thérèse, called "Little Flower," is said to leave
roses in the path of those who pray to her. How many of us
call on the help of St. Anthony when we lose something?
"Tony, Tony, turn around. What is lost must now be found."

All Souls' Day, November 2, is a day when the Christian
church remembers people who have died. Some people place
lanterns and candles in their windows to guide the spirits of
those they loved to food and drink that has been prepared for
them inside. In Mexico, some families make an altar in their
homes for deceased relatives. They decorate the altar with
marigolds and sweets. How might you honor those in your
family who have passed on?

Raksha Bandhan is a festival celebrated by most Hindu and Sikh families. It's a day when families remind one another how much they are loved. On this day, a sister ties a plaited bracelet, called a *rakhi*, around her brother's wrist, and he promises to look after her. Perhaps your family could create your own Raksha Bandhan, and plait fabric, string, ribbon, or wool into family bracelets.

Kwanzaa is an African-American harvest festival that celebrates the values of traditional African customs. Kwanzaa was first observed in 1966 and is now celebrated each year from December 28 through January 1. Seven candles are lit during the Kwanzaa celebration to represent traditional African principles. A Swahili word is used to name each of these values. For example, *kuunba* means "creativity," and *umoja* means "unity." Maybe your family can have a Kwanzaa celebration and light candles to honor and represent your own family values.

Save holiday artwork from each child and reuse it the following years. Children can see how they have grown and changed, honoring who they used to be, as well as feel the support from parents who have kept and cherished their efforts. Perhaps you could begin a mural that symbolizes a particular holiday; children can add new sections each year. Or trace your children's hands on colored paper and cut them out to make a paper chain of hands to hang across the holiday mantel or above a door. Add a new cutout each year—what fun to see the size progression of colorful hands.

Many religions have their own calendars, which means that people celebrate the New Year at different times. The Sikhs celebrate their New Year, Baisaikhi, in April. The Hindus celebrate Diwali in October. The Jewish New Year festival, Rosh Hashanah, happens in September or October. Each New Year festival has its own traditions and customs. The Chinese name each year after one of twelve different animals. How do you celebrate the beginning and ending of a year—both the calendar year and your chosen religious New Year? Perhaps your family can create a tradition of writing down all the exciting things about the year that has ended. Stop for a few hours and think about the times you have spent together over the past twelve months. What stands out, good and bad? What are you thankful for? What are you each proud of? Mark the time that has passed. What did you do that really mattered? What did you learn? Write it down. Not only does it mark the achievements and progress children have made, it honors the year God has given you. Think of it as writing an annual Christmas or New Year's letter to God. Take stock in the year and sum it up. Growth, change, tears, joy. Write a prayer for the New Year. What would you like to affirm? Use your imagination and endow your vision of the upcoming months with rich details. Pour chilled sparkling cider in beautiful champagne glasses and toast one another! Mimi involves her young children in a New Year's Eve ceremony:

> *We write down what we want to let go of from the past—then we throw that paper in the fire and release it. We then write down what we would like to manifest in the new year and put those pieces of paper in the center of the table in a beautiful bowl. We all pray over these affirmations. We might not stay up until midnight, but we celebrate our spiritual renewal in our own way.*

Some families even make a ritual out of burning the passing year's calendars on New Year's Eve. Rolling up the calendar and tossing it into the fireplace or outdoor bonfire symbolizes letting go of the old and beginning the fresh new year.

Our tradition for New Year's is to sit down with the kids and go through the pictures for the past year. We pick out our favorite ones and set up a photo album for the year. We also go through the kids' boxes of artwork, schoolwork, etc., and make scrapbooks for each of them. It's a lot of fun and makes for good memories to look back on for the years ahead. (Father of four)

Celebrate Be an Angel Day on August 22 by becoming someone's angel. Don't forget to celebrate holidays like St. Patrick's Day, Valentine's Day, and Arbor Day. A family we know has honored May Day (the first day of May) for many, many years:

Every May Day, our family and our cousins, grandmas, grandpas, aunts, and uncles all get together for the May Day Maypole party. We make wreaths for everyone and we gather a bucket of petals. We do the Maypole dance and then we make a big circle and pass the bucket of petals around; everyone takes a handful of petals and makes a wish for the coming summer as they throw them in the middle of the circle. It is such a joining experience for the whole family!

Family Phases

Create ceremonies, rituals, and toasts to acknowledge the important phases each family member is going through. It is a real touchstone to the soul. Mark the bridges in the lives of those you love. Applaud their stages of life with custom-made ceremonies that provide the opportunity for your child to bask in his growth process. Create rituals to observe baby's first step, the first day of first grade, adolescence. The Christian sacrament of baptism asks the child's family and selected god-parents to accept spiritual responsibility for the child. Perhaps you would like to design your own ritual to illustrate your acceptance of this sacred commitment. Family and the chosen godparents could each say a blessing to honor the spiritual life of the new baby. These blessings could be written down and kept in a special box or book for the child to read when she is older. This minister told us about her church's way of honoring a new child:

The Unitarian ceremony for children is called a Child Dedication. It is a welcoming into community and a pledge to guide and support the child in her or his own spiritual and personal development. I use the water from our annual Gathering of the Waters ceremony (after summer vacations, everyone brings back water from all the places they have been and things they have done, including water from a new puppy's dish, swimming lessons in the local pool, and a bit of an iceberg from Antarctica . . .) This water has been gathered (and sterilized) for many years. (Mother of one)

First communion marks a child's link with the sacred rituals of her church. Bar mitzvahs and bat mitzvahs are really rites acknowledging the young adolescent's passing to a new level of responsibility in faith and life. Celebrate these rites of passage with special details that lovingly honor the sacred life of your child—their spirits yearn for markers and celebrations as they emerge into new phases of their lives.

When my oldest son (now twelve) started kindergarten it just tore me apart that my baby was going to school. I was working at the time, so I took a long lunch hour,

*picked him up from school (he only went half-days),
and we went to a diner. I let him order anything he
wanted and we talked about school. Then on the last
day of school we did the same thing and talked about
how much he had learned that year. Well, we've done
that every year since. He really looks forward to our
lunches and we have included my younger son (who is
going into second grade this year). I even tried to
change restaurants, but he wouldn't have anything to
do with that. "This is a tradition, Mom, and you can't
change traditions!" In two years we will be including
my youngest when she goes to kindergarten. I only
hope they go to college somewhere close so I can continue it then too!* (Mother of three)

Birthdays are our own personal New Year. One mother calls
her son's birthday his "Earth Day," as it is her celebration of
her child's entry to the earth. What special customs does your
family have to celebrate this thrilling day? Can you steer away
from the commercialized, plastic, overused modes of celebration and create some of your own rituals? Build and fly a kite
for the child born in the spring—it can be a symbol of freedom
and flying high during the upcoming year.

How about a short hike through a nearby forest with a
group of playmates? Bring out the picture albums you've accu-
mulated and tell stories about when she was born, and how
she's grown. Congratulate her on how much she can accomplish now.

Measure your child's growth on a designated "Family
Growth Board." Ask your child to compose three wishes or
affirmations or visions for the upcoming year and say them
together as a family. Place candles in more places than just on
top of the cake. Light is a symbol of illumination—fill your

home with it to mark your child's spiritual progression. Designate a special birthday candle that is lit only on the child's date of birth. How much has it burned down since last year? Could you make sure it is lit all day if you are home to monitor it?

Plant a fruit tree as a birthday ritual. As the tree grows, so does the child. In South America, children are given "God's eyes" on their birthdays. These are sticks fastened into a cross and woven with colored wool. Each different color of wool stands for a year of the child's life. Perhaps you and your child can make tiny God's eyes from toothpicks or bigger ones from bamboo canes and craft sticks. This could be a great activity if you have planned a birthday party—children could take their sticks home. In Cuba, a birthday child is allowed to stay home from school—would that please your child? The Filipino child is decked out, head to toe, in completely new clothes. Can you plan your yearly clothes shopping around your child's birthday?

Birthdays are perfect for self-reflection. Ask your child to sum up his past year in a story or poem. Can you write a bit about the year you have spent together? Perhaps you can create a display of symbols that reflect the birthday child's interests and accomplishments over the year. The kitchen table's centerpiece could be pictures, statues, toys, and other objects to represent the birthday child. As part of your child's birthday celebration with his friends, pass a blank book around so each guest can write what he likes or admires about the birthday child. What a great way to begin a yearly journal—with glowing comments written by your friends. Have fun and create special birthday rituals.

My mother always brings me breakfast on a tray on my birthday. (Age thirteen)

We have five children and have specific gifts to honor birthdays. For every sixth birthday the children receive their first watch. At eight they get a camera and at ten a beautiful pen. When our children become teenagers, age thirteen, they receive a weekend away with Mom or Dad. There is a lot of excitement and expectations about these clear age-defining gifts. (Father of five)

The everyday happenings are every bit as important in nurturing your child's soul as the big events. Create a serene environment for your family; let your home be a spiritual sanctuary. Your home reflects and mirrors your consciousness. Perhaps you want to have it blessed by your priest, minister, or rabbi, or put a mezuzah, cross, or other symbol on your doorway. Have a house- or apartment-blessing ceremony. Even if you've lived in the house for years, you can bless it now. Use your imagination and invite your friends. Children can help create the ceremony and be a part of it. Burn candles, select a special rock from outside the house, make up a prayer, call upon a special angel who is designated to watch over the space, come up with a name for your home, sprinkle "holy" water throughout the rooms, burn sage to clear out any negative energy that might be left behind, ring a little bell, spritz water scented with essential oils throughout the house, play happy music, and fill your home with laughter. A friend of ours has moved five times in six years. She has created a ritual for claiming her new home:

The first thing I do when I move in a new place is buy a bunch of eucalyptus leaves. That pure smell fills the house and I feel at home. (Age thirty-five)

Include spiritual and religious symbols in your furnishings, whatever these may be for you. Allow your children to place their own important spiritual objects and pictures in their spaces. A six-year-old uses her deceased grandfather's glow-in-the-dark rosary for a cherished night light. One family we know keeps lucky shells and rocks on the windowsills of every room in the house as visual reminders that each room carries a blessing. The family blessed the shells and rocks together, giving each one a specific blessing—the pretty pink shell in the living room holds a blessing of laughter, the rose quartz in the youngest daughter's bedroom carries blessings of love, the black shiny stone in the kitchen is endowed with peace and tranquillity.

Explore the eastern concept of feng shui, which creates balance and harmony in your environment. The idea is that there is ch'i (pronounced CHEE) or energy in and around our physical world, and the way we place objects affects the ch'i. Many children seem to know intuitively where they want things to be placed in their rooms. One little girl pestered her father for days to help her rearrange her room—for the tenth time. Her patient father put her ideas into action and she was finally happy. "You know, Dad," she said, "it just feels better with the bed on that wall."

Turn Down the Volume, Turn Up the Peace

Make a conscious effort at times to lower the household noise, including voices, music, movements. Notice how it changes the atmosphere; things seem to slow down. Calm returns as noises dwindle or are replaced with quiet. Even in an active family, there can always be times carved out for this restful peace. Some sounds are in themselves gentle: the wonderful tone of children's voices, the cooing baby, or the conversation between two happy toddlers. Encourage these by mirroring gentle words and a quiet voice as much as you can.

Color and art can add to the calm and peacefulness of your home. Become aware of what colors and forms quiet your mind and body and incorporate them into your special retreat area. A friend of ours painted her home office a soft yellow color after unsuccessfully trying to run a business in the gray room. She found that the yellow lifted her up and made her feel positive, and her business flourished. Buy some large stretched canvases and ask your child to paint a serene picture—then hang it in a prominent place.

Some other ideas for adding magic to the ordinary include:

• Hold hands and give thanks at the evening meal. Perhaps each person can say what he is grateful for or you can use a traditional grace. This is a simple and lasting ritual. "Bless this food and the hands that made it" is a nice concrete blessing that can open the door to a conversation about all the many hands that had a part in the food we eat, the farmer who grew it, the truck driver who hauled it, the store worker who put it on the shelf, the cashier who bagged it, and the daddy who made it.

• Designate one night a week as "Family Night." Let your child hear you decline invitations because you are committed to your family every Sunday night. You have prioritized the most important people in your life and they know it, which makes them feel great.

Friday night is our Family Night. Family Night is when we show all our artwork or our homework from school from the whole week to our family. We have pizza that we make together and special drinks. I wait all week for Family Night to come. (Age five)

These Family Nights should be easy and happy for everyone. Play charades, checkers, or an imagination game. Dance together or roast marshmallows in the fireplace. The important thing is the ritual, the repetition, the predictability. Whatever seems fun to your family is what will flourish.

How do you start a Family Night when Dad would rather watch TV or sleep than spend time with the family? (Mother of three)

Perhaps Family Night could be tied into watching one program together that you all agree on and having pizza, then off goes the TV and you start a circle story or play a game. Come together with open hearts and begin some of your own magic rituals.

• Circle stories are wonderful magic for children and build great, often funny, memories. One person begins the story and one by one the others add to the story line. The person who ends must tie it together somehow. This can adjust for any age and works very well with mixed ages. Take the idea a step further and start a circle letter. Begin a story on paper and stop mid-sentence. Mail it to a grandparent, cousin, or friend to add to and then send on. Keep it going. Your child will receive a patchwork story from the imaginations of those he loves.

My mom's family comes to our house for Christmas every year. Every Christmas Eve before the kids go to bed we tell a big story. We turn out all the lights, except the tree's lights, and we pass a candle around to the person telling the story. My uncle tells great stories. I remember circle stories from the past two years. (Age eight)

- Bedtime is one of the big events in a child's life. If you choose to read to your child at night, select something comforting, spirit feeding, a book with beauty to carry into her dreams. Help your child say prayers, or simply listen to his. Encourage your child to talk to her angel or guide who will be with her during the night. Sing to her, cuddle with him, make falling asleep a gentle, peaceful time. Create a magical threshold to help your child enter dreamland. Be careful to make these rituals fairly simple so that you will enjoy this time as well. Encourage your child to establish his own ritual for going to sleep, one he can use even when you cannot be with him.

I am going through a divorce, working full-time, trying to start my own business and be a good mother. I am overwhelmed most of the time. I have found, however, that my daughter's bedtime is a special time for us to connect. One of the things I have done lately is have her imagine getting a hug from someone she loves who isn't nearby. She squeezes her little eyes shut and pretends that she is being hugged. It's my way of showing her that love isn't earth-bound, it's in the spirit, and it's always there for her even when we're apart. (Mother of one)

I kiss my eleven-year-old son good-night and sing a silly made-up song that we've been singing for years. He has a hard time getting to sleep without it. (Father of one)

We gather together each night as a family before we go to bed and we take turns thanking each member of the family for something specific that they did for us or helped us with that day. (Father of three)

• The ritual of dress is comforting for many children. Putting on a special pair of socks or dressing in a certain predictable order can be a daily ritual that comforts the child and often makes the parent crazy!

I have four boys and they all play ice hockey. Getting ready for practice or a game is an incredible ritual. They suit up in the family room and it's like the Native American chief putting on face paint for battle. They dress with ceremony and have a ritual to the order of donning their apparatus. (Mother of four)

• Create your own special way of saying good-bye as your child leaves the protective nest of home. A special signal or sign that says, "I love you," a wink, thumbs up, pulling your earlobe, your hand on your heart. A silent signal can be a warm transition into the world out there.

• Teach your children something you enjoy: gardening, sewing, playing the piano, tennis. The time together can be magical.

I can still remember my great-aunt Anna teaching me to fish and play Skupa (cards). It's a memory that has staying power! Anna is in her eighties now and not well. Through my memories she will always be with me. (Mother of three)

- Get out the little white lights you might use at Christmastime and let your child decorate his room with them. These sparkly lights can be enchanting night lights. Wrap them around the bedposts or drape them around a large plant. Why wait for a holiday to decorate with magical bits of light?

Finally, let's remember to give the magical gift of expression to our children. Encourage them to write, paint, sculpt, or dance their emotions and thoughts. If they can translate their feelings in special, individual ways, they can nurture themselves and enrich their sense of beauty. We can better understand their inner lives when we allow and affirm their expressions. Accepting children's vision of their world, not blocking their natural tendency to observe and revel in the moment, takes a lot of patience. It's planning an extra ten minutes when we take a walk with a toddler to stop and marvel at the spider's web. It's declining the dinner party because you are committed to Family Night. It's leaving the kitchen a mess so you can go outside and see the mud cakes the children have made. It's spending time enjoying life instead of teaching about it. It's remembering that no one on his deathbed ever said he wished he'd spent more time at the office or cleaning the house.

PARENTS' INSIGHT-BUILDING EXERCISE

Think of your past. Place yourself at a younger age and remember magic moments. What images do you recall? Who was there? What did they do? How did you feel then? What have you brought with you into your adult life from that experience? Now think back to an ordinary event in your life with your children that became special, became magical. Did you join with your children in celebrating the magic? How did they respond? What did you do to create the magic? Ask for guidance on ways in which you can turn ordinary days and events this coming week into special celebrations. Stay open for opportunities to turn the mundane into magic. Be prepared to see the magic in your own life. Acknowledge and give thanks for these small miracles.

Parents' Check-in Questions

- What have I done this week that added enchantment to my soul?

- What would I like to have done?

- What have I noticed about my child's sense of beauty?

- Did I slow down, call a time-out to the rush of the day, and make some magic with my child? How did my child react?

- Where could I add some small object that would reconnect me to spirit? A stone on the windowsill above the kitchen sink, a favorite poem pasted in my daily planner, an affirmation stuck to my computer monitor, a picture of my child mounted on gold paper with star and moon glitter stuck to my car dashboard.

CHILDREN'S GUIDED JOURNEY

(Note to parents: You may want to meet your animal guide. If so, join your child in this journey. Perhaps your animal has advice for you.)

Sit or lie down, making yourself very comfortable. Close your eyes and let your hands drop down to your sides with the palms facing up. The upward-facing hands are open to receiving all that your spirit has in store for you.

Take a nice deep breath through your nose as if you are smelling the most fragrant flower on earth. Now exhale out through your mouth. And again. Inhale deeply and let the breath out, sending with it all your worries or busy thoughts of the day. Gently shake your legs, shaking off all the tension and tightness. Now your arms. Shake your arms and hands and wiggle your fingers. You are now so relaxed, so quiet.

Imagine that you have a special animal guide or animal friend who watches over you. This animal is just for you. He is a kind and loving friend with extraordinary powers. If you would like to meet your animal, ask him or her to come to you now. Picture yourself in a safe and beautiful garden. It's a warm day and the sky is so blue. You are sitting in the garden waiting for your animal, who has promised that he or she will come today to meet you. You see this guide approaching now. What do you see? What does your animal look like? Picture the head—now the body—and the toes. What does your animal guide want to say to you today? Listen! What do you want to say to your animal guide? Talk to your animal. Now thank him or her for coming to your garden. You can come back and play with your guide anytime you would like. Slowly open your eyes and come back to the room.

Some examples of children's animal guides:

A green parrot—he talks for me. (Age five, boy who never spoke in his kindergarten class)

The cheetah is mine. He came to me to say, "Don't underestimate the power of us." My cheetah is a big one. He is fast and fierce and very rare. These are all things I could be with his power. (Age seven)

A dog came to me and licked me. It was a kind dog. It came to me to feel happy. He came and I got on his back and rode away. (Age six)

Children's Check-in Questions

- What is beautiful to you?

- What special family tradition do you like?

- What would be a good tradition or celebration to start?

- Where do you see God's magic?

Affirmations

ADULT

I let go of the "shoulds" today.

Life is exciting and filled with marvelous surprises.

Today there will be joy.

I recognize the magic and miracles in my life.

CHILD

Beauty is everywhere.

I look for surprises.

Today is filled with happiness.

The universe sends me a wonderful gift today.

CREATE A FLEXIBLE STRUCTURE

There is never enough time to be quiet and all by myself. That's because we are always going on errands, or picking my brother up from a lesson, or going to soccer practice, or driving to my grandma's house. (Age six)

Children of all ages need predictable structure in their daily lives. Rules give them limits in a limitless world, which in turn create emotional security. The trick is to be structured without being rigid and to be secure while remaining spontaneous. Life is dependable when boundaries and expectations are clear. Within these rules flexibility can exist for the child's expression of individuality and spiritual exploration. Can you recall the thrill of freedom when you were all on your own but knew your parents were waiting right around the corner? A flexible structure creates that balance of independence and security.

Children also need rhythm in their lives to maintain psychological and spiritual harmony. Rhythm lives in nature; our heartbeat is rhythmic, our breathing is rhythmic. It is not always the same, but it is always rhythmic. The sun rises and sets in rhythm. When a child's inner wisdom tells her she is out of harmony—the rhythm is upset—she will let us know.

Creating a flexible structure entails examining and becoming clear about our own spiritual, ethical, and moral beliefs. Every so often it's a good idea to give ourselves a personal refresher course on all those basic "rules for living" that we have been using since childhood. If we can be clear about our own beliefs, we can include them more easily and more authentically in the framework of our children's lives.

We should design our family's structure with thought, as we would a fine, strong, and livable home, not haphazardly, as if it were an overnight campsite. The underpinnings of the family give our children a safe and consistent base, so as they come and go from home they feel secure and rooted.

This structure will be stressed, stretched, and shaken; therefore it needs to be flexible. When the family system is predictable and yet pliable it permits children to swing with life's surprises, successes, failures, miseries, joys, and disappointments. It is your privilege as parents to make the center of your family structure your own—composed of your values and rules and driven by you and your techniques, but allowed to bend and move with your family's needs and changes.

You may wish to take some time to focus quietly on this idea, to become mindful of what your soul holds as valuable. It often helps to make these personal concepts more tangible if you imagine you have been asked to explain a particular belief or value to another person. See what you find as you search your spirit. Begin by listing your five most important personal values, writing whatever comes to mind. You do not have to meet someone else's standard, although you will probably hear a parent's voice in your ear as you reflect. (Your children will likely hear your voice in years to come.)

Honesty is a basic value that I stress with my kids. No lies. I trust them and they have never let me down in that area. Of course I always have to be straight with them and in front of them. No more fibs about a sitter who didn't come in order to get out of an invitation.
(Mother of two)

Structure and flexibility are partners in spiritual parenting. Structure is the framework of your child's environment. Rules are the guidelines for staying within that framework, whether it be family, school, or community. There are some obvious directives: "We always say 'please' and 'thank you.'" "Hitting is not allowed." "Wash your hands before you eat." "We don't talk with our mouths full." "Call if you will be late." "Look before you cross the street." "Hold hands." "Wear your hat." But there are also more subtle, perhaps unspoken, directives about sharing, accepting people, being kind to animals, speaking your mind, working hard, and the value of material things, which frequently form the bedrock of the family structure, often without our even putting them into words.

I never realized how important it was for my daughters to look out for each other until the youngest joined her sister at elementary school. The first day riding the big yellow bus my little girl felt proud and confident as she sat next to her experienced sister. I didn't need to ask the older child to help her sister, it came naturally.
(Mother of two)

I really wish my dad would make some rules for me, like curfews and chores. It's like he doesn't tell me what to do, so how do I know? (Age thirteen)

Adults who do not recognize a child's need for structure often label a child as irresponsible, inattentive, or distractible. Rules enable a child to know where the perimeters and boundaries are in his family and his world. A child feels safe and free to be himself when boundaries and expectations are clear, but not rigid. Parents adapt and vary the rules for individual children and for different developmental stages, but if the structure is to stand, there are always rules and standards.

Perhaps you can bring your children into the rule-making procedure. When they are a part of the process children feel a sense of ownership and pride in cooperating. Learning to make and keep agreements is an important structure for any family—it involves trust and responsibility. What rules or agreements would your children like to see as family regulations? Clear communication about what the agreements are comes first.

Bending the structure gives children freedom to develop as individuals, to be themselves with all their miraculous dimensions revealed. Flexing the rules and regulations means accepting your child's ideas, feelings, intuition, intellect, physical needs, and comfort level. Remaining flexible in your approach to parenting enables your child to steer clear of the "tribe" mentality for a bit longer, or so we hope. He can blossom fully into who he is, secure with his integrated internal structure as a base. The mother of a teenage son told us:

> *I wish I had it to do over again—I'd make very few, but very firm rules and give lots of support in between. I missed so much of who Luke was because I was so hung up on drawing the line and making him adhere to rules I'd made up for the children. Looking back I realize by trying to make him behave like everybody else I*

missed out on enjoying my original, creative son. I never got the tricky balance of structure and approval right. (Mother of three)

Finding the perfect mix of flexibility and structure is not easy. Life keeps changing and children keep developing. The best way to keep tabs on how things are going with your children is to listen to them and observe their behavior. Ask how they feel and watch as they play, work, study, and daydream. You may find their answers sometimes upset the routine, as did the mother of this seven-year-old. Ask anyway.

I feel like I'm in prison. Everyone tells me what to do. My mom, my teacher, even the bus driver tells me where to sit. Then I go to Sunday school and I have to glue the picture just like the teacher's. I feel just like I'm in prison. (Age seven)

Then again, you may be delighted!

We have pretty strict rules at our house, but we've been bike riding after dinner, before we do the dishes! Two nights in a row! It's fun! (Age twelve)

You may function best when there is order and routine and feel uncomfortable when you try to be spontaneous. Go easy on yourself; honor your comfort level, as well as your child's. In a harmonious family the preferences of each member, child and adult, are respected—ensuring that individuals will remain spiritually intact. If you focus only on your child's spirit and needs, ignoring your own, you will soon resent your child, and your spirit will wither.

CREATING A FLEXIBLE STRUCTURE

A child needs to think, "Just as we have breakfast in the morning, or as I make my bed before going downstairs, so too will my dad always love me and care for me." Through this dependability we show our children the face of a trustworthy God. They can trust us; they can trust God. This is the lesson that frees the child to develop in a spiritually healthy way. With the comfort of a predictable structure, children can reach out and take risks, trusting that there is safety and security in their home.

Small children need to have the structure created for them by responsible and loving adults. If this is done well, if limits are set with love, the child will gradually begin to set her own boundaries.

It's easy to become frustrated with our kids when they have trouble focusing on the routine and rules of daily life—doing homework, brushing their teeth, picking up their things. They so easily become sidetracked. They need our love, acceptance, and incredible patience so their behavior doesn't become a reason to criticize them repeatedly, thereby creating that soul-crushing "inner critic" voice inside them. We can bring order to our children's lives without stamping out their natural enthusiasm and spirit. Let's bend the usual routine sometimes and examine God's surprises.

I am very behaviorally oriented. We have a firm schedule about bedtime, but last night, after dark, we sat outside on the curb and watched the bats swooping. My son is very interested in bats. (Mother of two)

We say prayers every night. We have to, but we can say anything we want to God. (Age five)

Creating a flexible structure makes life smoother for everybody. When the rules are clear and understood, we can get on with other important parts of our lives. We have more time for swimming when we already have our towels and sunscreen with us. A child can spend time with Dad after he has finished his homework. We will learn something new and wonderful if we are welcoming to new people. Our actions and thoughts will not be in conflict because we are conscious of our need to tell the truth.

Trust grows inside a solid, clearly ruled structure. When the six-year-old remembers, "Mama said I could always tell her my feelings even if I can't always get my way," he trusts that this will continue to be true. He trusts in the structure of his family. He can then move out to trust others.

Living within a structure that stretches allows a child to take some risks. She can venture away from the safety of home and try things, knowing she is tethered to the strong and predictable framework of her family. The need to feel physically and emotionally safe is vital to a child. Because of the flexibility of her environment she can take a chance without overwhelming fear. The child knows, "It can be fun to try! It's okay to try. It's okay too, to fall on my face. God and my family will still be there." For our children to survive and thrive they must remain curious and flexible—curious about why things happen, and emotionally, intellectually, and spiritually flexible in dealing with life's events.

One of the toughest issues for a spiritual parent is freedom. We wrestle with trying to respect our children's freedom while preparing them to live in this world. "If I tell my child what to do, I interfere with his freedom; if I do not tell him what to do, I neglect my duty and show myself indifferent." How do we solve this dilemma? As we watch our children's emotional and physical development and remember that freedom and personal responsibility are partners, we can use that awareness as a guideline for increasing freedom while decreasing parental rules. We must also trust our intuition, pray for guidance, affirm divine order in our actions, and aim for harmony between respecting our children's freedom and loving concern for what they experience. We can think back to our own childhoods and remember the times we felt truly free. Where were we? What were we doing and how were our parents involved? How might we create such times for our children?

Staying Open to God's Plan

I believe we can always go to God for help and that He hears us and helps us sometimes even when we don't ask. (Father of three)

Creating a flexible structure means being attentive to the flow of your family life. Are things going smoothly? If so, you probably have a nice balance between structure and spontaneity. Is there room for a bit more structure in the tenets of your spiritual beliefs? Do you have enough fun and impulsiveness in your family life? We all need a good dose of play. Is your home a place where your energy is restored and your faith deepened, or do you feel dissipated and exhausted from the demands? Perhaps it is time to remind ourselves that family is not "work" and parenting is not "baby-sitting." Let's try to put aside the tensions of our careers or responsibilities and let the pure joy and delight of our children wash over us.

God's plan for our family is even bigger and better than we can imagine. Let's remember this when we pray and remain open in our expectations of the outcome. Our lives unfold in absolute order; because God takes care of the details, we can let go of our worries as we help our children release theirs. It can be a tremendous relief for children to know that by turning over problems to a loving God they don't have to figure out all the answers themselves. Is there a time and place in your family life for turning worries over to God?

Set aside specific spiritual times within the structure of your days—these can become the frame of your life. A morning meditation walk, calling a housebound neighbor each day at noon, or reading a section of an uplifting book before bed each night can become a daily spiritual practice. Adapt these practices for your children: a few minutes of silence before eating breakfast, reaching out with kindness during the school day, writing in a prayer journal before bed.

To us it was important that the whole family go to church together when the children were small. We thought children needed that structure to form a spiritual habit for later in life. They have all grown up to be intensely spiritual people. They celebrate their spirit in different ways and with different religions, but they each have a rich relationship with God. (Mother of four)

We don't always go to church on Sunday, but we always take time to give thanks and celebrate our many blessings. Our favorite thing to do is to go into the woods and let the children lead the ceremony. They seem to repeat many of the same rituals each time we come. Everyone brings sketch pads and we fill our souls with nature and the magic of worshipping together in our own way. (Mother of two)

If you attend a religious service on a regular basis, could you be flexible on the times and days you attend? Would it be comfortable to visit another church or try a different service time? What if you let your child choose?

Attending church or temple is certainly not the only spiritual time in a family's life. Daily prayers, seasonal ceremonies, rituals and celebrations around big and little events are all ways to include spirituality in your life. The important thing is to plan and set aside time for these activities for yourself, for your children, and for your family. The time can be flexible, as can the prayers, conversations with God, and meditations. Some days there may be time and energy for a long and intense conversation with God. Your child may chat with her angel for ten minutes one evening. The meal blessing might be inventive and wordy at one dinner, while other days may only allow for a quick "Take over, God, I'm too rushed to pray." A now-and-then prayer thrown in is a simple and short way of chatting with God. The security of the structure remains, molded a bit to accommodate the day.

Remain open and in tune with your child's most comfortable way of praying. Silent prayer with closed eyes works well for some people; others prefer to pray in a group. Ritualized prayer with rosaries, malas, prayer wheels, prayer sticks, horns, cymbals, or drums is the way some people reach Spirit. For others, prayer is a simple moment-by-moment awareness of God's always-available presence. Sometimes a child may like praying out loud or sitting on his bed or in the yard. Whatever works is fine. All prayers are heard.

In my family we spend some quiet time talking to God at least one time each week. This week I made up this song I sang to God:

The mountaintops are covered with snow
The valleys nice and green.

You created it.
You created it.
You created you and me.
It might be hard to get to church.
It might be hard to pray.
But we still are so thankful
For what we have today. (Age eight)

Sitting on my bed listening to music with my cat, that's how I feel closest to God and all those kinds of things. (Age seven)

Prayer need not be a rigid, forced activity. A ten-year-old we know decided he no longer wanted to join in the evening prayer of thanks his family said together. His mother panicked, thinking this meant he had turned away from his family and God. In fact, the boy was exploring his own connection to spirit and was more comfortable praying silently. He sat with his family during their prayer time but chose not to join in. When his mother calmed down and accepted his choice, everyone was happier.

For many families a special solo quiet time alone is reenergizing both spiritually and physically. We call this oasis "Quiet Time," a sort of positive time-out. It provides a rest from the daily activities and a time for privacy. So try to include it in your child's daily routine. If your child is in day care make sure there is a peaceful nugget of time built into her day. If possible your child should take his Quiet Time away from you and from other children. This offers you both a breathing spell. Try to establish a regular schedule for quiet time so it can become a habit. Adjust the length to your child's age and situation—as little as ten or fifteen minutes may suffice. Quiet Time creates an environment at home that allows children to develop the habit of taking time for themselves. It builds a child's comfort with silence, and in the silence there is room to listen to the voice of God. It lets children explore their inner lives, their imaginations, their ideas and thoughts. Creativity grows from this personal Quiet Time. Quieting your physical body enables your spirit to come into your thoughts. Then later, when you come together again, ask your child how she felt.

Quiet Time is when you stay in your room and you can't talk, except to yourself. It's when you can play quietly or rest in your bed. When I have Quiet Times I whine and I fuss and then when I am done I really like it and I want it to be an extra hour. (Age five)

A timer is often helpful to signal that Quiet Time is over. "It's quiet time. Let's all go to our rooms until the timer rings." This time, if it is part of the routine of your day when your child is young, will become a habit in later years. Children may do whatever they wish during Quiet Time as long as it is a calm, quiet, solo activity. Young children may fall asleep. Older children may read, work on a puzzle, daydream, pray, write a letter.

Thank God for Quiet Time. I have three young children and I need the time! We each go to our rooms. The baby goes down for a nap, and since the boys share a room I let one of them rest in their little pup tent. They take turns. I find we all come back together much happier. Everyone needs a break from one another. I meditate and the boys, who are four and five, hum, sing, draw, and sometimes actually say they talk to God. (Mother of three)

Take a Break from the Usual Pressures and Distractions

Another way to change and flex your structure is to do something very unusual—shake things up a bit. Neglect some of the tedious errands that can fill your hours. Put aside your to-do list and inject the unpredictable into your family's life. Turn off the phone for a day. Hang a "Do Not Disturb" sign on the door and let everyone paint, color, or draw. No coloring books! Instead initiate freedom with order. "You have thirty minutes to create something you like." Give yourselves time to get used to this looser expressive style if you and your children have not had such freedom before. Sadly, many school-age children have not been offered open creative time. Encourage and mirror for the kids. Schedule spontaneous time for yourself—whole afternoons to do whatever whimsy dictates. Tap into your own wonderful spiritual resources and open everyone's imaginations.

We are in a society of overscheduled kids with packed agendas. Just because everyone else is signing children up for soccer, art, dance, ice skating, computer, and piano, you aren't doing something wrong if you don't choose that road for your kids. Scheduled events and classes often substitute for play in the lives of today's children. Where do we strike a balance between overscheduling and providing children with stimulating activities? Find the answer that's right for your family. Ask yourself if your children have time to play, explore, dream, draw, pray. Do you have open-ended opportunities to interact as a family? Downshift into your child's rhythm rather than always imposing your own. The payoff? Your stress level simmers down and time begins to feel like an abundant resource, instead of a limited commodity. While it is true that we want our children to find success, we don't want them worn out. Most families and children we know are desperate for more free time.

I guess the only time I have to relax is when I'm sick and get to stay home from school. (Age seven)

I relaxed once at my grandma's house. We sat on a bench and watched the birds fly. I felt so good and peaceful. It's too busy at my house to relax. (Age seven)

Try not to get caught up in the competitive rush to sign up, join in, and push harder to give your child a leg up on the other kids. His childhood is an important time all on its own— it's not just the preparation for adulthood. The best possible edge for your child is your sensitivity to his fragile inner life. A child's freedom to imagine lies at the root of a happy and well-balanced attitude toward work in later life. More important, kids need to do what comes naturally to them—play. Find other families who are providing open-ended time for their children. Support one another. Studies show that 96 percent of American families complain of not having enough time in their days. Keep time open for your children to experience inspiration, intuition, reverence, and wonder.

In heaven no one gets hurt. They have lots of time there, lots of free time. (Age six)

I call this "Nature Art." I come outside and use whatever the earth leaves for me. Then I scoop with an acorn and pat down the earth or place a stick in a little hole and put small stones around it in a circle. Then I tie a flower that I find that has fallen on the ground on the top of the stick like a flag. It is a nature sculpture. I kind of leave these sculptures around places. (Age six)

Take time out just to "be." This can be the very best block of structured time in our hectic scheduled lives. Loosen the edges of the structure and relax. Let the children lie on their backs outside and look at the clouds or the stars or the tree-tops. Watch the busy bugs. Pretend you are ants and imagine how the world would look. Imagine you are clouds or trees or birds, and see the yard from a different perspective. If you need to schedule this time off, then do so.

> *I remember when I was little I was really happy during the summers on the farm with my grandparents. I played in the barn, helped with the animals, and ran free all day. I wish I could go back to those days.* (Mother of five)

> *There is so much to do with my dad and my mom working all the time. I don't have time to go to my thinking place. Like today I have to go to a friend's because my dad has to work, so it will be too dark when I get home to go to my special place.* (Age six)

Allow school-age children to select an agreed-upon number of "personal days" each year. These are days when the child isn't sick, but feels he needs some time to relax. We all occa-sionally need time away from our structured days to free our spirits. Use your best judgment and instinct on the timing and use of this escape from routine. A mom we know acted on an inner cue and gave her daughter a much-needed quiet day:

> *One morning my daughter was acting unusually crabby and short-tempered. Impulsively I asked her if she wanted to stay home from school. I work from a home office, so I could do this. She was thrilled and spent the*

whole day reading in the hammock and puttering around her room. The next morning she was back to her old self. Of course I had to be clear that this wasn't an ordinary luxury, but every now and again, as long as her schoolwork was going well, we could arrange an at-home day. (Mother of two)

Some other ideas for creating a flexible structure include:

- Help your child listen to the signals from his body about food, rest, play. A baby has no problem responding to his body signals, but as he grows he is expected to adjust to the messages from family and community. Help him out with this. Try to find appropriate ways to balance the child's rhythm, flow, and needs within the family structure. The more a child listens to, and trusts, his own natural signals, the more he will respond to his body's healthy flow.

- Alter the daily routine. Take a recess from dishwashing for a night. Change the bedtime "just because." Sleep upside down in your bed. Switch rooms for a night or day. Have a long walk after breakfast and before chores. Turn the lights out and just use candles—on purpose! Get up very early to watch the sun rise or stay up late to see the moon. Just keep in mind that some changes in structure and routine are scary and unsettling for children. Use your good sense and your knowledge of your child.

- Evaluate household rules. Rules are important for the structure of the home, but can become tired and outdated as families change and grow. Can you discuss some issues that were dogmatically imposed last year? What about allowances, treats, food in the living room, owning a cat, taking your shoes off, cleaning your room on Saturday, calling your friend after nine? Maybe new rules need to be made or old rules dropped. Be flexible, but maintain the structure. Don't forget to ask your kids about their rules.

If my parents said I could change the rules in my house I don't think I'd change any except maybe I'd be able to eat in the chair my grandfather gave my mom. It's so comfortable. (Age nine)

- Vary meals. Maybe your family would have fun with a monthly dinner with international cuisine and music— wear clothes to fit the country. Let the children pick a country and plan the menu. There can be music, traditions, and food from that country. Have tea in the afternoon (old-fashioned chamomile tea has been known to calm the wildest child) in the bedroom on a tray. How about breakfast in bed on an ordinary day? It needn't be complicated or elaborate, just a change from the usual routine. Let the structure be flexible and enhance your children's sense of wonder.

Helping Your Child to Make Choices

It is important for children to have the opportunity to make choices and to learn from those choices; it gives them a sense of control over things that affect them. It may rock the boat a little, but choosing and learning from the consequences are necessary parts of growing up. If Susie takes swimming lessons she may miss going to her friend's house for a long weekend, but she will be able to swim without water wings in the big pool. Let Susie decide, then help her accept the consequences on the sad day when her pal goes off for her long weekend, or when she has to put on her water wings. Remember not to overwhelm children with too many options. "Do you want to wear the green shirt or the yellow shirt?" may be simpler for your four-year-old than "What do you want to wear?" Remember also to strike a balance between giving children a say in their lives and honoring your own needs and choices. Be flexible to the child who really needs some direction rather than the opportunity to make a choice. Strike a balance between respecting children's feelings and giving them some direction when they need it.

When your child is faced with a decision, invite her to ask God for help. Perhaps she can think about all the possible outcomes of her choice and try each one on for size. What does it feel like in her body when she imagines each outcome? God is working with us and through our bodies and our minds to give us clear clues about our decisions, both big and small. Decision making with God as our guide can be less stressful.

Remind your child to think about what he believes in when he makes a choice. Connecting with our value system leads to creative solutions. When our choices are structured by being kind, staying honest, not hurting anyone, taking the high road, it becomes obvious what we must do. If your child is having trouble making a specific decision, ask him to step back from the dilemma and ask himself questions like: "What's the right thing to do in this situation, according to who I am and what I believe in?" Then remind him to listen to the answer that is generated.

Pay attention to the differences in your children. Allow each to be who he really is. One child may insist on order and ritual and feel panicked by the simplest change, while another is always wanting to push the limits and might need a firmer structure. The child who today clings may tomorrow push away. Being open and responsive to the particular quirks and needs of each child is essential, and not always easy! Just when you think you've got it—the behavior changes! If you are confused about what your children need or how they are different, take a moment to focus on each child's individuality. Observe and listen to the ideas that come. A father of five has a wonderful philosophy about his children's individuality. He tells us: "I treat my kids as equals but not the same."

Notice and accommodate the child who needs more time alone, the one who likes to snuggle, the child who keeps her distance. Be alert to your children's responses to new situations and support their individuality. Accept the differences in your children so they need not spend their time trying to be what they are not. Celebrate who they are! Praise their different approaches to life while keeping the family boundaries clear.

Cultivate your children's individual talents and try to be flexible enough so that these talents find expression within your home. Maybe your child can select the color of her bedroom or paint the inside of her closet with the colors and pictures that make her soul sing. Or if your child has an interest in plants, perhaps he can grow tomatoes or herbs from seeds. The music fan may choose to have his radio on with music too loud to bear—okay with headphones, in his room. Flexibility.

I've let my nine-year-old son, who has real inner vision, decorate and arrange our living room. He naturally began doing this at a young age. It mattered to him where things went and how they looked. It's not House Beautiful, but it's our interesting home and there is a lot going on. (Mother of three)

- Many kids love team sports, and thrive with that kind of structure. But children also love to make up games, and flex the rules according to the situation or whim.

When my children were younger they played "night games" like Kick the Can and Hide-and-Seek. They made up the rules depending on who was playing. These loosely run games lasted until organized games, Little League and such, took over. I think they missed those "night games." (Father of three)

- Stay open to the idea that your family is living a spiritual experiment and it is in the ebb and flow, the yin and yang, the ups and downs, the openness to change, that you grow closer to one another and to God.

- Get creative with your family's entertainment and take turns deciding what you are going to do for fun. Perhaps assign an "entertainment director," taking turns each week or month. What does each family member love to do?

I'm happy to sit quietly and read a book. (Mother of two)

It is sheer heaven to be able to get out my easel and paints and have an entire afternoon to paint. (Mother of two)

I love to go to the park with my sister and my mom, who can push me for hours on the swing—really high. It's scary but fun. (Age four)

- Take local field trips. Let your child choose the direction and take a walk for ten minutes that way. See what you discover. Go to a new shop, church, museum, football game, playground, friend's house, farm, train station, neighborhood, town, state, place in your yard, beach, or mountain. Let an older child select a place on the map and visit the library to find information on the place—an adventure in travel at home.

- Learning is marvelously entertaining, especially if you steer away from the "assignment" mode and explore fresh subjects with your child. Look up information about a bug found in the grass, how a bike works, or where water comes from. Research what kinds of clothes children wore when Mommy was a little girl. Have you met or read about a person from a different country? Investigate that country's culture. Learn about your town's history, or your family's background. Encourage your children to ask questions, then show them where and how to find the answers.

- Be flexible with clothing. Haven't we all had those days when we want to snuggle into our pajamas? Give it a try. Make sure you each have enough comfort clothes—the kind that make you feel cozy and at ease.

- Choose family fun and togetherness for some part of each weekend. If it is necessary to schedule it, then do so.

Weekends are about catching up and planning for the upcoming week. It's usually a blur of rushing around. We have started to block out specific times to be together, even if it's just for breakfast, and it's forced us to pause and slow down. (Mother of three)

- Our spiritual dimension includes humor. When your children get silly, get silly yourself, let go of your grown-up side, and have fun. Talk in a silly language if "ou-yay ancay emember-ray"! (You remember pig Latin, don't you?)

Let your child's joyful spirituality be free and reclaim your own spontaneity. God's world need not be always solemn; laughter and fun enrich the soul.

I don't have money for toys for my kids and our VCR is broken, but we still have fun. We acted out Gilligan's Island *the other day. Everybody laughed.* (Mother of three)

I played jacks with an eight-year-old today. I haven't done that in forty years! I was pretty good. (Grandfather of two)

• Add a new twist to relationships. Trade roles with one another for an evening. Let Dad braid hair one day. Have the youngest child take on the role of eldest for a few minutes while the eldest gets to be the baby. Mom assumes the child's role—the child becomes the dad—Dad becomes the mom.

• Allow time for your own needs. Nurturing yourself, tending to your own spirituality, is so very important, for it allows you the energy to enjoy raising your spiritual children. Within the structure of your day take time for yourself. Practice yoga, pray, meditate, refresh your soul. We've included some affirmations and exercises just for you. We encourage you to add these, or your own, to your personal, spirit-enriching list of to-dos.

• Ask your kids to make a list of all the things they "have" to do. Some of the things might be "Go to bed at nine. Make my bed in the morning. Be kind to my sister. When I make a mess I have to clean it up." Next, ask them to write down things they "choose" to do. These could be "Play with a friend. Read *Little House* books. Wear black overalls. Play with my brother sometimes." Discuss these lists together. Which one is longer? Do they have enough choices in their lives?

- Avoid getting into a rut. Take a risk and try something new just for yourself. Take that writing class that calls to your heart or arrange for a weekend away to think and plan. Leave room for your child's sudden inspiration too.

Being flexible is more than just bending the schedule, it is really about accepting your child for who he is right now rather than imposing on him some standard that suits your own needs at the moment. Children are beings of light and love who want to spread their joyful abundance of spirit. Does the schedule of your family allow your child's light to shine and you to bask in it?

Parents' Insight-Building Exercise

Outline a typical weekday in the life of your family. Take three sheets of paper, and label them "Morning," "Afternoon," and "Evening." Fill in each sheet with the normal events for that time of the day. What does each member of the family usually do in the morning? Who wakes up first? Who makes the beds? What goes on at breakfast? What is eaten at breakfast? How do the children get off to school? Just write down images as they come to you. If you children are in school during most of the day, write down what happens when they come home on the "Afternoon" sheet. Who picks them up? Do they let themselves in the house? For "Evening," write about the dinner hour, homework, bedtime routine, and other events in your home that end the day.

Now look over these typical weekdays and see what stands out. Is there a routine? Where could adjustments be made to add flexibility if it looks too structured or to add order if the pace is frantic? Reflect on this information.

Take three more sheets of paper, again label them "Morning," "Afternoon," and "Evening," and rewrite your typical weekday. How would you like the days to run? What do you visualize as the perfect scenario for a normal day in the life of your family? Write it with as much detail as you can imagine. Have fun with this. If your "inner critic" is telling you, "Are you kidding? Your day could never look like that," block it out. Tell yourself that this is the reality you see for your life. The pictures you visualize can and will create your reality. Ask your kids to try this exercise. How do they interpret a typical day?

Parents' Check-in Questions

- If I could spend a whole day doing anything I wanted, how would the day look?

- How are the rules of our family working?

- Do my kids have reasonable choices in their lives? Do I set wise limits?

- How flexible have I been today?

- In what ways have my children changed in the last three months?

- What part of my family structure needs work?

- What values and beliefs am I seeing in my children? Do I like what I see?

CHILDREN'S GUIDED JOURNEY

Close your eyes and let your body become soft and relaxed. Sink into the floor and grow roots right through the floor and down into the ground. Feel yourself safely attached to the earth. You are secure there. Now let your mind focus on an imaginary sky full of hundreds of colors. You can see green and yellow, pink, fuchsia, orange, purple, brown, turquoise; you can see whatever colors are glorious and beautiful for you. You can see all God's magic colors. You can see the light of the sun as it shines through the colors. What wonderful shimmering colors are above you!

Now imagine you have a giant paintbrush and the colors and light of the sun and sky are your paint box. Think of the space around you as drawing paper. Take that huge paintbrush and dip it into the colors you love, bring it down to the paper, and paint in those shiny colors. Swish your brush into some other colors and put them on the paper. Paint and paint and paint. Use any color you like. Use all the colors mixed up if you wish. Dip and paint. How beautiful your paper is. See it all around you. Colors of beauty everywhere.

Look back up at the imaginary sky. Do you see sparkling sunshine? Touch it with your giant paintbrush and scatter the sparkles onto your paper. Use as much sun sparkle as you wish. This is lovely. Your paper is beautiful and shiny and sparkly. Continue dipping and painting until your paper is just as you like it. Amazing, beautiful colors. Look at it. You are a wonderful artist.

When you are ready to put away the paintbrush and paper, imagine you are placing it in a very safe place. Maybe you can give it to an angel to keep for you. When you have finished cleaning up your wonderful painting tools, take a few moments to remember the colors. You can paint with them again whenever you wish. Now open your eyes and slowly bring your mind back to this room. Shake your body a little—gently—to loosen the roots you have put into the ground. All loose? Okay, now slowly sit up. That was a lovely adventure and you can have it again whenever you wish.

Children's Check-in Questions

- What's fun about our family?

- When do you relax?

- What kinds of things do you like to learn about?

- What is your favorite time of day?

- Let's discuss our family's rules. What do you think of them? How can we make things better?

- Do you like the pace of our days? How could we change it so as to be more comfortable for us all?

Affirmations

ADULT

I move within God's secure structure. I am safe here.

I am free and unlimited and flow with the moment.

I set clear limits and expectations for my children.

I am open and adaptable to change.

I live fully in the present.

CHILD

I have enough time to get everything done.

I have many unique talents.

I am safe within my family. I can try new things.

I take time each day to listen to the silence inside me.

BE A POSITIVE MIRROR FOR YOUR CHILD

My husband and I believe that our spirituality must be evident in our daily lives. We try to live so that our children will be able to see God through us. (Mother of five)

We are mirrors for our children and show by example how spirituality and daily life merge. Everything we do or say, every habit we have, our tone of voice, our expressions, all teach our children what the world is and how they fit into it. What they see in us is a mirror of the bigger world. What they see in us is a mirror of who they are and who they are to become.

My whole, entire family likes to pray. I guess that's just who we are. Maybe it's part of us—like in our blood or something. We gotta sing it out and say "amen" and "alleluia Lord." It feels really nice—comfortable—you know. (Age ten)

What you do now, for and with your child, is very important; what you do with your own life also sends profound mes-

sages that will remain with her throughout her life. This
responsibility need not be a burden; instead it can be a joyous
adventure for you both. What the child sees in the mirror of
you, she sees as herself. She forms her earliest ideas about God,
the world, people, and trust from what is mirrored from you.
Do you see the world as safe or dangerous, a place to take
from or give to? How do you wish your child to see God?
How do you wish your child to see herself? How do you live
and demonstrate your spirituality? Is this the way you wish her
to experience her connection with the Divine? If you believe in
unlimited good, and focus on the positives in life, chances are
your child will too. As you put your spirituality into everything you do, you turn each experience into an opportunity for
increased good; you create your reality and your child wit-
nesses that miracle.

You are a specific and custom-made mirror, a mirror with
feelings, judgments, and intellect. As your child looks toward
you for his identity and his impressions of the world, he sees
the reflection as it has filtered through your belief system.
Become aware of what your child is seeing. Take some time to
look inside your heart and examine your soul's deepest long-
ings—your intimate connection with spirit. This is not about
being perfect, so go gently. Be mindful of your spirituality as it
manifests in your daily life. Are you following your intuition,
trusting in God's divine plan, eliminating judgments, flowing
moment to moment? Is your spiritual path crossing over into
your role as a parent? Increase the positive messages you mirror and work on the not-so-positive ones. What is your child
observing in your mirror of faith?

Don't be afraid to ask God for help. Look inside, pray, meditate, keep a journal, find role models. Begin to nurture an intimate relationship with your soul so you can forge a spiritual

path that is personal, creative, life-affirming, and joyful. To support the spiritual lives of our children we must first find a way to nourish ourselves. What feeds your soul? What people or events uplift you? Do you have resources for the times you feel empty? Look carefully and then attend to your needs as best you can each day so you have the energy to mirror your true self to your child. Everybody benefits as you gain insight into yourself.

Life is busy. You may be a single parent, a grandparent, a working parent, an out-of-work parent. Whatever your life situation, remain attentive to the signals you send. Put yourself in your child's body and look out. Does she see herself as a chore or a delight? How does your state of body, mind, and soul impact your child's view of himself? Are you too frazzled at the end of a day to nurture yourself, much less your child? Look carefully at your life and where you could change things to send more positive light to the child in your world.

I pretend to be grown-up. I worry if I get things wrong. I cry when I am sad. (Age six)

One mother of a seven-year-old was concerned about her son's hope for "piles and piles of money." When she explored it a little further she came to the realization that she grumbled about money—and the lack of it in her life—quite often. Could her son have felt that if he had "gobs of money," his mother would be happy—or home with him all day? Look at the subtle messages you mirror to your child. Study your child carefully. Do you see yourself anywhere? Do you like what you see?

When my mama laughs and smiles it seems like the sun comes out inside the house. (Age five)

*I say hi to Daddy just like my mama does. Sometimes I
hug and kiss him, but when I'm mad I just say nothing.*
(Age six)

It is a huge and blessed honor we have as parents. We are
given an opportunity to help shape the life of another human
being. Our children, equipped with their own remarkable gifts,
are in our care for better or worse. With the help of God we can
make that caring magnificent. Let us choose to mirror love, joy,
optimism, faith, hope, kindness, generosity, understanding, and
forgiveness, and in so doing nurture our children's souls.

*When it comes to honoring my son's sovereignty, I bal-
ance my absolute respect of him as my brother with the
practical lessons of dealing with authority that it's my
job as his earth mother to help him learn. My experience is that there is not a wrong or right way. If I listen
to my heart, pray, and meditate, I make fewer mistakes,
and am able to allow myself to be guided in this area. I
pray with my son often, "God, help me to be the mom
you would have me be today. Thank you for this angel
you sent to earth." My kids are definitely my teachers,
bringing my unhealed places to the Light, and showing
me how to enjoy life.* (Mother of four)

BEING A POSITIVE MIRROR FOR YOUR CHILD

*Be careful the life you lead, you may be the only Bible
some people read.* (Author unknown)

Like it or not, we are it! Scary and exciting and true, we are
mirrors for our children; we are the one big reflection of life

for them. Let's present an uplifting mirror, one shining with our own spirit.

When I grow up I'm gonna be a mama and all my babies is gonna be girls and they are gonna be exactly like me. (Age four)

Think about the way you feel when you are with positive people, people who are interested in life, curious to learn, excited by the magic around them. Do you catch their outlook? Do you feel more energized and enthused about the possibilities in your life? Optimism, a positive outlook, is contagious. Draw more of these enriching people into your life and join them in becoming someone who energizes others. Allow optimism into your days, then spread it around. It's a great mindset from which to parent.

If possible, let go of the people or situations that drag you down. Christine Lavin, a popular folk singer, calls these negative people "energy vampires" and sings a funny song about how they can "suck you dry." You know the ones—they call you just to complain about the weather and conjure worst-case scenarios for each new risk you take. Why let these people deplete you when you have so much to give your children and your world?

Use the following powerful affirmation for releasing negative situations in your life: "I let go of everything and everybody that is no longer a part of the divine plan of my life. I forgive and move forward with the light of God guiding me. I release any negativity I may have held. I have all the energy I need to live my life's purpose. I have all the energy I need for my children, and myself." Adapt these words for your kids to use.

Children look to us to show them the best way to live. They see how we behave, believe, and talk, and they take it as "the way it should be done." We have an opportunity to teach them valuable lessons about perfection. None of us is faultless, nor is our world. Each day we grow, improve, and come to terms with imperfection. God doesn't expect us to be perfect, nor can we expect it of our kids; but we can strive to do our best while keeping our lives in balance. Do your children witness a parent who is never happy with himself? Are you your own worst critic? What if your child heard you applaud yourself for trying, for risking, for dreaming, for relaxing? If you aren't enough for yourself, how can your child ever hope to measure up?

The world seems to move faster and faster each day. Stimuli and messages bombard us from all directions; media, traffic, entertainment, medicine present more and more "important things we must do." We live in an age of "instant information" and "immediate satisfaction." This ongoing stimulation is difficult for children—as well as for their parents—and the ability to maintain balance becomes a valuable strength. If we are able to achieve a healthy equilibrium, we can more honestly mirror it to our children. Are our days run by the clock, lists, and schedules? Are our routines devoid of peaceful times and flexibility? How about our children's days? Are they packed with things that must be done, people who must be heard, and places where they must go—school, teachers, bus drivers, day care, extra classes, camps, baby-sitters? Do we control our children's wardrobes, choice of friends, activities, hobbies, chores, food choices, reading options? When our kids get home from school, is there enough time for them to unwind before beginning homework, chores, dinner? Do we allow them to relax or do we see that as "goofing off"?

A family we know recently purchased a puppy for their two children. The truth about their hectic schedules was clearly illustrated by a crying puppy who received little attention. The children had limited free time for the puppy—a few minutes in the morning between piano practice and the arrival of the school bus. Most afternoons were filled with ballet lessons, Girl Scout meetings, church choir, play dates at friends' homes. Weekends were packed with swim lessons, soccer games, birthday parties, grocery shopping, science projects, horse shows, and often out-of-town guests. The puppy spent more time in his crate than living the vision the family had of him leaping and running in the backyard with squealing children. The puppy was the impetus for this family to slow down their lives. They declined weekend parties, cut out swim lessons, woke up an hour earlier in the morning just to play, put guests up at a local hotel, chose only one activity or class a week. They took evening walks together and spent time frolicking in the backyard with their adorable puppy. This doesn't mean you should go out and get a dog, but do take inventory of all the to-dos in your family's life. Are you enjoying simple, stress-free activities together?

> *What is important to our family? Being together and doing things on our own schedule. If my children want to play soccer or basketball they go outside or they find their dad. On weekends we go camping or play outside, going for bike rides and in-line skating. In the fall we signed up our ten-year-old for soccer. What happened? He wanted his freedom back. He didn't like having to go to practices. He wanted to play outside with friends or do other things. I had guilt, but no more.* (Mother of four)

You can begin by examining all the areas of your life, all the "things" you carry. Is your load too heavy? Are you saying "yes" to things that pull you away from your family or your goals? Would you like to let go of some obligation? What can you drop? If you release some duty or problem, your child will observe and perhaps follow your example. Go ahead, unload a little. Forget the quarrel with the neighbor that zaps your energy, decline the dinner party that you dread attending, resign from the school board and spend the time in your child's classroom instead, turn on the answering machine after nine P.M. and soak in the bathtub. A busy mother we know had a harsh realization about all the "things" she was involved in:

> *I realized I was doing so many things for my children that I was never home with them. When I got home from work I was on the phone arranging things for all the committees I was on at their school, coming up with Sunday school lessons, baking for bake sales, finishing up business so I could go in the next day and parent-help in their classroom. I was short-tempered with my kids, I was so exhausted. One day it hit me that this was a crazy way to live. I wasn't really helping them, I was just busy trying to enhance their activities. It has become easy now to say "no." I have gotten off all committees and only volunteer one day a month at their school. Everyone is happier.* (Mother of two)

We show children that we have the potential to change, the power to move forward, and the ability to improve with God's help. If our minds are full of love, peace, and abundance, those concepts will reflect back into our lives and into the lives of our children. Our kids watch closely and absorb our "lessons" and actions. As we reflect positive and healthy beliefs and behaviors, we open their futures. By showing them how we are courageous, committed, spiritual, kind, and imperfect individuals, we present children with an encyclopedia of healthy, reachable behaviors. When our kids see us standing up for someone who is being put down, they will do the same thing. When we go the extra mile and reach out to someone who is alone, our kids will take the same risk. If we witness injustice and take up a pen to write a letter of complaint, our children will become empowered to voice their opinions. If we give our word to someone, or to ourselves, and keep it no matter the situation, our kids will honor their commitments. When we ask ourselves aloud in the morning, "What is it I might do today for you, dear Lord?" our children will go into their days with the same awareness. If we ask for forgiveness when we make mistakes, our kids won't be ashamed to take the high road.

Whatever we treasure deeply we reflect to our kids. If we treasure a connection with God, our children will value God. If we treat family members and friends with respect, so will our children. Let's demonstrate these behaviors and beliefs, not simply talk the good line. We can begin with loyalty to our extended family as these two women did:

I insist our kids visit their grandmother once a week. She lives close to us, so it's not difficult, but they don't always like to go, and I believe in family members supporting each other. The other day my seventeen-year-old daughter told me she had really learned a lot from her grandmother and liked talking with her now. The other children haven't fussed about the visits since. (Mother of three)

I watched my grandmother take in her two brothers when they became unable to live alone and saw my own mother bring her mother into our home. It seemed to be the natural thing to do. Mother lovingly cared for Gram until she died, and we all participated in that care. In looking back I recall how Mother allowed Gram to maintain her role in the family long after she was incapacitated by poor health. I like taking care of family, so I guess I'm lucky, and we learned by example that families take care of each other. (Mother of five)

Living a life with integrity will win your child's respect. It is earned daily, as your child observes you. Are you consistent and valid? Do you say and do the same thing? Are you a mirror reflecting the person you wish your child to imitate? If good sportsmanship is important, are you a sore loser? Is it a rule in your family to respect others' property? Do you get away with sneaking chocolates out of a Halloween stash that's clearly not yours? How about the little white lie you tell the neighbor? Do you ask your children to respect others, then cut off another driver in traffic? Do you tell your children it is wrong to steal, then show them a grown-up who gets away with copying videotapes? Of course you will find flaws here and there; we are all flawed. We are changing, exhausted, excited, defeated, wondering, worrying, courageous, joyful parents. We are marred human beings able to do marvelous things when we have God as our guide and parenting partner. The goal, however, is to operate our lives with the intent to become the kinds of persons we would like our children to be—for our actions to be consistent with our values. This father adjusted his actions after his son called him on an inconsistency:

Last Sunday after church we were all loading into the van to come home. It had been a long service and I was really looking forward to reading the newspaper and having some downtime. As we were about to pull out of the parking lot my wife remembered that I had a church committee meeting—right then. "I'll just tell them I forgot about it," I mumbled. My eight-year-old son, who doesn't miss a trick, piped up with "But, Daddy, that's lying, didn't we just talk about honesty in Sunday school?" I teach Sunday school. I was so embarrassed I had to laugh and admit he was right— that was a lie. I decided I would tell the committee head the truth, that I was tired and wanted to go home. That is what I did. I called him that evening and told him why I wasn't at the meeting. My son quietly observed every minute of the call. (Father of two)

Your beliefs determine what you will find in your world. If you focus on negativity you experience negative events. Do you wake up expecting the worst, spend your day looking for problems and usually finding them? Or do you look forward to a day filled with successes and unexpected surprises?

Understand that we create our experiences by what we think; what we say to ourselves becomes our reality. Try to say positive things and focus on assets rather than deficiencies. Rather than thinking, "I'll never be able to learn how to budget my time," consider, "I'll focus on one thing at a time today and get things done easily. I have all the time I need." It doesn't hurt a bit to request a little assistance in this: "God, can you give me a bit of focus here please." Or, "I could use my angel's assistance with this work today." Help will come in some way at some time and your child will repeat the behaviors you have mirrored to him.

Why be a positive mirror?

- Love needs to be reflected as a multifaceted, all-embracing, enriching virtue. Children who see this kind of love in the mirror of their parents learn early how tenderness satisfies their souls. If Mom and Dad demonstrate love by respecting and appreciating each other and their children, that loving energy resonates in the household. As we speak lovingly about absent friends and family we mirror a message of kindness and affection.

• Your role as a mother or father is the first and most influential reflection of God's world to your children. It is the parent's behavior that the child uses as a benchmark for the world. His spirituality, already within him, can be welcomed and enriched, or ignored and diluted. How fortunate the child with a spiritually positive parental mirror!

MIRROR A POSITIVE AND SPIRITUAL DAILY LIFE TO YOUR CHILDREN

I think we are all setting examples for our children if we know it or not. When they see the types of lives we are living, our spirituality shines through. I work with seventh graders. One of the rules in class is to be positive and not put other people down. I know how difficult junior high is and I feel that is important to give them a safe environment where the energy is positive. It takes a lot of decreeing some days to get it that way, but I try to have that as a goal. My point is, we don't always have to talk specifically about spirituality; children begin to get it by the example we set. (Father of two, teacher of twenty-two)

In this chapter we are focusing primarily on you, the parent. Your children copy what you do, what you say, how you interact. What a surprise when your child uses the same words you do, responds in a familiar way to a situation, or makes a choice using your logic. Here is an opportunity to enrich your child's life and spirit while watching the results of your efforts live and in living color. The relationship is a symbiotic one; as the inner lives of your sons and daughters blossom in the reflection of your spirit, your own soul flourishes. A rather lovely reward for parenting well, don't you think?

Our spirituality is always available and need not be partitioned away, closed into a closet to be brought out and dressed up occasionally. Rather it can be the driving force in our lives. Accept and incorporate this philosophy into your being, and your parenting will be smoother—choices and decisions will be made easier as you approach them from a spiritual and example-setting perspective. Did the cashier give you too much change? This is a great opportunity to show your child the right thing to do. Is your father recovering from an illness? Instead of silent words of thanks, can you stop what you are doing and together with your children thank God for answering your prayers. "Thank you, God, for helping Poppy get better. We know you are at work and your divine order is being established." Are you at odds with your child today? Is his behavior driving you crazy? Instead of reacting to the behavior, use the moment as an opportunity to pray for guidance— maybe even out loud? "Okay, God, I am really angry at Mark right now because he is teasing his sister, complaining, not cooperating, and hurting my feelings. Is there something I can do to help him or can you give us both guidance in this moment?" Then follow through on God's inspiration.

Imagine for a moment how our world would be if everyone embraced a spiritual philosophy for living. How do you think the next generation would change if today's adults parented from a spiritual base, living their lives with meaning and purpose, actively expressing positive ideals and values? If we all were to live a spiritual existence, people would be happier, kinder, more fulfilled, patient, and honest, and less anxious. One six-year-old expressed it this way:

> *God could make everybody happy if only people would listen. We always know deep down what to do. It just depends on how deep you decide to listen.* (Age six)

As you become a positive mirror for your child, remember it's okay to make her aware of your negative feelings—when you feel stuck, overloaded, inadequate, or just plain cranky. Your spirit is sagging and you reflect that to your child. Fine— in fact, excellent. Talk with your child about your mood and your accompanying behavior. "I'm tired and I know I'm being cross and impatient this morning, Tim, and you really want me to help you build that bridge. If I can have about twenty min- utes alone with my book and my tea I'll be a happier partner for you." In explaining your situation you have done several positive things.

1: Dad has told me that he's crabby today because of some- thing in his life. I'm not responsible for Dad's mood.

2: If Dad gets cranky it must be okay for me to be cross sometimes too. Dad's not perfect, so I guess I don't have to be perfect either.

3: Dad talks to me about how he's feeling, so it's okay for me to do the same.

4: There is something Dad does to help himself feel better. Maybe I can find things to help me when I feel bad.

All of us have a spiritual toolbox for any situation we encounter—our own equipment for tackling life's ups and downs. What is in your box? Prayers? Meditations? Affirmations? What happens when you are faced with a painful decision? Do you find comfort when you go to church, read a religious or spiritual book, get out into nature, go within and ask for God's help, call a dear friend, help someone? There is a great deal of giving involved in parenting—how do you replenish yourself? How do you give thanks for the blessings in your life? Find your tools and let your children know how you use them. Share the valuable lessons you have learned through life with your personal stories that reflect ways to deal with real challenges.

> *When I feel overwhelmed I take a walk and try to talk to God. Sometimes I need a loving pal, often one of my grown children, to listen before I can get clear enough to chat with the Holy Spirit to find the answers.* (Mother of four)

> *I have an easier time praying and connecting with God in my everyday routine. When disaster strikes, as it has recently, I am stunned out of my habitual spiritual practices. I can't meditate in the morning because I'm at the hospital with my husband who is ill. I find I am searching for a way to reach God. I am full of panic and want something concrete to hold on to. My kids are looking to me for ways to get through this time. We talk to God at bedtime; those standard prayers have helped them have some level of normality.* (Mother of three)

We have a friend who practices what she calls "insurance prayers." She prays in front of her children constantly. She blesses the driver who patiently allows her to pull out of a parking space—without honking. During the holidays she praises the creativity of those who have decorated the outsides of their homes. "Thanks for adding extra light and sparkles to our holiday. I send you light and sparkles back so you may be filled with the love of God." This mother blesses her children's friends when they come over to play by complimenting them and pointing out their positive qualities. When times are tough and she has trouble praying, all those little "insurance prayers" float back and lift her up.

Your own spiritual growth is a gift to your children—as you grow spiritually, you will connect with them in deeper, more meaningful ways. Spiritual growth, like spiritual parenting, is a process. We experience life, we respond, we learn. Our soul's development continues throughout our lives. We have the opportunity to talk to our kids about this maturing process without preaching or pontificating. When we give them information about our spiritual path we offer them a precious intimacy into our lives. If we're lucky they will return this gift and we've become dual nurturers.

I have been spiritually pragmatic most of my life— always searching for intellectually acceptable answers. I found many and incorporated them into my life, but it wasn't until I was well into my mature years that I began to understand faith and the reality of the unanswerable questions. (Father of four)

Celebrate mistakes as opportunities for learning. If you flub up in your child's presence, use it as an example of acceptance. "Oh my, this meat loaf is truly awful! I must have left something out. Next time I'll try not to rush and read the recipe better." Or, "I guess I spoke harshly to Uncle Ed on the telephone.

I need to say what I mean instead of getting angry." Or, "I'm going to keep trying to cross-country ski—even though I couldn't get the rhythm of it today." Your children will remember your relaxed behavior, your lack of embarrassment about failure. They will see that you are willing to risk and try new things without worrying about failing along the way.

Acknowledging mistakes doesn't weaken our authority; it teaches children to own up to their own. "Oops, I missed on that one" or "I'm sorry I hurt your feelings" are important words for children to hear from us. When we fall short of our own expectations we can let our kids know about it. As a family we can strive for the best, but support and encourage one another when we don't quite make it.

> *More than anything else I try to live by example for my kids. I make many mistakes each day. God has taken to reminding me that there are times I must go to my children and ask them to forgive me—sometimes for being overly cross with them, yelling at them when I'd rather be yelling at my husband. I let them know I make mistakes; I let them know I've asked God for forgiveness, and I ask them to forgive me too.* (Mother of three)

We can't be flawless, we make mistakes, and many of us learn the most from these mistakes. Create an atmosphere at home where mistakes are accepted as signs that learning is going on. Sometimes we might even applaud mistakes as these parents do:

> *People always think I'm nuts but I want my children to learn that when you make a mistake, it's okay. So, if they spill the milk, we sometimes clap and say, "Yeah, you made a mistake!" and giggle a bit. I always follow*

up by teaching them to repair their mistakes, like, "What have you seen Mommy do when I spill something?" They say, "Get the sponge?" and I say, "Go for it!" (Mother of three)

I try to make a point of putting up pictures that aren't the "perfect" illustrations or spelling tests with a few incorrect answers. My son is really hard on himself and I want to make sure to display work that isn't considered "the best" so he learns we value all aspects of him, not just when he is perfect. (Mother of two)

Show your child you are human and imperfect, just as are all people. Let her know you try continually to improve, but accept failings as part of your humanness. When you accept the inevitable flaws, life will be easier for you both. As you acknowledge your own inadequacies, release any expectation of perfection from your child. Let him be who he is and not who you think he should be. By relaxing into this acceptance you release a struggle you may not even know was there. Try to do this internally, for yourself, and externally, for your child. Tell him he is wonderful as he is, and when he learns to ride a two-wheeler he will be a wonderful kid on a two-wheeler. Let her know you don't care a whit that she can't stand on her toes like her sister, or that she spills things or falls over her feet or has red hair instead of black like her friend who is *perfect*. Let her know she is as she should be at this time, and she is a most delightful child. Not the perfect anything.

I try to be good, but I keep being bad. Sometimes I just think it's too hard and stop trying. (Age five)

Demonstrate to your child that challenges, things we don't do well, are not bad, but are simply areas that need work. As your child sees you accept your own shortcomings, she'll learn that imperfection is not something to criticize ourselves about. Let her see that you, like everyone, have strengths and weaknesses, and in working together, cooperating with each other, we can make use of each person's gifts. We can look for help from another person who might be strong where we are weak, and from God, who points us in the right direction when we listen. Combined with one another and with God we can do anything.

Accepting Our Differences

Mimi was recently the designated driver for a car full of nine-year-old girls. A purple-haired, wildly clad, nose-pierced teenager crossed the street in front of the car. Comments from the girls were fascinating. "Oh, gross—look at that weird girl," shrieked a child. "Go, girl, go, express yourself," proclaimed a usually shy and reserved girl. What are our attitudes about appearances? An attitude of acceptance allows us all a broader view of life's intricate nuances. So many opportunities are cut off when we demonstrate criticism and judgment to our kids. Reach beyond your cultural norm and expose your child to the brilliant dimensions of other cultures and other worlds through books, museums, magazines, music, travel, discussions, videos, exchange students. Reach out and your child will journey with you.

Children learn about acceptance by your demonstration, not just by your words. They will be the first to call you on your inconsistencies. When children see that you are not interested in specifics about people, such as what they wore or who said

what about whom, they have a pure blueprint on how to interact with the spirit in others rather than the petty human quirks
we all fall into judging and measuring.

Use your own divine sight to find God's spark within each
person. You will find remarkable hidden surprises and maybe
turn this way of thinking into a habit—one your child might
mirror. It is possible to bring pleasure into the most mundane
duties of our days. Most personal exchanges are opportunities
to share the light of God. Open yourself to each encounter and
pass along that wonderful light. Imagine your typical errand
day—a stop at the drugstore, another at the cleaners, at the
library, at the grocery store. What happens when you deal with
the people at these places? Are they warm and helpful? Do
they smile and seem glad to have you there? Think next about
how you respond to others. Are you a messenger of kindness,
of spirituality? Or are you a grump who barely speaks?
Certainly there are individuals who seem miserable doing their
jobs and act that misery out on us. Others shine their joy
toward us. Everyday life brings both responses and choices.
The circle of kindness can grow larger if you offer a gentle
word or a lovely smile. Ask for light, accept it, and mirror it
back to your child. Others too will see the reflection, for it
spreads onto many faces.

> For me, one of the most wonderful things about living
> in the South is the way people treat one another during
> the routine interactions. It is rare to pass another per-
> son on the sidewalk without a smile or a "Good morn-
> ing." A discussion about the weather is always a part of
> a grocery store checkout. Since so much of our time is
> spent doing errands, this charming attitude makes life a
> whole lot more pleasant. (Mother of four)

Be genuine in all areas of your life. Behave in a way that is consistent with what you believe. Live honestly. If you find you are having trouble and come across as someone other than who you truly are, it may be time to reevaluate your goals, beliefs, and priorities. Find your own spiritual center and let it direct you. Live in accordance with your inner truth and act on that in the world. It's a boundless, authentic, invigorating way to live. Your children will see any insincerity or artificiality very quickly. They love you for who you are.

Reveal Your Struggles

We pass down from generation to generation a moral and ethical code of sorts that can guide our children, give them a sense of belonging, and provide them with a framework for life. What did your parents give you? Are you living by that code now or have you modified it? Do you follow society's moral code or your own inner sense of right and wrong? Society's code might say it is okay to fudge a little come tax time, inflate your earnings on a résumé, flame someone on the Internet, or boo the opposing team. Our cultural mantra seems to be "Look out for number one," and we admire celebrities and athletes who have parlayed grossness and outrage into lucrative careers. How does today's promoted value system fit with your personal moral framework?

Because we are all stressed for time it becomes easy to drop the inconvenient courtesies, lose patience with the clerk who chats with the customer ahead of you in line, berate the waiter who made a mistake on your order, or ignore the car trying to merge into your lane. It's easier to "do what's right," however, when we remember our children are absorbing our actions as the moral code to live by.

I wrote a letter to the manager of a restaurant that I frequent a great deal. I named the waiters and waitresses who had been particularly kind and helpful over the year and wrote specifically the things they did that I was grateful for. It just took a few minutes to type up. I found out my letter was read at the restaurant's annual Christmas party. This was over a year ago. I ate at the restaurant last week and after the meal I thanked our attentive waiter. "You might not remember me, sir," he said, "but you mentioned me by name in a letter you wrote. It meant a whole lot." (Father of two)

It is a good idea to let your child know you frequently have difficulty making positive choices. "I would really love to go to the neighbors' party next week, but it is being held on Good Friday and that is a very holy day for us." How do you deal with routine choices? Share your strategies with your children; they are confronted early in their lives with the need to make choices and decisions. When your child faces a difficult challenge, suggest she draw or paint the two roads she could take, illustrating the picture with the situations or opportunities she finds on each road. Make it fun, not a task. Even young children like to do this with help from an adult. An older child can make a pro and con list for decision making. Applaud your child when she has the courage to make a choice that honors her personal values or intuitive guidance. Acting on her inner strength isn't easy when the choice goes against "what everyone else is doing." Your example and support are vital.

Another way to help your child make choices is to have him visualize a time in the future—a month, a year, five years, ten years from now, after he has made a particular choice. How does he feel about himself and his decision from that perspective? Now have him visualize how he might feel with a different choice. Is he proud of himself as he looks back at his decision? You can adapt this for the age of your child. It's effective for adults as well. The exciting thing is that when we choose an action that is consistent with our value system our spirit is at peace. If we act in a way outside our personal beliefs we're usually uncomfortable. Our spirit is unsettled.

Celebrate Your Spirituality

Participate in your chosen spiritual and religious rituals. Celebrate in a way that works for you. Look at your faith with a fresh eye. Sing hymns, drum, chant, or pray. Religious rituals can help keep you focused on the spiritual center of your life, and mirror a powerful message to your children. Symbols, stories, and myths feed children's imaginations. The spiritual stories and images you embrace will be captured by your child's memory. As modern Westerners we have allowed our symbols to become commercial icons to serve the economy, rather than images that relate to nature, the elements, seasons, history, or religious traditions. The symbols your children see you celebrating will provide them with meaning and comfort for a lifetime. Investigate your heritage or connect with the beliefs of ancient people who listened to the spirits of the natural world for their traditions. Reawaken and recapture the spirit and secrets of your childhood that nourished your young soul. Those images may be with you today—buried beneath the surface of your busy life.

> *I'm not much for churchgoing, but I find a lot of spiritual help from wandering in the woods, I have since I was a kid. It is a prayer for me.* (Father of two)

Establish routine prayers and meditations. Ask the blessing at mealtimes, say good-night prayers, ask for a safe journey as you get into the car and buckle everyone in, write a prayer to say at the beginning of each month and each school year, institute a few moments of meditation after school and before homework or other activities. These habits will stick with your kids. Say some traditional learned prayer when you feel unglued, or create a repertoire of song lyrics, poems, or prayers you have written for specific times. If nature is a spiritually rejuvenating tool for you, regularly include some exposure to the natural world in your life. Take the time to discover what nurtures your soul—explore. Your child will notice your search for spiritual fulfillment, and her own quest will unfold naturally.

Connecting with God in a comfortable and ongoing way is a wonderfully nurturing habit to incorporate into your life. This relationship need not be brought out and shined up only on Sundays, Shabbat, or holy days. Bring spirituality and religion into your everyday world where it belongs. Use your connection to gain strength and comfort all the time. Children raised in an open spiritual environment—where people appreciate and honor the spiritual dimensions of life—find the encouragement and support to develop the natural mysticism of childhood.

A concerned mother of two asked us, "How do I care for myself—my own soul—without being selfish?" What about opening your celebration of spirit, at times, into a soulful circle to include your children? Hike together and delight in the wonder of nature's gifts, practice yoga together, grow a garden that you design and tend as a family, learn a new skill you can bring your spirits to, such as playing the harp or piano, meditate together, attend your chosen church as a family and become involved in the outreach activities, be together in silence. Share what is joyful to you with your children—in doing so you bring God to your children and to yourself.

Be spontaneous in front of your kids. Exclaim about a lovely cloud or a funny dog. Sing out loud and dance with the baby. A mother we know tells us she gets through the chores of life by remaining open to the glory around her:

Sometimes the colors of Mother Earth are so vivid and I'll ask the children "What does that color make you think of?" or "Listen ... what do you hear the earth telling us?" (Mother of two)

Life is joyous, not dour. Laughter refreshes the spirit. All babies are spontaneous, but often adults are intolerant of this behavior in older children, and the children suppress their natural excitement. You can nourish that joy and excitement by mirroring your enthusiasm to children. If you feel moved to chat suddenly with God, go ahead. If you have the thought to dance wildly on the patio, by all means turn up the music and dance! Loosen up and respond to the wonderful world around you and the spirit within you. Become aware of the energy of life and let it flow. Trust yourself and act spontaneously on your feelings. The more we feel, the more alive we are with the creative force of the universe moving through us.

Each of us is made up of many different aspects. Not only do we want to be good parents, but we want to have successful careers, be good friends, make names for ourselves, write books, run marathons. It is important to acknowledge and balance all the parts of ourselves. It's okay to goof off, hang out, and relax sometimes. It's also okay to want to win the race, be successful, home-school, drive a truck, open a shop, be a dancer, or trade bonds. The ultimate desire is to come to know and love all the many facets of our beings. When our children see us exploring and expanding our lives, they too will be free to explore their complex personalities, instead of limiting themselves by one definition. Take a moment and think about what you truly love to do. Are you doing it? What are your fantasies, dreams, and visions? What makes you feel more alive? Take small steps each day that bring you closer to your heart's desire. God will guide you by making your way clear.

God gives me all the energy I need for my own creativity and my family's well-being—wholeness and creativity live together in me.

I am a limitless being filled with light and love.

As we change, our children change, and as our children change, the world around them changes. One move toward the light causes a ripple effect of good. Here are some further suggestions and practical methods for reflecting the image we wish our children to embrace and mirror in their lives:

- Develop the courage and trust to follow your intuition. Become aware of the subtle energies operating in your life. We all have internal strengths and wisdom about certain things. At particular times and in specific situations we know we are making the correct choice. Our spirit is wise and we must listen to its voice. The most important thing we stress in our work with children and adults is to listen, to reconnect to that inner voice. It guides us through our lives. Mirror this behavior to your children early on and perhaps they won't have to struggle to reclaim it.

You know, the most valuable thing you have taught me is to listen to my own intuition and heart. I have made the most important choices of my life by doing that, and I thank you for the lesson. (Age nineteen)

- Life is filled with opportunities for taking both necessary and unnecessary risks. A spiritually secure parent knows when it is safe to try new things. Sometimes you can consciously let something happen primarily for the learning experience. We do this all the time—by trying a new sport, taking a different route to work, meeting a stranger, starting a business, buying a dog, traveling to a foreign place—and learning from the outcome. It is often frightening for parents to encourage adventure for their kids, but without risk there is no change, and without change there is no growth. If too protected, the flower and the spirit die; if too free, they float with the wind; firmly planted and gently nurtured, they grow.

- Bring more light into your life. You have the power to call in light anytime. You can be driving to a Boy Scout meeting, attending a conference, cooking dinner, or sitting with a sick friend and still call in light to feel peaceful, calm, and protected. When you want to help someone, send her light. As you practice this powerful technique, describe it to your children—they will pick it up easily. When you leave for the day, picture your house or apartment surrounded by light. Bring light into your body when you are feeling sick. Picture the light going directly into the place of discomfort. Children love this technique—approach it as a child would, with wonder and an open imagination. You will experience amazing results.

- Accept your child as a beautiful and miraculous gift, a loan from God. See the best in him, for he will then see the best in himself. Praise and encourage his positive qualities. Feed his spirit by making sure he knows you love him, flaws and all. He is worthy just as he is. How you see your child expands into how he sees himself.

- Bring God to your table. Pause together before you eat and thank God for the food that nourishes your bodies. Create a serene dining experience, enjoy your food, eat slowly, and appreciate the taste. Just as we nourish our souls, we also feed and support our bodies with healthy foods. If our children see us eating and drinking in a balanced way, they too will value their bodies.

I think that Brussels sprouts are the most delicious food on earth. When my children were little I would tell them that the sprouts were just for Mommy, but when they were a little older they could try one. I built up such a mystery around Brussels sprouts that when my daughter was four she begged to try one. I gave her a special bowl of melted butter to dip the sprout in and told her she was now old enough to have the privilege to try one. She loved them and to this day Brussels sprouts are her favorite food. She even grows them in our garden. (Mother of two)

- Be in the moment with each task, give it value and meaning. For example, try to be fully present when preparing meals. Some believe that the energy we put into our cooking is transferred to those who eat our food. Play some soothing music and think serene thoughts while you chop those carrots.

- Be attentive to small choices that create your child's values. Notice if they show respect for people, animals, the environment. If you think they need a nudge in a different direction, model the behavior in an obvious way. Quietly comb the cat's fur, water the plants, fill the bird feeder, pick up litter as you come across it.

- Mirror commitment. How well do you keep your promises to people? What kind of action do you take when you feel strongly committed to a cause or a belief? When you are in a group where negative things are being said about a person, idea, or belief to which you are committed, what do you do? Doesn't it feel great to stand up for something you feel passionate about? Do it often and with vigor!

How do I deal with relatives who feel different and others who have an influence on my kid? (Mother of three)

It's tough to be a spiritual parent when my partner thinks the only way to relate to our boys is through dumb jokes and Nintendo. (Mother of two)

- You aren't able to control how your spouse, partner, or relatives live their lives and mirror to your children. "My husband's eyes just roll when we light the candles and start meditating." But you can boldly live your own spiritual truths and talk to your kids about the different approaches to life they observe.

- Make an attempt to change some behavior or habit that you are now ready to release. Your child will feel the benefits of your increased energy and determination. Are you honest? Do you sometimes misrepresent the truth? Are you critical of others? Do you use blame as a way of making yourself feel better? Can you admit when you've made a mistake? Want to give up smoking? What about beginning an exercise routine?

- Show your children how you handle your worries. Give them an example of a parent who tackles her problems head on, but doesn't brood over them or dwell on the negatives. This doesn't mean you should burden your kids with issues inappropriate for them—use your good sense.

- How do you deal with money? Do you look at money as energy, flowing in your life as you need it? Or do you feel pinched and confined around money issues? Have you tried the spiritual concept of tithing 10 percent of your income to the person or place that enriches you spiritually? Do you pay your bills with anger and fear or do you bless each check as you write it out? Take a look at your prosperity consciousness and the messages you give your kids.

My daughter had a loose tooth—it seemed to be hanging by a thread for days. When a friend commented on it I said, "Well, we're hoping it falls out because if we go to a dentist it will cost fifty dollars to pull it." My friend later said to me, "I know you didn't mean to, but I think saying that in front of your daughter made her feel guilty about costing you money." (Father of two)

- List five traits you liked about yourself as a child. Were you tenacious, bold, creative? Write the first five qualities that come to you. How did your parents cope with these qualities? Do you see any of these characteristics in your life right now? How about in your child? Ask for guidance and insight on ways you might reignite your inherent strengths. How can you mirror a grown-up who has maintained her natural qualities?

- Let yours be a home where it is okay to talk about what you are feeling or sensing. If you truly allow free-flowing conversation and opinions to have a place in your home, the stress that comes from holding back will disappear. What about releasing some outmoded ideas, opinions, feelings, assumptions, biases, attitudes? Can we open up and let go of these limited feelings? Can we clean out the clutter of our minds so we bring ourselves to our homes and families without all the stuff and baggage that may have weighed us down?

- Are you in touch with your healing power? All of us have the potential to send healing energy to ourselves and those we love. A child will naturally place his hands over a skinned knee or rub his tummy when it aches. Instead of reaching for the bottle of aspirin when you next feel the first twinge of a headache, try taking some deep breaths and rubbing your temples. Ask your child to place his hands on your head and together feel the heat travel from his body directly into yours. Call on the power of healing light and incorporate healing visualizations. If your child has a skinned knee, together picture the energy of her hands placed over the knee covering it with a net of protection, an invisible bandage of light. Then picture the blood traveling to the knee to speed the healing, fresh new cells growing with the help of this magical net of light. Can she feel the tingle of the energy entering?

- Get creative with encouragement—support and cheer on others. Go to a friend's soccer game and yell or hold up cheering signs. Ask about the project a friend has begun. Offer to help a family member with a new skill. Your children will follow your lead and reach out to others in his life.

- How do you handle grief? Do you, as a friend of ours advocates, grieve as you go? Or do you stuff the pain and try to keep a stiff upper lip? We hope you aren't dealing with any grief now, but if so, know that it's okay for your child to witness your sorrow. She will understand that you too feel deep sadness and perhaps you can cry together.

When my grandmother died I was so sad it got stuck in my throat. I didn't want to cry because I was afraid my brothers would tease me. My mom didn't talk much about her mother's death. I still feel all bottled up when I think about my grandmother. I never grieved her death. (Mother of three)

- Model empathy. When you are reading a book, for example, where the character is left out of a party, you could pause and comment on how sad and lonely she must feel. Or as you stand in line behind an elderly person searching for change, smile at her, allowing your children to observe your patience. Explain that the car going so slowly might be a student driver or that the man with the loud voice may have a hearing problem.

We went to see a movie today and just as the feature was starting, an older couple shuffled down the aisle in the dark. Unable to see, they couldn't find a seat right away, and they were blocking the view. All of a sudden a young man about sixteen stood up, walked over to them, and asked quietly if they were having trouble seeing. He quickly and quietly found two spots for them. Such a simple, yet thoughtful gesture. (Mother of two)

- Make a "Life Balance Sheet." Use columns headed with the different segments of your life—social, spiritual, physical, intellectual, family, friends, professional, aesthetic—

then under each, list how you nurture that particular part of yourself. Are there empty spaces? Is there balance? If not, can you think of ways to fill in? What about the amount of time given to each area? Your child will take your Life Balance Sheet as the way to live.

Enjoy becoming a positive mirror for your children. Remember that just as you are able to pick up on their feelings, they too can tune into yours. As you remain calm, peaceful, full of light, and focused on God's love, your children will share in the peace you experience. They will feel peaceful. As you grow closer to the light, so too will your children. What a wonderful reason to nourish your soul and allow the love of God to enfold you.

PARENTS' INSIGHT-BUILDING EXERCISE

Take the time to clear your thoughts and become quiet and relaxed. Now picture yourself as you are today. What do your children see? Do they see a loving parent who creates time to be with them, or a tired, stressed grown-up who always seems to be rushing? Begin to focus on the person you would like to be. What reflection would you like to create? What vision do you have of yourself? What kind of parent do you want your child to see? Visualize yourself as patient, calm, open, and loving. See yourself waking up with joy and calmly going through your day. The picture is coming to you easily and comfortably. Look at yourself joyfully greeting your family in the morning, your friends at work. See yourself gently speaking to the people you meet throughout the day. Notice how you are looking at the beauty in your visualized day and commenting on it. How are others around you behaving? Are they in harmony with you? As your day ends, visualize your

family happily together—lovingly interacting. Feel the peacefulness of your home. Can you see the light surrounding you and
your family? What color is that light? Take a moment and
brighten the light.

Take a look now at your child's view of the same day. Get
inside her body and see out into her world. What is she seeing? What does her behavior reflect? Has she felt love and
serenity? Does she seem calm and content? Is light flowing
through her day?

Now take a moment to create more light in your child's day.
Picture the same events you saw earlier but enhance them. See
her smiling face and her open, loving spirit shining—sparkling
with light.

As you quietly return to the room and the world around you,
think how you as a mirror might reinforce the positives you see
in your child and change what you find troublesome. How did
you feel as you imagined order, calm, and love? What you
imagine can be real. You can create your world, and your child
will feel the effects.

Parents' Check-in Questions

- What is one thing I could show my children that
  demonstrates I have the power to improve myself?

- Does my child demonstrate a quality that I see in myself—
  easily frustrated, judgmental, short-tempered? How might I
  begin to make changes in myself in this area?

- Who modeled anger for me as a child? Am I reflecting that
  way of expressing anger to my kids?

- What strong beliefs do I have? What about important
  values? Am I reflecting them well?

- Who and what am I using for my support system? Am I drawing on my spirituality and my religious beliefs for strength? If not, why not?

- Is there a spiritual practice or philosophy I would like to know more about—yoga, shamanism, fasting, keeping kosher, retreats, tithing, journaling? Where can I begin?

CHILDREN'S GUIDED JOURNEY

(Note to parents: This journey can be an eye-opener for you if you listen and watch carefully as your child acts out the mirror imagery. Use a light touch with the journey so it is fun for your child and illustrative for you.)

Breathe slowly in and out, in and out. Relax and let your body become limp and loose. You feel very calm, relaxed, and peaceful. Now imagine you are in a lovely room filled with mirrors. There are mirrors on every wall. You can see yourself wherever you look. This is so much fun. You jump up and down and all the mirrors show you jumping up and down. You make a funny face and so do the mirrors. You can dance and laugh. The mirrors dance and laugh. This really is fun. Now look and see your mother (substitute any other appropriate title or name) in your mirror. When she smiles, the mirrors smile. See her wiggling her nose? The mirrors are wiggling her nose. Anything you do, the mirror does. Anything Mom does, the mirror does. Play in this mirrored room for a while. Play and watch. This is fun for you and for Mom. You can play a game of copying each other and the mirror will copy you. Stay here a while, and when you are ready, slowly come back to this room. Open your eyes. If you would like to talk about your trip to the mirrors it is fine. I will listen.

Children's Check-in Questions

- Is there anyone you imitate? What do you imitate most? Why?

- What do adults say or do that lets you know you are special to God and to them?

- What do you learn from me about God? What do you learn from other people?

- Is there anything about me you think you will see in yourself when you are grown-up? What?

Affirmations

ADULT

I am a loving mirror for my child.

I find my own peace today.

My life is balanced and full of abundant blessings.

I am strong, successful, and courageous.

I am a creative channel for God's good—my children are living reflections of that divine energy.

CHILD

Love surrounds me like a warm, snuggly coat.

I love and respect myself.

I can try again and again.

I am a positive model for other kids.

When I look in the mirror I like what I see.

RELEASE THE STRUGGLE

I always have worries. I write them on a piece of paper in my mind, then crumple the paper and throw it in the trash! (Age six)

Can you recall an occasion as a young child when you struggled with a task or a problem and found yourself frustrated and angry? Maybe it was a physical skill you had not yet mastered or a school assignment you couldn't understand. Can you remember how you stewed over these things? Perhaps you can also remember someone who recognized your dilemma or to whom you went for help. What a relief to get some support. What a joy not to struggle alone.

I had a terrible time with geometry in high school—just couldn't get the concepts. I struggled and worked and finally asked my dad for help. He showed me a really logical way to do the problems and it suddenly became clear. All that semester he helped me with the math. I'll never forget the relief. (Mother of four)

We have the same feelings as adults and the same need to find a "helper" when we encounter life's problems. We have God—who can give the support we need if we only ask.

Many of us would vehemently say, as we dance along nicely to life's harmonious music, "Of course I am living my spirituality and parenting with spirit." But how about the times when we hear only discords? Sometimes there are days or even weeks when we struggle just to maintain the routine of our lives. There is too much to do, life is too busy, too scary, too sad, too lonely, too overwhelming; events are out of our control. During these times we realize we cannot do it all ourselves, we don't have all the answers, for us or for our children. We struggle to get it all right, to meet conflicting obligations to our children, friends, jobs, extended family, communities, and ourselves. Full, burdened days exist for us all and we need help.

When we turn toward the Divine Parent to help us release this struggle we are led to the power of God within us. This power can support us and our children throughout our lives. We are not parenting alone; we share the job with God. We can give up the struggle to find fulfillment outside ourselves and instead go to our spiritual centers—attainment is not out there somewhere, but inside. When we search outside ourselves to feel complete, we only extend our struggle.

Our concerns have many themes. Often we become driven by specific ideas of how places, occasions, and people should be. Many of us have specific and distinct expectations of who our children are and who they will become. Chances are they can't possibly meet these expectations. Perhaps we need to be honest with ourselves—in what ways are we disappointed in our kids? How do our children measure up to our image of them, and in reality whose image are we using as a standard? Probe a little into why you hold these expectations. Is it a result of your own failed attempts, your family's definition of success, your image of what a girl or a boy should be like, your concern over what others will think of you? Take a moment, after you have become clear on where your expectations have come from, to release them. Rip up the paper you've written them on or say "I let go of old, outdated, limited definitions of my child. I am open to the unique spiritual being he truly is." When you revert to your old expectations, ask for the limiting images to be healed and for light to fill your consciousness. See and accept your child's changes. Approach him with a fresh mind and a clean slate. Be open to what he is today and put away your old ideas of who he is. Be surprised by your child and revel in his newness.

Some of us live through our children. We offer them as trophies to our family and friends, as if to say, "Look what I have done." But we are only custodians for these souls, who have their own path, a path not meant to be measured and judged. Each stage, each place along that path is important in their growth, and our role is to accept our children and allow them to be right where they are, rather then hurrying them to the next stage. Give them the gift of freedom to be anything, rather than limit them by labels, roles, and expectations. Pray to see the beauty and individuality of your child as he is, flaws and all. If the flaws are out of proportion, it is your vision that's flawed, not the child.

Katy was born with Down's syndrome. We were devastated, but through spiritual struggle and growth I have come to a place of total acceptance. Isn't it ironic, since Katy's whole way of being is to accept; she is a divine spiritual child. She lives in the moment, finds humor and joy in the most ordinary things. (Father of two)

*If my teenager flips her hair one more time or uses the
word "like" another time today I might scream. But
she's a good kid and this too will pass.* (Mother of two)

Releasing the struggle means watching as your child makes
her way in the world—makes her own mistakes and decisions.
Letting go implies that you can loosen your grip, knowing that
God is gently holding her for you. It means trusting that you
have given your children firm roots so they can fly with their
spiritual wings. Freeing your child is easier when you remember that you and she are connected by a strong spiritual bond
that will never be broken.

No one's life is free of pain or disappointment, but we can
choose how we carry that suffering. With God's constant flow
of energy and love we can accept, adapt, adjust, and grow. We
can choose how to handle challenges, struggle with them, or
resolve to give them up to God. This doesn't mean we accept
limitations or turn our backs on responsibilities—we strive for
the best. But it is okay to take a rest from our challenges and
allow the power of spirit to come through so we can find the
answer, the direction, the information to move us forward.
Next time you are locked in a conflict or can't find your way
out of a problem, take a deep breath and say, "I let go of my
struggle to make things happen and I surrender to the intuitive
voice within me to reveal the answers for my greatest good."
Then wait with the faith that divine order is at work and
answers will come.

Let's admit to ourselves that we are not perfect parents and
allow God in to help. The buck does not stop with Mom or Dad;
we don't have the responsibility of making everything okay for
our kids. There are also a couple of messages children need to
hear—first, Mom and Dad can't fix everything all the time, and
second, the child can go directly to God to meet his needs.

When we remember we aren't the ultimate authority for our children or always responsible for their behavior, it is easier to let life flow. The same is true with other areas—when we decide to go with the events of our lives, instead of struggling against them, we can claim some peace. When our children begin to embrace life with an acceptance of what is, they won't allow problems and worries to paralyze them. The presence of God is so great and so ever-present that when we struggle we disconnect from that loving source. Ironically, it is when we release the struggle that we become free.

RELEASE THE STRUGGLE

Marsha's father, Mimi's grandfather, is ninety-seven years old. On a recent visit to his home we noticed a torn and tattered piece of paper taped to the wall above his desk. The words on the paper were: "Fear came knocking on the door. Faith answered, no one was there." This wonderful man has not had a headache, he claims, his entire life. We think we now know why. He discovered this saying, of unknown origin, over fifty years ago, carved into the wooden beams of an English pub, and it sums up his approach to life. Release the struggle— rest in the arms of faith and lose fear. Mimi's two young daughters quickly memorized their great-grandfather's favorite saying. It will live on in a new generation of parents.

Parenting can be overwhelming and frightening. There will be bumpy days, days when you may find yourself off balance and losing hope. Perhaps you're working on ending a negative habit, or adding a healthy one to your family's life. Maybe your goal is to reduce the friction between siblings and increase cooperation. These are everyday struggles for most parents, not extraordinary, but annoying and continual. These are the little drip, drip, drips of life that eat away at our serenity and make us want to scream. How lucky for us as parents that we can give up the big and little struggles and have faith in God's guidance. It is equally valuable for our children to understand they too can release their struggles and hand them over to God. Doing so sets them on a lifelong course buoyed up by trust in the ever-present guidance of their connection to the Divine.

Every one of us has an individual purpose, we are each becoming ever-improving spiritual beings, we need not run a race against our brothers and sisters. When we do our best and trust in God's help we release the stress associated with winning the race. Who and what we are is enough.

As we release the struggle and allow God's light to take its place, many things in our lives become less complicated.

- Instead of reacting with emotion to things that happen around us, we can respond from our spiritual centers. We can't control late airplanes, snowstorms, a declining stock market, the tummy bug. We can focus on the presence of God within, however, and trust the divine order in our lives. When we encourage our children to approach their lives with this attitude we give them a tool to release their struggles. Now might be the time to teach your child the Serenity Prayer:

  God, give us grace to accept with serenity the things that cannot be changed, courage to change the things which should be changed, and the wisdom to distinguish the one from the other.

- We are on an adventure with our children—an adventure full of unexpected twists and surprises. Giving up the illusion of control and trusting in the power of God helps us enjoy the ride.

- Our children are not always going to please us. We can feel tremendous anger and frustration in our role as parents. It is important to take time to let go of the anger in appropriate ways and move on.

- When we acknowledge that we can't do it all, that life is too much sometimes, we allow room for grace to come in—that extra breath, the answer to our prayers, the ability to go on.

- When we accept our circumstances, our children, our feelings, our problems, and release the struggle of denying what is, we soften and relax.

This letting go is a much healthier state of being—it also allows us to open to God for guidance on our next step.

Instead of hurrying through life, we can slow down and enjoy the magic of the "now." Remember the pleasure of dancing to great music, the enjoyment of the dance as the music plays, how freeing it is to move to the rhythms? We're not in a big hurry to get to the end of the song, we simply flow with the sound. Life can be the same way. We can flow with its song if we remember to let the exhilarating feeling of God's love wash over us, easing our worries and tensions.

WAYS TO RELEASE THE STRUGGLE

It is really very simple to release our struggles; all we have to do is to trust in a caring God and ask for that sacred power to illuminate our darkness. The obstacle for most of us is that our egos fool us into thinking we can solve all our problems with the right books or professionals or tools or skills. We think we would be happier and our children "better" if only we had more money, more time, fewer hassles, a better past, were younger, or were married to someone else. It seems to take forever to accept that we cannot fix everything and, furthermore, that we don't have to fix everything; we can leave a few things for God. When we finally catch on to this truth, things go more smoothly for us and for our children. Our struggles in the physical world can be quieted when we go within and tap the power of the universe for comfort and guidance. Remember, you have God as a partner in parenting; you are never going it alone. With God there is a way out of every challenge and a way into a blessing. Embrace every opportunity to let God move in and through you. If you make connecting with your inner wisdom a comfortable habit, consulting with the Divine Parent on a regular basis, you will find that your stress level goes down, your parent comfort level goes up.

It is tough to admit that we cannot solve all our children's problems or make all the hurts go away. We want to make things okay for our beloved children. The truth is that children come equipped with spiritual tools and an internal spiritual power. The most helpful thing we can do is to remind them of that connection and those tools when problems arise. Remember they are sacred beings—try not to discount their wisdom. As one insightful six-year-old said:

I know a lot. I'm a wise old genie. (Age six)

Release Guilt and Perfection

Guilt is the huge enemy of contentment. "If I had just stayed home from work a month longer," or "If I hadn't spoken so quickly." "If only I could have known what she was thinking," "If I had been there to catch her," "If I cooked healthier foods she might not have gotten sick," and on and on we berate ourselves for our oversights, our imperfections, our lack of knowledge. Release thoughts that lock you in self-pity or blame and move ahead resolved to live each day as best you can.

Trust that you are enough and your family is the right one for your child. A loving father felt terrible guilt over his choice to have only one child. This burden blocked his total enjoyment of his daughter.

> *We have a two-year-old and do not plan on having any more. Do you think raising an only child is fair to the child?* (Father of one)

Release your image of an "ideal" family. This vision can set up disappointments and unattainable desires. See the best in what you are given—your reality today. Pay attention to what is happening now, not what you wish could have happened. The past is over. Live in the here and now without the pull of "I should be doing . . ." When we choose to keep the past more alive than the present we block the energy of the moment and create a struggle. Create and craft your present moment and fly into a joyful future.

> *I'm a working mother and I feel this incredible guilt about not being with my son. I tried staying home and felt awful about letting my talents in the business world go to waste. I am always being pulled and really want a way to get a grip on life.* (Mother of one)

Sometimes it seems we spend the entire day trying to mold our kids into "ideal" little beings. "Use your manners." "Let's even off your bangs." "Those are new sneakers, don't get them dirty." "Pick up the towel." "Don't begin eating until we are all seated." "Shake hands." Decide that just for today you aren't the almighty-their-destiny-depends-on-me parent. It is liberating to decide that just for today you will bite your tongue and rechannel your energy by notching a mark on a piece of wood or drawing a star in a notebook rather than nagging or controlling your kids. Pretend that you are the baby-sitter and Mom is coming home tonight after the children are asleep. No directives, no disapproval, no threats today. "With God's help there is order in our home today— God's in charge."

Start by letting go of the little things. Try to stop nagging, which is really a veiled way of criticizing. There are other options for eliciting cooperation. Visualize your child picking up his room, picture his room neat and tidy, visualize him becoming responsible for his things. Continue to hold this image of your son. When you are about to scream from the sheer horror of seeing piles of clothing on the floor, shut the door and go back to your image. Try it—you may be surprised by the results! You and your child may have different priorities. Can you ease up on your need for absolute order in the closets as you realize your son is absorbed in learning about the earthworms and frogs in the backyard?

Do these sound familiar? "She looked at me." "He touched my cereal bowl." "She's on my side of the car." "He is making faces at me." For many of us the tension builds as our kids, in their fatigue, impatience, fear, and anger, pick at one another. How can we release this struggle? Try this: "Today I let go of the exhausting effort to control the interactions between my children. I entrust their complex, lifelong relationship to a special sibling angel I'll call (choose a name). I trust in this angel's help to improve the harmony in my home. I'll bite my lip when I start to jump in and fix things between my kids, the squabbling, the wants, hurt feelings, and slammed doors. (Angel's name), surround these children with your crystal energy of healing light, ease their hurts, and connect their hearts with love."

Maybe you could visualize or picture your children connected by a golden cord of brilliant light. See the light coming from their hearts and linking them in a beautiful way. When there is tension between siblings, try closing your eyes and picturing this light. You might even ask them to do the same. "Did you know that our family is connected? We are all joined together by a sacred cord of light. What color is the light that connects you to your brother? What happens to the light when you fight? How might you guys solve this problem other than hurtful words, mean faces, and coming to me to intervene? Let's ask the light to help us reconnect and come up with some ideas for solving the problem."

You may even wish to begin the week using this centering, unifying exercise with your family. Sit together in a circle and close your eyes. Each of you picture radiant light that connects you all; this light comes from your heart and goes directly to the hearts of the others in the circle, tying you together—perhaps with a luminous bow—and with each breath the light becomes brighter.

Trust in the natural flow of the universe; accept and move with the rhythms of life. Today may be a slow-moving day when your child seems content to do little.

Sometimes I just want to sit quietly and look at books, not be running everywhere all day. (Age seven)

Maybe he needs a quiet day, a relaxing time, a little less striving. Follow his lead and facilitate some gentle time for him. If it is an impossible day to do so, let him know exactly when he will have time to relax and "just be." When we "go with" instead of "push against" our inner promptings, rhythms, and intuitions, struggles will dissipate—we are in the natural flow.

I am always tired. (Age nine)

Whenever I shut my eyes to go to my peaceful place, mist comes and sends me to the clouds. And I take the secret key out of my pocket and I unlock the secret lock and open the door and step inside and I'm there. (Age eight)

Build Quiet Times and Activities into Your Family Life

Somewhere really nice and peaceful, that's heaven on earth. (Age six)

Slow down and moderate the pace of your children's lives. Try not to hurry them through childhood or get caught up in preparing them to be adults. Instead, enjoy and accommodate their current levels. This may be your only opportunity to be a hugging mother, a movie pal, a secret keeper, a football spectator, a traveling companion. You may not again see your child so freely display the silly games, the soft sadness, the learning excitement, the love of you, the free-moving dance, or the conversations with invisible friends. Don't charge through the days without treasuring them. Rushing creates disharmony; it goes against the natural flow and cheats us of the joy in experiencing our children's day-to-day growth. Living with a constant dialogue of what's to be done, what hasn't been done, what you don't have, what you must have, and who is doing, being, or having more yanks us from the present moment and dissipates our energy. Yes, children also need time to loosen up. Pay attention to the unique way your child relaxes, then supply him with frequent doses of it.

I feel relaxed in the summer when I can lie on a float in a pool and just float there. Aah, that is really nice. (Age seven)

Before dinner I relax. I wish I had more time, but I'm so busy. (Age six)

I put my head under my pillow and it is so quiet and my mind finally stops going so fast and the noise of my sisters and brothers is blocked out. I need those pillow times a lot. (Age seven)

Help your child to create a peaceful place in her mind. By closing her eyes and imagining a restful setting—complete with details of smell, color, and sound—she can picture herself in this tranquil place whenever she needs to become renewed and relaxed (see Children's Guided Journey). Join your child in becoming still and going within—doing so will help you put on hold the striving and pushing you may have become accustomed to. You may have to schedule time to get to the calm, but it's well worth it. Create your own peaceful place, a place that allows you to get centered and quiet, then talk about your experience with your child.

Mimi leads "Peaceful Place" workshops in elementary schools. Children respond to this visualization and carry it with them into their lives. A seven-year-old was having a hard time focusing in the classroom and was a constant challenge for his teacher. His parents and teacher reported that an amazing calm settled over the child as he used the peaceful place visualization in his life. He wrote Mimi a letter:

Thank you for helping me find my peaceful place. I think about my place when I am tired or when my brother is bothering me. I think about my place on the bus and before I start studying my spelling words. Thank you because I like it there and it makes me feel better here on earth. (Age seven)

Here are some examples of children's imagined quiet places:

My peaceful place is at the beach at sunset. It's peaceful in the weeds and the waves lull me to sleep. The sand makes me a blanket and the wind blows my hair. The beach is a peaceful place for me. (Age ten)

My peaceful place is up in a hammock that's hanging on a tree in space. There is a pillow, all my stuffed animals, and my blanket. When I look down I see sky and clouds. When I look up I see the moon. Only whales, horses, and dogs and myself can go there. I smell my mom's perfume. (Age seven)

My peaceful place is at the sea on a tree. There is a purple sky as I lie on a limb and the sun warms me up. (Age eight)

My peaceful place is where cats are. There are flowers too. It is always hot. There is a stream with ducks in it. All you can hear is meows and purrs. (Age six)

With so much going on in our lives it pays to remain calm. We can stop worrying about the outcomes of situations and instead allow the universe to handle the details. When we remember that we are living in God's orderly world, our thoughts remain serene and we move gracefully beyond life's small annoyances. This doesn't mean we throw caution to the wind and pray our way to success. We have to do the legwork and "show up" in our lives. But we cannot figure everything out. God can create situations beyond anything we can ever think up.

Light—A Powerful Force

Release your child into the divine light of protection by picturing a cocoon of light around him. Imagine this beautiful light, pinkish in color, surrounding and enfolding your child. This is a wonderful way to replace worry with a specific image. Another idea is to sit quietly and imagine your child standing in a pool of light and love. See him as calm, peaceful, harmonious, happy, and confident. This pool of light is like a spotlight shining directly on your child.

Teach your child how to put on a coat of light each morning. Have fun with this image. Explain that he can create the coat in any colors imaginable. Maybe he would like to imagine he is weaving light from the moon, the sun, or the stars into his coat. Strong, radiant colorful light vibrates from this magical coat and keeps him safe and snug. We know families who like to swap their coats. Knowing your child is going out into the world wearing a magical coat of light can help you surrender the need to take care of and protect your child—it helps release the struggle.

Visualize a brilliant white cloud of light and then successively, one at a time, place in this cloud the faces of your children, thinking their first names as their faces appear in the cloud of light. This is a strong method for sending your child healing, empowering energy and light.

Pay attention to the changing patterns of light throughout

the day, dawn, noon, dusk, sunset, night. Light is a powerful energy to which your child can become attuned. Have her take a sunbath and picture the healing light filling her body. Don't forget the sunscreen.

Ask your child to place his hands on his heart. Feel the beating. Have him imagine his heart sending blood, healthy pure blood, throughout his body, filling him with light, renewing him.

Any time you need to become centered, stop what you are doing and put your hands on your heart. Feel the warmth from your hands and imagine your heart filling with light and love. Breathe deeply. Picture beautiful light pouring into your heart. Feel the calm, steady beat. Affirm that you are ready to love, nurture, and awaken the spiritual life of your child. A spotlight of healing love beams onto you as you open your heart to spiritual wisdom. Draw the light into your being and pour it out onto your children. Imagine that you are parenting in the light.

Some additional ideas for releasing the struggle include:

- Help your child create tools for handling stress and worry. Remind her she can talk to God anytime, day or night. Teach him to picture light around your home, your car, his school, his school bus, you, his pet, his problem. Suggest she lie down and imagine the ocean is washing over her. The waves rushing over her body leave behind the power of the ocean and wash any negative feelings out to sea.

- Show her the techniques you use for releasing stress: walking, meditating, writing, playing tennis, practicing yoga, swimming, playing music, taking a long hot bath.

- If a child is worried about a test, teach him visualization techniques to see himself calm and focused, easily completing the test, retrieving all the information he has learned. Of course, couple this with good study habits—but help your child, from an early age, learn how to manifest his good by first picturing it.

- A great tool a child can use to release teasing or negative words from others is to pretend the words are rain bouncing off his body. He has the power to keep the negative words or intentions from seeping into his consciousness. Or he can imagine a shield of light around him to turn dark words into bright ones.

- Accept that there are some things we just can't understand—situations, people, events, obstacles with no obvious logical explanation. "Why is my child ill?" "What reason is there for my terrible financial loss?" "How could this disaster happen to all those good people?" We are inclined to think, "If only I knew the reason I could better accept," but the reality is, we may never know the reason and it's only in trusting divine reasoning that we might truly give up the struggle of figuring everything out.

How can we explain to our thirteen-year-old why a hurricane has killed the entire family next door? I didn't have any answers for myself, let alone my child. I still don't, but have had to accept that these things happen. I move on loving God and my child and living each day to the fullest. (Mother of one)

Let your child see you accept the small and large unexplainable events in your life and she will follow your example. Maybe her sadness at not being invited to her friend's birthday party or not making the team may be lightened if she sees how you handle disappointments and release the struggle of discomfort. Help her trust that from all events, no matter how painful, good can come. Help her move forward and let yesterday's mysteries unravel in God's divine way.

- Listen to your heart when making parenting decisions. Your heart knows what you should do—tune in and follow your gut feeling. No one knows your children as you and God do. Center yourself in God—clear your mind and ask for grace, light, inspiration, and direction in the decision you face.

- If you work outside the home you might create a ritual for yourself to release the struggles of the day by sitting quietly for a moment in your car before entering the house—slow down, let go of the business of the workday, and put on your parent hat.

- "Right place, right time" can become your mantra whenever you feel trapped in the wrong place at the wrong time. Try it the next time you're running late or stuck in traffic, and discover how quickly you can arrive at a place of calm and acceptance. No tight shoulders. No tirades. No sharp words misdirected to your children—just "right place, right time."

- What ritual or prayer do you have in your religious tradition or your family's routine that allows a child to rid himself of guilt, confess, and move on. How do your children cleanse their spirit? Is there a way for them to let go of distortions they have made or to ask God to forgive them for things they have left undone?

- Act with a peaceful heart and rise above power struggles. We often push to make our point and demand our children hear our way of doing something. Our definition of the "right" way might block the avenue of discussion. What if we shifted our thinking and stopped trying to "win" or always be "right" and instead practiced being compassionate? Suspend your own ego—just for a day, not forever if that feels too overwhelming.

- Form a parent group. Get together with like-minded parents and support one another. Perhaps you could visualize, affirm, and pray together. There is power in numbers—individuals united in a focused prayer create a powerful force. When you have a support system of kindred souls you can often release a struggle or worry into the group. Find people who are positive, reliable, and committed to parenting from a spiritual perspective. Often when we give spiritual parenting talks, participants exchange names and form ongoing groups so they can meet to support each other in this new way of parenting. Perhaps you can create a group to meet on a monthly basis and focus each meeting on one of the principles presented in this book. That gives you ten meetings a year. The other two can be opportunities to bring your children along and have a party or invite a local rabbi, priest, teacher, or expert of some kind to speak to you. Don't worry if you can't think of more than one or two friends who you believe parent as you do. Put the request out to the universe, through affirmation and prayer, to connect with like-minded parents, and they will be supplied to you. Stay open to the ideas and the people that are sent your way.

- Kids have to release their energy throughout the day. Before dinner push the furniture back, blast some music, and allow your child to "dance it out." Run around the block, invest in a trampoline, install a basketball hoop outside, get down on the carpet and roll around with your children. Find ways for you and your children to let it all out without being judged or reined in.

One morning a few years ago, my rugged little boy draped himself in some of my cheap beads and declared, "I must dance." He naturally felt the primitive impulse to dance, to express himself unabashedly to the universe. (Mother of one)

- Create your own "angel committee" to assist you in your role as parent. How about the angel of patience, the angel of focus, the angel of health, the angel of humor, and the angel of imagination? When you need a little help you can call on a member of this divinely appointed committee to come to your assistance. "Dear angel, I am asking you to take over these worries and problems and help them to get worked out for everyone's highest good." Thank your angel at the end of the list. "Many thanks, dear angel, for taking over this list and for finding the best solutions." Your angel will help you release the struggle in an angelic way. Call on your child's guardian angel to be a part of this angelic group. When you would like insight or to speak directly to your child's soul, her angel can assist you. You can't always make things okay for your child, but you can send an angel to help.

My son feels so lonely in third grade. He says no one plays with him at recess. It breaks my heart. I have tried to tell him things to do, like ask to join in a game or reach out to another child who is alone. The other day I paused during my busy day at work and whispered a prayer to any angel who wanted to help. I asked that angel to be with my son at recess and help him. It made me feel much better and my son has been having an easier time of things since. (Mother of one)

Your child can also call upon the help of his angel to release the struggle. Children often see angels with clear vision.

Angels are in the fairy family. When there is danger I get on my angel's back. It's a white horse. The tail is brown. I've seen it for five years, every hour. Its name is Vanilla. It flies like Pegasus. I'd say it's my guardian. (Age eight)

My son was about eighteen months old when he appeared to see things in the air around him. He kept pointing up and would say "there" or "see." I also caught glimpses of sparkles in the air when I glanced sideways quickly. I think that "guardians" were with him. I believe that the young, without jaded views, can sense the comings and goings of angels. (Mother of one)

God has a lot of helpers and servants. The angels are the guys who shine the stars and help God out with other important stuff. (Age seven)

• Rather than worry and fret about your children, picture them as healthy and whole, living a free and full life. Replace anxiety with positive visions. It's a habit you can begin right now.

It is so hard for me to be in a relaxed state—I am a born worrier and get stressed out a lot of the time. My kids see a frazzled, tired, worried mother. (Mother of three)

• Make a list of all the baggage you would like to release: problems, worries, fears, past mistakes. Then speak words of release to shake them out of your life, "I disengage from these things or conditions. I let them go and move forward in my life." Children can use a simpler affirmation to release the negative roadblocks from their lives: "I move ahead and leave (problem, worry, bad situation) behind. I am free."

Make your home a peaceful sanctuary. Get rid of clutter and organize the necessary tools for living. Remember not to invade your child's private space. If he is not in favor of organizing his room, so be it. Begin with the other living areas. When your home is tidy, chances are you will internalize that sense of calm and organization. Children need order, it allows them to feel in control and centered.

You might approach "room cleaning" by explaining to your children how free and uncluttered they will feel when their belongings are organized. Instead of "nagging" your kids to pick up their rooms, ask them to try a spiritual "cleaning" experiment. See if they don't feel a release from cleaning out old belongings and putting things in order.

Recently I heard an interesting story. There was a woman whose whole life was messed up and she was praying for God to help her. And you know what he said? "Wash the dishes." So she did. Then she mopped the floor, washed the clothes, and vacuumed the floor.

She eliminated the clutter. Suddenly the kids came home to a house that wasn't a disaster area. Once her home was organized, then her life became more organized. If you aren't self-disciplined enough to clean the house, then how can you be self-disciplined in other areas of your life? Well, yesterday I began realizing the effect this has had on me, my marriage, and myself. I started throwing things out left and right. The living room looks completely different. There is so much space now that newspapers, magazines, and knick-knacks never used are gone. Next is the kitchen. I feel like I am cleaning out my life! (Mother of four)

Keep It Simple

Try putting away all your young child's toys in a closet or a place where she isn't distracted by them. Start the day in a focused new way. Each day when you awake, put one item out for your child to focus on as she begins her play day: one toy, one doll, one book, one game, one beautiful picture postcard, one lump of scented clay. Put the featured object in the middle of the clean room; it takes on a kind of magical quality. Your child can focus on the day's new object and see it with clear eyes. You will find that she attends to that object as if it is magnetized; old toys take on a new delight. Her attention can be fully devoted to one item instead of all the plastic, neon, puzzles, gadgets, and toys that scream for attention when cluttered around a room. Replace the featured toy when you sense she is ready to move on to something else.

Thank God for simplicity. Whenever my life starts to become too chaotic, the first thing I do is clean and reorganize my house. As strange as it may seem, it's the

first step to clearing out the unnecessary things in my
life. Almost immediately I regain focus and peace, and
can then reorder my life. (Mother of three)

Think of even more ways you can simplify your life.
Consolidate children's wardrobes—perhaps you could organize clothing so each piece is interchangeable with all the others to give kids easier choices, more variety, and less laundry.
Get rid of junk; clean closets; organize shelves; give away outgrown clothes, toys, books; stop junk mail from coming to
your mailbox. As a result of this effort you might unearth hidden treasures like the earring you thought was lost, and you
will certainly feel liberated as you look at life in a fresh, clear,
new way. Notice your child's changes as a sense of order
enfolds your home. Small simple things take on a new signifi-
cance when you have an organized backdrop.

Small things are becoming special at our house lately,
since I have simplified our household. Making home-
baked beans from scratch and eating them by candle-
light was our weekend adventure. Living simply means
pride in achievements like a pantry full of home-canned
foods from food we grew all summer or picked at local
farms. But most of all, it means being here, home with
my child while she is small and looking at life through
clear vision. For her, life boils down to this: "Can I
have chocolate milk?" "Can I hug my friend?" "When
will Daddy be home?" Spirit has a shining place in this
new simplicity. I realize this isn't the right choice for
every family, but it's working for us. (Mother of one)

Make sure your child has a real place to get away from it all,
a quiet corner, a peaceful chair that is designated for serenity, a

nook under the stairway, the foot of a bed with pillows, under the kitchen table. Maybe your young child's car seat can double as his "thinking chair." Bring it in the house when it's not needed and tell him he can use it when he needs quiet and space. No one is allowed to speak to him when he is in his "thinking chair." Even the youngest children need ways to release the struggle, and when we show them how to do so we might find their crying and whining quickly declines—they now have other options for letting go.

In the back of my yard there is a place where I go to be alone, it is a little muddy and it is my thinking place. (Age six)

You could go a step further and designate a room that is your "simple, quiet, calm space" where nothing noisy is allowed. In this quiet room you might provide good inspiring books for all ages, comfortable pillows, potted flowers or plants, an air purifier, an altar, fresh fruit and flowers, peaceful drawings, relaxing music, whatever nourishes the spirit of your family. Anyone can go to this room when he wants to relax and refresh himself—as a family or solo. Take away the clutter and focus on what is meaningful. You'll find that children gravitate to this place and use it often. Serenity is a soothing balm for everyone.

Our children seem so sophisticated. They want everything they see and our lives become so cluttered. I struggle to keep it together and give them the material stuff they want. (Father of three)

Material things complicate life. Our society has made everything awesome, cool, over the top—to such a degree that we feel inadequate if we can't have it for our kids or ourselves. That in turn has put so many of us in debt, and the financial pressures cause us to be confused about values in general. It's difficult to find your spiritual creative core when much of the time you're negotiating with yourself or your child about the "haves" or "can't haves." Make a commitment to move away from "things" and focus instead on order and simplicity. Your older children will balk at first, but soon you all will be relieved at the new focus your lives take.

Release Fear and Find Images of Comfort

The powerful web of fear can zap our serenity. Many kids struggle with vivid, fearful pictures springing from their imaginations. As they grow older their fears grab them in different ways. They are fearful of the world—their imaginations continue to spin a gripping web fed by stories they hear, television, real situations they encounter. Fear can paralyze us all, no matter our age or our fright. We can help children release the struggle of fears. Begin with the idea that he can replace the struggle with love. Explain that love is like a fluid. Show children a clear glass of water and say, "The water is like love filling up the glass—you. It is there naturally, God supplies it. Fear pushes the water out and leaves us with an empty glass." Then illustrate this idea by putting lots of ice cubes in the glass and observing the water spill out. "That's fear and it keeps God's love out. When we allow ourselves to feel the love we know we are never alone and God always loves us. When love cannot fill our hearts and our minds, we are disconnected from our souls, which consist of total love." There is always a way out of any situation, because divine love does move through us. Assure them that when they call on God they can find respite from pain, worry and fear; they won't overflow.

Maybe your child can write what he's afraid of on a piece of paper. Ask him to feel the feelings as he writes—breathing into them—and allow the fears to go through him and into Mother Earth. Or designate a special box as a "fear box," and your child can pretend he is putting his fears in the box for the night and then placing the box outside his door. This box works well for all of us. Could you put your "inner critic" in the box when you begin work on that novel you want to write? Perhaps you could encourage your daughter to put her "limited thinking" in the box so she can get on with her history project.

Brainstorm other ideas with your child, on ways to release fears. Often just by sitting down and taking the time to imagine options your child will come up with his own unique and powerful solutions, as did this six-year-old:

> *When scary pictures come in my head—like a witch, a monster, a bully, or our house burning down—I pretend it's from a photo album and I turn the pages until I get to a picture I like.*

Mimi's six-year-old daughter's fear of fire and robbers was keeping her from sleep. Mimi asked her child to get quiet and look inside herself to see where these fears might be coming from. She then listened and acknowledged her daughter's response:

> *I was a Native American woman in my last life and we used fire for many things. We cooked with fire and I was badly burned. I am also afraid of robbers because my tribe robbed other tribes for their blankets and hides and things to keep us warm, so now I am afraid that will happen to me.*

After this conversation Lillie no longer seemed plagued by these fears.

Find an image that's a comfort for your child—a picture of Mary, Jesus, angels, a magic unicorn, a sunset—and let her carry the picture in a pocket during the day or put it under her pillow at night. Relics, rocks, medals, statues, pictures of saints, an altar in the corner of a room are all comforting, concrete objects that can be used as touchstones to the serenity and peace within. Touching the crystal that hangs around his neck can remind your child to breathe deeply and know God is with him. She can carry a special crystal in her pocket and pretend to rub her worries into it, thereby letting them go. He can imagine that the rock in his hand is his link with the earth and through that link he is grounded and firmly rooted in the here and now—releasing what has happened in the past or is coming in the future. For young children, you can buy or make a "worry doll." This tiny doll can become a silent, comforting friend that holds the child's fears for her. You could be your child's pocket pal. Tell him that you will shrink down and ride with him in his pocket all day. If he becomes afraid he can feel you right with him and draw from your strength. It worked for us. When Marsha returned to school after her children had grown she was the oldest student and had some fears about a new area of learning. Mimi reminded Marsha that she wouldn't be alone—Mimi would be right there with her, a silent pal, riding in her pocket. From time to time we are pocket pals for each other and it's always the extra support to get us through—and we're grown-ups. Imagine how helpful it might be to your children.

Find what works for your child to help ease him into sleep. For some children the image of angels flying around the room keeping monsters away may help; for others the solution is imaginative and unique:

God asked this nice witch named Maggie to sit at my door at night and protect me. Maggie is very pretty— she has long hair and she sometimes tickles my back after my mom has stopped. (Age six)

My angel is a pretty butterfly—a girl—she flies in my room at night. She helps me fall asleep when I have a hard time. She's big with beautiful colors around her. She looks like stained glass. She makes the stars and the moon. (Age five)

I've had this guy named Mr. McDougal around at night for a long time. He is super scary. The thing is he goes away when any piece of light hits him—so I make sure to leave a light on and I remind my mom every night to leave the hall light on. (Age nine)

I'm embarrassed to talk about this because it's really babyish. I have an orange and yellow monster with millions of long legs living under my bed. He is all wrapped up, but at night his long, pointy arms and legs can come up through the crack between my bed and the wall and grab me. I stuff my dolls and pillows in the crack to keep those slippery fingers from grabbing at me. (Age nine)

Remember that to children dreams are very real—don't deny that by insisting that "it's only a dream, it's not really happening." Let your child know he has the power to stop a dream if it is scary. He can say "no" and wake himself up. Another technique kids have fun with is to rework the frightening images before they fall asleep and make them humorous. If he dreams of robbers sneaking around, could he turn them into bumbling idiots who split their breeches? If he dreams of an awful monster, could he try to become the monster's friend and even offer him an imaginary gift? Many kids like the idea of finding and using a dream stick. Take a walk in the woods with your child and encourage her to look for a stick that could travel to dreamland with her. You could have a little ceremony to affirm the magical dream powers of the stick. Your child can paint it in her unique way if she likes and place it next to her in bed, or on the floor. When she goes to sleep the stick can go with her.

Foot or hand massage before bed helps children unwind. Try making some scented oil using a drop of essential oil such as lavender or chamomile mixed with a base of almond oil. If your child is comfortable having a massage, make time to give him one—especially when you sense he is holding stress. You'll see his body relax and release the tension.

Additional ideas for releasing the struggle:

- Crying isn't all bad—it lets feelings out. "Crying lets the hurt out" can become your mantra with children. Pretty soon you'll see them comforting their friends with these same sage words. Crying is one way a child releases the struggle.

- Make a "worry-wish tree" for your child. He can write down his worries or wishes on a card and hang the card on the tree. Tell him to let the worry go—the tree will take it for him. The tree is strong with deep roots and can take all the worries or wishes a child wants to give. Use an actual tree that grows outside your home or an inside plant. You can construct a tree out of construction paper and hang it on the wall, or your child can create a tree in his imagination and place his worries on it, then drift off to sleep, unencumbered. The worry-wish tree is very helpful for nighttime when so many thoughts and worries swirl around in a child's head.

- Come up with a spiritual habit that connects your family and helps with any struggles or issues that naturally occur. Perhaps at noon each day you will all close your eyes for a moment, no matter where you are, and send light to one another. Imagine you are zapping your child a beam of pure, white, healing, empowering light. It may be just the boost she needs to get through her math work or make a friend on the playground.

- Maybe each morning before everyone departs for work or school, you can take five minutes to pray together for that day's specific needs. If Sam has a test at eleven, you can pray for him in the morning. You may all pause at eleven to send Sam good thoughts. It's helpful to go out into the world as a team, supported by God and your family.

- Act as if what you want has already arrived. Experience the bliss of living the dream. Use your imagination to picture it. Children love to use their powerful imaginations and are quick to "pretend" an emotion or an outcome. What a great way to experience our desires as reality. So next time your five-year-old is upset and unable to find her center, ask her to "pretend she is relaxed and calm." See what happens.

- Learn to release anger in appropriate ways and observe how your child imitates your techniques. Next time you are angry use *your* words: "I'm really angry that you didn't do your homework again and I have to be homework cop. I want to let it out because when I hold it in it makes me sick. I love you, but I need you to know how angry I am feeling right now."

- Yoga can help children release the struggle. Try the woodcutter and rope pull poses to release negative energy, fatigue, stress, or worries. To do the woodcutter put your arms above your head, interlock fingers, and thrust yourself forward as if holding an ax and chopping wood, throw your arms down, bend your knees, and exhale your breath. Kids love it. To pull rope simply raise your arms in the air as if you are pulling ropes above your head. Reach up and pull the ropes. You can imagine a huge church bell will gong with each pull. Exhale your breath with each release of the rope.

- Remind your child to pray in the midst of big and little struggles. Prayer connects our children to a reality beyond their struggles that is bigger than they are and where they can find comfort and rest. Help your child to trust in prayer as a means of listening to God.

- Help kids to eliminate envy. Be happy for the person you envy and know you are being given a sign of what is possible. Let go of jealousy or envy for someone else's good and know that when you get in touch with the essence of that longing you can draw it to yourself. Help your child do this. "Why do you think you'd like to live in such a big house? Is it because you would have more room to play? How can we make more play space in the house we have now?"

- Use visualization to find lost items. Close your eyes and "see" the misplaced item in your mind's eye. Where do you see it? This is such a simple technique and consistently works to help kids focus, go within, and discover their lost object. It sure beats the "Mom, have you seen my sneakers?" that some of us hear all too often.

- Help kids let go of a struggle by reminding them to breathe. Often when we are tense we hold on to the breath—remember the purple-faced two-year-old having a tantrum? Ten deep cleansing breaths work like a charm to diffuse exploding emotions or calm bedtime fears.

- Make sure you have a drum around for your kids to use when words just won't do. Loud drumming can let their anger or frustration come thumping out.

- We can give children tools to use as they struggle with conflict. Teach conflict resolution. "Conflict is when things get all mixed up, your idea of what you want and my idea become entangled and we both become confused and angry." Early in a child's life, at home and at school, we teach them to "tell a grown-up" if there is a conflict. All of a sudden, about third or fourth grade, kids hear, "Figure it out for yourselves." Somewhere, between those choices, somebody must teach the child how to "figure it out." A loving parent is the best teacher.

- Enjoy each day to the fullest—don't focus on what you didn't accomplish. Release the pressure of fixed schedules and constant future planning—be in the now. Remember that people are more important than things. Can you approach holidays and big events from the perspective of spiritual fulfillment, instead of what expectations you must meet? Could you ignore what the neighbors do or the products commercials tout as important?

PARENTS' INSIGHT-BUILDING EXERCISE

Relax, breathe deeply, and bring your attention inward. Let your worries and concerns of the day drift through your consciousness. Allow the thoughts gently to float away as you clear your mind. You are deeply relaxed and at peace.

Now picture a beautiful kite designed in your favorite colors and with a gloriously bright cloth tail. Put any symbol or design on this kite that represents your essence or just feels right. Now write on the kite a descriptive word or two for any struggle or worry you might have. Use big letters, writing boldly and clearly. Take the string of your kite and run with it, letting it go behind you, and up, up, up above you into the beauty of the sky. Let the breeze take it higher and higher, carrying your struggles into the clouds. Let go of the string! Watch the kite become smaller and smaller as it rises. With it go your concerns. Let them go for now. Release the kite. Release the struggle and move on with your wonderful day.

Parents' Check-in Questions

- Where am I holding tension in my body—right now? What happens when I pause and send light to that place?

- Is there something going on in my relationship with my child that I would like to release? Are there control issues or power struggles that I'd like to dissolve and replace with harmony?

- What about the outside world? What am I struggling with in my life right now that I might surrender?

- What helps me release the struggle? How can I include more of that in my life?

- How can I show my child my techniques for letting go?

- What spiritual habit might I begin with my family that would connect us all with our inner light?

CHILDREN'S GUIDED JOURNEY

Picture a place that is all your own. This is a place where you can go anytime you want to be alone and quiet. This is a safe place where you are able to relax. It could be in a meadow, a field of flowers, on a beach, in a cozy cave—create a peaceful place all your own. If you want to bring something from home to have with you in this place—a stuffed animal, a blanket, or even a pet—you are welcome to do so. What does this peaceful place look like? What are the smells? Create a spot here where you can lie down if you would like, a cozy bed or nest. This place is filled with love and harmony. Just rest here and let any thoughts that come up gently drift away. The breeze gently brushes you as you relax.

This is your peaceful place where you can come anytime you need to relax, get quiet, and let your struggles and worries go. You can imagine swinging in your hammock or lying in a nest of eagle's feathers. You can see yourself drifting along on a cloud or swaying on the branch of a weeping willow. Whatever you have created as a peaceful place can change and evolve as you do. So enjoy this place and remember it awaits you at any time. If you would like to talk about your peaceful place I'd love to listen.

Children's Check-in Questions

- What bothers you the most these days? What can I do to help?

- Do you have an angel or an animal spirit that guides you?

- If you could dig a deep hole and bury any worries or bad feelings, what would they be?

- How do you relax and let go?

- When are you the most comfortable?

Affirmations

ADULT

I let go and let God take over.

I am guided and supported by the universe.

Everything I need to know for my peace of mind and my calm interaction with my children is being revealed at this moment. I listen.

CHILD

I let go of the day and drift away.

I fall asleep easily and peacefully.

God's hands are on my shoulders—guiding me with love.

I forgive myself for any mistakes I have made.

Principle 10

MAKE EACH DAY A NEW BEGINNING

*In the new morning I remember what I did yesterday
and then I do something new. I forget yesterday's stuff
and start all over again.* (Age five)

Life is a series of beginnings and endings—of work never
completed, new problems, and ongoing frustrations. Luckily
we've been given the grace of dawn. Nature gives us respite in
sleep and renewed energy in the new day. The cycle of the natural order of things shows us we can always start again. We
are not bound by the past—we get another chance. We know
the sun is behind every cloud, that the storm will always pass
to reveal a new day. As the clouds disappear the world is again
filled with light. What a remarkable and repairing design is
God's world, filled with the light of new opportunities. We
share a circular, ever-evolving creation. Everywhere we look, if
we examine carefully, we find a beginning, a middle, and an
end. What we make of this gift is ours to choose.

Once we become parents we enter an endless union. We can
look at parenthood as a series of tasks to be completed, as in,

"Whew, she's out of diapers," or a continual journey with softly rippling phases. Let's celebrate the cycles and honor the newness of each day—each moment. Most of us are living lives very much of the world; we are not sequestered away in monasteries where we spend our days in meditation and prayer. Ours is a walking prayer—a real-life meditation. It is a challenge to express our spirituality when we are immersed in the mundane details of life; yet when we connect the spiritual to these everyday events we are able to experience exquisite miracles. Not flashy, walk-on-water miracles, perhaps, but the holy moments that come into our lives with our children.

You can't control your children in the big sense, but each day you have a choice about how you respond to unfolding events. You may select delight and wonder or drudgery and disgruntlement, focus on your child's limitations or celebrate her strengths. You can become angry and resentful or choose to let the little things go, forgive, and move on. Your ability to select your reactions is as simple as the predictable morning light. "He's digging through trash again, making messes for me to clean up." Or, "He is joyfully exploring—fully in the moment. I'll show him how to clean it up in a minute." We're not advocating social chaos with your little cherub as dictator, rather we're giving you the eyeglasses and letting you choose the lens color. How do you see your world, rosy or gray? Do you view each day as a new start or look for the problems lurking around the corner?

Henry David Thoreau once said, "If the day and the night are such that you greet them with joy, and life emits a fragrance like flowers and sweet-scented herbs, that is your success." A joyous attitude ensures a creative, uplifting life and is one of the greatest and most constructive gifts we can give our children.

Every day the universe gives us gifts of pure energy and limitless opportunity. You can remind your children of this always available spiritual power, and encourage them to tune into its guidance. The more they do, the less they will feel the victims of circumstances. When they believe that each day is a new beginning, with energy and miracles awaiting them, your children will feel liberated, with a sense of control over their lives. They will face each day with more joy.

I love the first day of school with new pencils and paper. I love to start all fresh! (Age seven)

Let's give each other another chance too, and start fresh with those we love—letting go of yesterday's hurts and living in the freedom of today.

Mom, I need a hug before I can leave. A hug is the key to the front door. (Age seven)

MAKE EACH DAY A NEW BEGINNING

Knowing that each day is a new beginning helps us and our children start our days with the faith that all will be well. It allows us to experience peaceful evenings when we know that tomorrow awaits—a new opportunity to begin again—and fresh assurance in the mornings that today is full of unlimited possibilities. We can remind our children the new day awaits them, so make it special, treat it with love, and see the goodness in it. Each day, each beginning offers the potential for bliss. Feel the magic of that possibility and your child will too. Today is sacred; experience delight.

I spent a wonderful Sunday yesterday planting pansies in my flower beds with my three healthy children and some of their friends. The sun was shining, it was warm, and the children were laughing. Before I die I want more days just like that! (Mother of three)

As you implement this principle your children will begin to understand and accept their successes and mistakes as a necessary part of growth. They will learn to say, "Okay, I goofed, but I can let go, for tomorrow is a new beginning. God forgives my mistakes as fast as I make them. Every second, every minute, every hour, every day I can begin anew." A seven-year-old girl told us, "Life is like stairs—whenever you are sad or scared, go up a stair." We recall her wisdom when our thinking needs to shift to a new level.

When dinner's burning, the baby dumps out your favorite bottle of perfume, and the phone is ringing, patience is hard. (Mother of four)

To be a parent is to live a balancing act. When our children are young we spend most of our time on family maintenance. We change diapers, buy food, make food, clean up food, wash clothes, pick out toys, pick up toys, put out toys, wipe away tears, wash clothes, drive to events, tuck in, wipe counters, pick up toys again, wash clothes, arrange appointments. The list is endless. How, we think, can we balance it all and attempt to nurture our children's souls as well as our own? The truth is, we may have to grab our sustenance while living an "on the run" life. A long hot bath, a walk around the block, five minutes of meditation, or three minutes of focusing on your breath can be soul-connecting nuggets slipped into your busy days. If we see the ongoing chores of family life as never-ending tasks, with no time for our own nourishment, we become frazzled and lose our spiritual center. But there is an ending. Each day we begin anew and are offered a fresh perspective on what lies ahead; we can recharge and start over. Release the old and embrace the new. Change will happen regardless of how tightly we cling to the familiar. It is only by living in the present moment that we have true stability.

Someone once said, "Lost wealth may be regained by working and being industrious, lost knowledge may be regained by study, lost health may be regained by medicine, but lost time is gone forever." The only time is now. Start fresh and savor the day, value the moment. According to recent research, inaction—failing to seize the day—is the leading cause of regret in people's lives over the long term. Carpe diem—seize the day! Treasure your child's morning smile and the pleasure of knowing she's safely tucked in at night. Delight in the moment, find joy in the present; be fully attentive to the "now" without rushing ahead to think of the future or lingering over what has past. Despite any hardship, worry, problem, or difficulty, celebrate your blessings today. Let the new day embrace and lift you into a place of comfort and peace. Each day is alive with the promise of discovery and the opportunity to act on the power of God that resides within. Do today what you will wish you had done fifty years from now. Don't live with regrets.

One thing that I find totally fascinating and totally frustrating at the same time is the realization that my children have chosen me in this lifetime for the lessons they need to learn—but what is it that I am supposed to teach them? One thing I try to do is to stop stealing energy from them. I work with that every day. A kind word, a gentle touch, even a smile can be a great energizer to children. I know this is my only chance to parent well, I can't do it over. (Mother of three)

In the early 1800s William Wordsworth wrote, "The world is too much with us." That is as true today as it was all those years ago. We feel swamped much of the time. When we make each day a new beginning, however, we might be able to relax a bit more, focus on the tasks at hand, live in the moment, enjoy the unexpected, and release tomorrow's demands or yesterday's issues. Our world doesn't have to be overwhelming for us or our children, when we let go and begin anew.

Serendipity happens when we are open to new beginnings. Creativity thrives on the unplanned and the unexpected. A researcher at 3M spills a chemical on her canvas shoe and discovers Scotchguard. The scientist finds penicillin by taking a new look at the mold growing on a lab experiment. When a child lets go of time limits he liberates a wellspring of original ideas and insights. So he can't figure out his puzzle—he can look at it with a new approach tomorrow. Try this affirmation with your kids: "There will be enough time for all my creativity because new understanding and ideas come in the fresh day."

When children are able to begin again they are not overwhelmed by bleak feelings. They can start fresh each day—knowing that big and little miracles await them. As they try new ideas and behaviors they need not be staggered by the thought of changing for the rest of their lives. When we approach the new with an "I'll try it just for a day" mindset we can take the risk, let go of limiting beliefs, or try the new behavior or idea with enthusiasm.

WAYS TO MAKE EACH DAY A NEW BEGINNING

Each day I get a new chance to start again. (Age seven)

You can make each day a new beginning for you and your child. Operate with a new sense of wonder as you begin each day. See miracles with awakened eyes—the bird's song, your child's soft skin, the breath you take for granted. Share this awareness with your child. Experience the amazing qualities of everyday events; know that your good is of God and is close at hand. Find this good in persons, places, and things. Affirm that only goodness can go from you and return to you. Allow your whole being to recognize this rightness everywhere and respond to it. Let God's positive energy envelop you and flow out in every direction. Spending time dwelling on the past creates an imbalance in our lives. We receive guidance each day and must be in the present to bring ourselves fully to the inspiration. When we remain fully in the present the past will be made clear—without strain or effort.

A five-year-old girl knew instinctively how to exist fully in the present. She was given a piece of chocolate for dessert after her family had dinner. She jumped up from the table, lay down on the floor in the middle of her hula hoop's circle, and began slowly to eat her candy. "Samantha," her mother said, "why aren't you sitting at the table?" "I'm savoring the moment, Mom" was the contented child's response.

Try being fully present to just one activity each day, washing dishes, making breakfast, reading one book to your child, pulling weeds in the garden, breathing. Bring your attention to the activity at hand and tune out your mind's chatter. Notice the details, smell the smells, feel the feelings. Focusing on the simple things can create a sense of calm and slow us down. Daily life, even with children, can be less frenetic. Perform the most ordinary tasks with love—they then become a kind of worship. Anything done with love is a form of reverence.

Encourage your child to try this exercise. Give him a warm cup of tea (peppermint and chamomile are nice) and ask him to describe the cup, notice the smell of the tea, and quietly allow the warmth of the tea to travel down his throat and warm his tummy. Being together without having to fill up the silence with chatter is a lovely experience. Try this exercise together and note how long you are able to focus on the tea.

> *Teatime with my mom each day after school is my favorite time of all. We drink tea out of real china teacups we have been collecting and talk about our days. It's cozy and peaceful and I have to sip very slowly or it will burn me. It's like the warm tea finally slows me down. I like that.* (Age six)

The child is the very symbol of the soul—unspoiled, open, nonjudgmental, appreciative, and loving. The child is whole and becomes divided as he grows. Our goal is to keep a spiritual wholeness intact in our children and in so doing help them remain God-centered. Try to focus on that objective and affirm the completeness of your child. Allow him to move smoothly through his days without being judged or evaluated. Most kids naturally begin anew and overlook mistakes, but our culture's labels and progress markers stymie their fluid expansion. Allow the child's natural wonder to flow as he anticipates good and revels in the moment.

Validate successes at the day's end, even small ones such as waking up on time, making the bed, completing a project, being kind to a sibling, completing homework without being nagged. When you take time to honor successes, your child will experience a sense of power and feel good about himself. Remember to shift away from comparisons. We live in a world where people are labeled "winners" and "losers"—sad but true. Teach that life need not be a contest where one is judged better or prettier or smarter than another. Be aware of this damaging quest for being "better than" and tune into your child's own progress and accomplishments for what they are—not for whom he beat or the "A" he received on a test. Most schools set up a system where kids work for rewards. We aren't suggesting you ignore rewards, but rather offer a place apart from the evaluated and judged growth environment of school. Make home a place where your children don't have the constant tension of measuring up to others, but can try something new without expectations. Home can be a place where each child can develop her talents without fear of judgment, a place where she is applauded for her efforts and where there are always new beginnings.

Use intention and focus to set your own priorities each day. It's all right to say "no." Choose what is important and what activities or commitments you can decline. If you are asked to do something and your heart says, "Ugh, no way," but your "shoulds" shout, "You must," stick with your heart. You'll find you have a lot more energy for the people and things that matter most in your life.

> *I was very involved in Girl Scouts, thinking it was a great thing for my daughter. I did it all . . . taught the girls, drove the girls, delivered cookies with the girls, camped, cooked, sewed, played, swam with the girls. I began to be more and more involved in administrative work. One day my ten-year-old said, "Mom, I really don't like Girl Scout stuff, but it's the only way I can ever be with you." And I thought I was doing it for her.* (Mother of three)

Just for Today

Just for today treat your child as if it's her last day on this earth—or yours. Your responses will be a bit more thoughtful, your attention more riveted on your child, your requests softer. Think of your child as a gift today.

If I could go back and replay the day Ted died I wouldn't have scolded him for spilling his morning orange juice or have so brusquely gotten him ready for swimming lessons. I was up late the night before and took out all my fatigue on this dear little five-year-old boy. I can't have that day back, but I can beg parents to really love their children each day. (Father of one)

Ask yourself what would happen if, just for today, you didn't fuss over the unmade bed, the spilled milk, the toys in the living room, the clothes that don't match, the inappropriate words said, the unbrushed hair, the crumbs on the kitchen floor. Don't sweat the small stuff; join your child in her exploration, fascination, and wonder. Rethink your priorities today. When it comes down to listing the most important things, people, events in your life, what makes it to the top five? Chances are it's not a new car or an updated kitchen. Make your thoughts and actions reflect your priorities—just for today.

No matter their age, hold your children. Let them know they are sacred beings and you love them. Some days this might be harder than others, but if you make loving your child a priority, the universe will give you the opportunities to do so. Make today a holy day. Don't wait for special occasions to observe the day's sacredness.

Play with the idea that today you have no limits. Ask your children to pretend they can do something they have been working on or hoping to accomplish. Open their minds and souls to all possibilities. Catch them if they utter an "I can't." Remember, today anything is possible. Very young children have this magical mindset; it is only as they grow older that they start to disbelieve. Help them trust in their own magical powers. "Today is God's day and I shine in it."

Miracles can happen each day when we take action. Today we have the opportunity to turn our inspirations and ideas into actions—as do our children. To translate spiritual ideas into actions is to perform an act that conveys the same meaning as the spiritual concept. An example would be to take our belief in God's generosity into the action of passing that generosity along to others. What can we give today? It might be as simple as smiling at the bus driver or putting an end to negative gossip. Perhaps your morning prayer can be: "Right now I decide that my actions will demonstrate my beliefs." Talk with your children about your spiritual beliefs and find ways to put them into action each day. One woman we met told us how important this idea was in her life:

Before I leave this world, I hope in some small way I have made a difference in someone's life. I hope to have left an imprint on someone's soul, lifted someone's spirits, taught someone something they didn't know. I hope to have gained a better insight into the meaning of things, and most of all I hope my children have learned valuable lessons in spirituality and pass that insight on. I hope to have loved completely and infinitely because there's more joy in giving than receiving. I hope to have been sensitive, kind, and caring. If I have made just one difference in someone's life, then I can leave this world without regret, because I have given little pieces of my soul and spirit away, and in a sense I would live forever in the hearts of those I touched. (Mother of three)

A Shift in Attitude

We can change our mindset and approach each encounter with our children from a higher place—a place centered in God and love. When we parent with love, our children take away a positive cherished feeling; actions that seem little or unimportant to us have the potential to cause a profound reaction in our children. Pay attention and counteract the harshness our world wants to impose on kids. Always remember children are citizens of the spiritual world as well as the physical world. You honor his soul as you acknowledge he is spirit in human form. It might take kids a while to get used to their cumbersome, limiting form—so have patience.

Enjoy what you have and remain aware of the abundance that fills your life. Point out all the wonderful bounty in your child's life. Be open to the gifts that are given to you. Look at your day as being filled with endless choices, endless opportunities, endless growth. It is indeed another day and there is always another way. Remember that abundance is a state of being—an awareness of the gifts right here, right now. Try a "gratitude attitude" and give your children the gift of "abundance thinking."

Accept the joy your child offers; doing so will allow the other areas of your life to blossom. Children don't take time away from us, they lend us their delight, fascination, energy, love, creativity, and light to take with us into our lives. Being with our children can wake us up to the feeling parts of our spirit; we can be more spontaneous, playful, and free. We experience joy when we love, and God is in that joy.

As much energy as our children share with us, it is also important we fill ourselves with energy from our own wellsprings so that we can begin anew. When we are centered and energized we are able to give to our children without draining ourselves and to receive without draining them. Our children need the same energizing tools. Being aware of breath is a simple but effective energy enhancer. Remind children to take deep breaths throughout the day. Whenever we are feeling tired we can breathe in the energy of the universe. Before each meal we can habitually breathe in and out deeply a few times. We can take breaks throughout our days and step outside to breathe the fresh air—feeling it flow through our bodies.

Try this gliding breath exercise with your kids to help release any tension stored in their bodies so they are able to move forward in their day. Stand in a place where you can stretch out your arms without touching anyone else, feet about shoulder distance apart. Close your eyes and become aware of your body. Find a way to stand so you are balanced and calm. Now take a deep breath and raise your arms shoulder height, palms open to the ceiling or sky. Breathe deeply in and out as you stretch your arms out as far as they will go. Take three deep breaths. Open your eyes if you are losing your balance. Now with each inhalation, raise your arms above your head, and with each exhalation, lower them back down to your sides. Pretend you are a bird soaring above your town, wind against your face. Don't forget the deep breaths synchronized with your arms as you glide into your new moment.

Morning Beginnings

In the morning I feel like I was just made all over again. (Age six)

Start the morning on a peaceful note. If it means making lunches and laying out school clothes the night before, do so. Try getting up fifteen minutes earlier than you usually do. Play soothing music and light some candles rather than turning on the bright kitchen lights and flipping on the television news. Encourage children to eat slowly and bring themselves gradually to the new day. It's amazing how, with a little thought, a normally chaotic morning, with everyone rushing through an untasted breakfast, then dashing out the door, can become a calm, soothing experience. Bring your awareness to each task this morning and approach it with a relaxed body, mind, and spirit. Your child will catch your pace and make it her own. She will begin her new day a bit more centered and a lot more relaxed.

Come up with some morning rituals to help your children start the day with an open, accepting attitude. A family we know sings "Day by Day" from the musical *Godspell* as they gather to eat breakfast. The lyrics begin, "Day by day, oh dear Lord, three things I pray—To see thee more clearly, to love thee more dearly, to follow thee more nearly. Day by day."

You might watch the morning creep in with your child snuggled next to you and together make a wish for something new and delightful to happen during the day. Or ask your child, "What color is this day going to be?" If it looks dark, brighten the picture by pretending to add white paint or light.

Bring your child's attention to the day in a fun way. Ask him, if he were a horse, what would he do today? What if he were the president? What law might he change? Or, if she had magical powers, how might today turn out? Then remind her she has all the magic she needs. You might even whisper into your child's ear that God's love surrounds him the whole day through—then wave your arms around him, spritzing water, and ask if he can feel the love.

After breakfast and before beginning the daily routine ask your child to draw a picture of what the morning looked like to her as she first saw it. Then ask if it has changed. Most of us are spiritually open during that short time between wakefulness and sleep—it's a dreamy kind of feeling. This is a wonderful time to say our affirmations, visualize scenarios, talk with God, surround ourselves with light, meditate. One seven-year-old we know writes magnificent poetry before getting out of bed:

First thing in the morning I usually write poetry. It just seems to come to me when I first wake up. (Age seven)

Ask your school-age children to think about their friends and teachers as they are on their way to school. What comes into their minds to say that might make that person's day a bit better? Starting the day thinking of how we might help others is a wonderful way to begin.

When you are taking your morning shower, pretend the water gently raining on your body is washing away any fatigue or worry that you might have carried with you into the new day. Let go of tension—imagine the water is washing it away down the drain. You can also envision light—pure, white, healing light—penetrating your body with each drop of water, filling you with energy. If your child takes a morning shower share this exercise with him. It can become a wonderful replenishing morning habit.

Write your family's prayer for the new day. Maybe you'd like to sing it each morning. The following are some traditional morning prayers:

This is the day the Lord has made. We will rejoice and be glad in it.

Everything I do today I do for you, dear Lord—let it be right and just.

Everything I do today I do with love.

**Dear God, thank you for this new day. I know you're
with me as I eat, jump, run, and play.**

Entice your children with the morning comment, "Walk like a
winner. Walk as if your spirit is surrounding you with light and
joyously pulling you through the day." Children are born with
natural charisma. It is the fear they absorb from adults that nib-
bles away at the strong, secure "don't you just adore me?" attitude. Encourage your children to push out their chests, throw
back their shoulders, and feel their power. Have them say to
themselves, "I have power and I walk with God today."

Don't forget to ask your children what they like to do first
thing each morning. This eight-year-old has come up with his
own beautiful ritual:

*I make a blessing each morning to the first plant or ani-
mal I see outside my window. It's the way I start each
day.* (Age eight)

Some more ideas you might try for making each day a new
beginning include:

- In the evening visualize how you would like tomorrow to
  turn out. What kind of parent do you want to be? Picture
  yourself with energy and patience, and fully in tune with
  God. Before your child goes to sleep encourage her to say
  out loud, write down, or picture in her mind what her
  tomorrow will look like (check the Children's Guided
  Journey at chapter end). Remember the words of Ralph
  Waldo Emerson: "The ancestor to every action is a
  thought." You live the life you imagine you are living.

Take the time to create first in your mind an image of your highest and best scenario; then be prepared to live it.

• Let go of media messages and follow your own heart and values. We have all the power, for we are God in action— we make our homes and our lives as *we* envision them each day.

Life has so many messages it is hard to connect to our kids. We go to movies (Hollywood values). We go to malls (Madison Avenue values, the same folks who bring us anorexic models). We buy magazines (and look at the images there brought to us by a select few in NYC). Our curriculums are regulated by a select few in Washington. If you disagree with any one or two of these, you stand out like a freak. Big money is spent on sports programs, but unless the competitive nature of that is monitored by caring adults, watch how that gets out of hand. All these messages . . . the pressure from us gets passed on to the kids. Who has time to be a spiritual parent in the pro-found silence it takes to listen to your heart? My channels are all jammed most of the time! (Mother of two)

• Who is the most spiritual entity you know? Look for help from these spiritual models: Mother Mary, Moses, Mother Teresa, Jesus, Buddha, St. Paul, the Dalai Lama. How did they begin again when problems seemed overwhelming? Reflect on their lives for guidance. Call on them to work through you and share this technique with your kids. A six-year-old told us:

I know what I'm going to be when I grow up. I'm going to be a mother, a saint, an actress, and a singer.

Oh and maybe a tennis player too. Right now I'm going for the saint. I ask for some of the saints from the olden days to help me out sometimes and I sure do feel their help. Especially the one for lost things, Anthony.

- Work with your child's unique rhythms; we all have dips and peaks. Just as energy wafts in and out of our awareness, so does frustration and anger. Kids will usually let their feelings out and get on with their day. Many of us aren't comfortable with displays of emotion, however, and insist our children "keep a stiff upper lip" or "grin and bear it." It's hard to start fresh when we've got all that emotion wanting to escape. It's much easier to move into the next moment when we've let feelings out in a safe and acceptable way; we are then free to operate clearly in the next adventure or task.

- Try the following exercise at the start of each week, perhaps on Sunday evening, after the children are in bed. Take a moment and get quiet. Close your eyes and take a few deep breaths. Picture your child in front of you.

  Take a few minutes to see her image clearly. What feelings, ideas, or words are coming to you? Don't judge, just accept whatever you are feeling. Imagine that your child is speaking directly to your heart and mind. What is she saying? If you have more than one child, be sure to focus on each individually. Trust the information or feelings you receive—this is a powerful way of tuning into your children's needs. These simple, gut-level impressions can shift you into a new awareness. Your child might say something as simple as "Love me—just love me." Whatever message you receive is valid. Make this part of your preparation for a new way to interact with your child.

- Live your life instead of recording it. Many of us are so busy capturing the big moments with video cameras that we don't experience them. Next time your child has an important event, leave the cameras at home and savor the occasion by being fully attentive. You can always ask a friend to do the picture taking.

- Focus on the positive; point out what is right with your family. Ask your child what the best thing was that happened during her day. You may get a big "nothing" the first few times you ask but keep asking. Highlight your own positive experiences to mark the day.

- Love the body that houses the spirit. Keep things in balance. Take time each day to relax and listen to your inner messages.

- Relate to your child from an inner knowing today. Give her exactly what you think she needs—based on how *you* would like to be treated. Don't do this for any specific outcome or behavior, but because of your deep love for her. When you shift into an attitude of "how might I show love?" you will receive the best intuitive messages and respond in the most loving way. Take a moment and think back to when you were a child. Place yourself at the age of your child today. Picture yourself then. What did you want from others? What did you most want from your parents? Just accept whatever idea comes to you and then bring that quality to your child today.

- Practice the following "L"s with your children each day:

1 Love
2 Listen

3 Let go

4 Light—send it out and accept it in

5 Learn

6 Laugh

7 Linger

- Never end the day with unresolved anger. Remember to communicate. When an issue concerns the entire family, take the time to talk about it instead of carrying the anger over into the new day. For every minute you are angry you lose sixty seconds of happiness.

- Remember the words of William Blake when you need to live in the present:

  To see a World in a Grain of Sand
  And Heaven in a Wild Flower
  Hold Infinity in the palm of your hand
  And Eternity in an hour.

- Sing the song, "This Little Light of Mine, I'm Going to Let It Shine." Discuss the idea that we each have our own special light—our own gifts that glow from within—to illuminate our way. We can take our light out into the world and let it "shine."

- Perhaps you would like to begin an evening ritual to celebrate the light we put out into the world. Come together at the end of the day and light a candle; native wisdom has it that the burning of beeswax candles purifies the energy in a room. Turn out the lights and focus your attention on the flickering flame. Ask your children, "Who would you like to send light to tonight?" and allow each person an opportunity to speak his names and situations. "For Mrs. Park's family to help them gain strength after her death, and for anyone who is sick." "For all the cold animals tonight and for anyone who has a dad fighting in the war." Each evening will be different but the ritual will remain. Before blowing out the candle say together, "We send the light of God out to all whom we have mentioned and anyone else who needs comfort. We ask for light to fill our hearts so we can begin anew tomorrow and take the light into our world."

• Write down all the things you would like to change about your child—behaviors that might annoy you. Now reword these traits so they are positive declarations. This exercise will help you shift from an opposition mindset to a positive way of seeing things. "She follows her sister around constantly" shifts to "She loves and cherishes her sister." This simple exercise can help you look at your child from a new perspective.

Trust Your Intuition—Begin Today

I have so many conflicting messages about how to parent. My parents live so far away and don't understand what I'm up against. Morals have changed since I was a kid. Then there are a thousand books on how to parent—most of them are about self-esteem. Now the kids have so much self-esteem—"Oh, Harry, you are a fantastic kid!"—and the problem seems to be that they lack self-control. Who is right? What is right for the long term? (Mother of two)

A parent's intuition about his child is finely tuned. Make the decision now to trust your feelings, hunches, sixth sense. There is no one better prepared to parent your child than you. When you follow your intuition about ways to best help your child, you are the "expert." If you sense your child needs more limits, he does. If you think he is self-absorbed, honor that inclination and follow through on ideas to help him move outside himself.

Dip into your intuition with even the most mundane choices, such as what to cook for dinner or which route to take to work. Tune into your gut feelings and see what turns up. Chances are the pasta and vegetables you make is just the nutritional requirement your child was needing, and the direction you took to work avoided a traffic jam.

Tell stories using intuitive language about times you trusted your gut feelings. "Good thing we gave Comet a bath. I sensed he might have a tick on him." "I'm glad I called Isabel this morning; she seemed kind of down and my call cheered her up." "Once when I was in college I woke up in the middle of the night and felt there was danger and I should get out of my dorm immediately. It turned out that the fire alarm went off as I was going out the door. There was a fire in the bathroom."

Give kids the opportunities each day to try out their intuition. "What do you think should go in this soup?" "Where do you think this flower ought to be planted?" "Why do you think your sister is upset?" "How should you handle the teasing at school?" Then reward them when they take their gut feelings out into the world and take action based on their intuition.

Spiritual Parent — Spiritual Child

Make today a new beginning. Become a brave parent and celebrate your child and your life together boldly. Parent from a spiritual perspective and discover the glory that choice brings. Remain aware and open for the incredible blessings and joy that come from living life in this way—for both you and your children.

Beginning today, refuse to hold any grudges. Forgive your child as God forgives us all—each moment. Teach your child to trust his intuition even when his world tells him to distrust anything but visible, tangible logic. Allow your child the room to discover who he is meant to be—paying close attention to your own guidance for information on your role in his journey. Create rituals, ceremonies, and traditions to nourish your child's soul. Construct a family life that makes room for silence. Keep your child's life in balance—learning, playing, praying, loving. Children are radiant spiritual beings, but they are also mischievous, energetic, testing, growing individuals who need their parents to help them live in this world.

Make the choice right now to release any struggle and instead make magic out of the ordinary. Participate fully in the present moment because it's what you have. Help your child understand his part in creation—his connection to all life. Remind him he is more than his body—he is a divine spiritual being just having a physical experience for a while on earth. Tell him how glad you are he chose you to be his parent.

Next time your child offers you her words, listen with your heart and your soul. Remember that children know much more than our society gives them credit for. The following experience helped wake us up. We were waiting for an airplane in a busy city airport. Across from us was a five-day-old baby, bundled up in his car seat on the floor next to his young mother. The crowds rushed by—hurried travelers moving quickly toward their destinations. A young boy of about three was walking past us holding his mother's hand. He made eye contact with the baby, dropped his mother's hand, and ran over to the car seat. He knelt down and gently placed his worn, well-loved little teddy bear onto the baby's chest. The baby became alert—eyes riveted to the young boy—tiny fingers reaching up for the bear. Not a word was spoken, but the recognition and love in the three-year-old's eyes was astounding. His anxious mother quickly grabbed his arm and the bear: "Come on, we're going to be late, hurry up, let's go." The boy's eyes never left the baby, but his smile changed to a resigned look as he allowed himself to be pulled back into the "real" world. The newborn's mother picked the baby up as if he needed comforting after an awful encounter. She brushed away imaginary germs that might have been left from the well-loved bear. To witness the exchange between the children was a privilege and a reminder of the wisdom and magic alive in all children. We all have to catch a plane—in one way or another—but to take a breath and allow our children to be who they really are, and enjoy the enchantment of that essence, is what spiritual parenting is all about.

You have all you need to be a spiritual parent today—right now. Wake up to the delights woven into your life today—right now. Reach out and love your child without inhibition; then accept his love back into your heart. Go forward joyfully and journey through life with your children and with God.

Parents' Insight-Building Exercise

Relax your body, slow your mind. Take a deep breath in through your nose, then out through your mouth. Again. Now picture yourself sitting or lying in a beautiful, serene meadow. You are safe here. See the beautiful blue sky and the green grass all around you. Picture this setting. Call now on your inner wisdom, picturing it as a loving and wise being. See this wise being walking toward you, full of love and light. Picture this light as white or pink, and as your guide gets closer, so too does this gentle light. As your guide faces you, the glorious light forms a cord between you and goes into your heart and then around you. You are both now surrounded in this light. Take a moment to feel this connection. Then, when you are ready, gently focus on a specific question or problem you are having at this time. See the problem clearly defined. Ask your guide to give you direction with this question or problem. "How can I be more patient with my child?" "What can I do to help Sam deal with the bullies on the school bus?" "How can I balance it all, my job, my kids, my own needs?" Ask your question now. Wait quietly, and listen for the answer. A soft inner voice will come as you continue to relax and remain open. It will bring a gentle kind of inner message. Trust that your answer will be revealed to you, if not now, then soon. When you feel complete with your guide, thank him or her for being with you and come slowly back to the room.

Parents' Check-in Questions

- How might I live more fully in the moment? Is there something I must let go of, such as a worry about money, control, caring what others think of me, perfection?

- How would I like to see my child today?

- What a blessing it is to know that I don't have to repeat the same mistakes over and over again. What would I like to let go of in my past to begin anew? How can I do that?

- Is there a way to find a new beginning in my current situation? How might I do so?

- Which spiritual parenting principle would I like to focus on today? How might I begin weaving some of the ideas into my family's life?

CHILDREN'S GUIDED JOURNEY

(Best used in the evening.)

Get comfortable. Close your eyes and breathe deeply. Count backward from ten to one. With each number you are becoming more and more relaxed. Thoughts flutter across your mind, then gently drift away. You are so relaxed.

Now bring to mind the events you have planned for tomorrow. What does your day look like? Are you going to school? If so, what is happening in the morning, in the afternoon, and after school? Now add more light to this picture. See beautiful light shining on your day. How would you like tomorrow to look? Create the day as you would like it to turn out. What happens in your version of tomorrow? You feel relaxed, creative, happy, and safe. When you have painted in all the details of your ideal tomorrow, come back slowly and open your eyes. As you actually move through your day tomorrow, don't forget to check in from time to time to connect with the vision you just created.

Children's Check-in Questions

- Is there someone you need to forgive so you can move forward into the new day? How might you do that?

- What are your ideas for starting the day on a more peaceful note?

- What might you do with worries or concerns so you can begin the day without anxiety?

- Will you help me create a prayer for our family to say in the mornings that starts us all off remembering each day is a new beginning? How might the prayer begin?

Affirmations

ADULT

I see new opportunities, doors opening, new beginnings clearly today.

My greatest good is happening now.

Today I release all sense of separation from God. I listen deeply to my inner guidance and know exactly what to do.

I evoke greater love, well-being, peace, and happiness in my life right now.

I am a blessing in my child's life today.

Today I receive new ideas from the creativity of God. My whole consciousness is alive, awake, and aware.

God works through me today.

CHILD

My life begins today.

God cares about me always.

Blessings on this day, may I make it special in some way.

Each day I am wiser, healthier and more peaceful. It's great to know this new person is the real me.

I choose joy today.

I open to the new day with a fresh attitude—anything is possible.

I am ready for the gifts God has for me.

Appendix

SUGGESTED BOOKS FOR YOUNG CHILDREN

Adams, Judith
 Looking for a Fairy
 Wyston Press

Baker, Dianne
 Ted Bear's Magic Swing
 Unity Books

Barker, Cicely M.
 A Garland of Flower Fairies
 Penguin Books

Baylor, Byrd
 Everybody Needs a Rock
 Aladdin Books

Bea, Holly
 Where Does God Live?
 Starseed Press, H. J. Kramer

Beckett, Sister Wendy
 *A Child's Book of Prayer
 in Art*
 DK Publishing

Berger, Barbara
 Grandfather Twilight (any
 of her books)
 Philomel Books

Bowen, Connie
 I Believe in Me
 Unity Books

Burnett, Frances
 The Land of the Blue Flower
 Starseed Press, H. J. Kramer

Carlson, Nancy
  I Like Me
  Puffin Books

Chanin, Michael
  *Grandfather Four Winds
  and Rising Moon*
  Starseed Press, H. J. Kramer

Cohen, Kenneth
  *Imagine That! A Child's
  Guide to Yoga*
  Santa Barbara Books

  Conari Press
  *Kids' Random Acts of
  Kindness*
  Conari Press

Curtis, Chara
  All I See Is Part of Me
  Illumination Arts

Doe, Mimi and Garland Waller
  Drawing Angels Near
  Pocket Books

Garth, Maureen
  *Starbright: Meditations for
  Children*
  HarperSanFrancisco

Greene, Leia
  Crystals Are for Kids
  Crystal Journeys, P.O. Box
  3452, West Sedona, AZ
  86340

Hamanaka, Sheila
  All the Colors of the Earth
  William Morrow

Jeffers, Susan
  Brother Eagle, Sister Sky
  Dial Books

Lehrman, Fredric
  Loving the Earth
  Celestial Arts

Lewis, Richard
  All of You Was Singing
  Atheneum Books

Loomans, Diane
  *The Lovables: In the
  Kingdom of Self-Esteem*
  Starseed Press, H. J. Kramer

McAllister, Angela
  The Snow Angel
  Lothrop, Lee & Shepard

McPhail, David
  Something Special
  Joy Street Books

Near, Holly
  The Great Peace March
  Henry Holt

Pandell, Karen
  By Day and by Night
  Starseed Press, H. J. Kramer

Payne, Lauren
  Just Because I Am
  Free Spirit Publishing

Rosen, Michael
  Elijah's Angel
  Harcourt Brace

Ryder, Joanne
  EarthDance
  Henry Holt

Rylant, Cynthia
  The Dreamer
  Blue Sky Press

Sasso, Sandy
  In God's Name
  Jewish Lights Publishing

Von Olfers, S.
  *The Story of the Root
  Children*
  Floris Books

Willard, Nancy
  Night Story
  Harcourt Brace

Wood, Douglas
  Old Turtle
  Pfeifer-Hamilton

Yolen, Jane
  What Rhymes with Moon
  Philomel Books

Zerner, Amy
  Zen ABC
  Tuttle

A blank journal for your child to write his own story is one of the best books around. If he is not yet writing he can dictate to you and illustrate the story himself. Guide your child gently—give him ideas to write about: "Angel Friends," "Quiet Time," "Meals on Mars," "Dancing with the Moon,"

"My Secret Place," "Stairs to the Clouds," "Swinging with the Fairies," "The Little People in My Woods."

VIDEOTAPES FOR YOUNG CHILDREN

Concert in Angel-Land (video stores) or 1-800-637-3555

House of Magical Sounds (video stores)

The Snowman (video and toy stores)

YogaKids, Living Arts, P.O. Box 2939, Benice, CA 90291

SUGGESTED BOOKS FOR OLDER CHILDREN

Berger, Barbara
  Gwinna
  Philomel Books

Brill, Marlene Targ
  Extraordinary Young People
  Children's Press

Burleigh, Robert
  A Man Named Thoreau
  Atheneum

Furlong, Monica
  Juniper
  Alfred A. Knopf

Furlong, Monica
  Wise Child
  Alfred A. Knopf

Hoffman, Mary and Jane Ray
  Earth, Fire, Water, Air
  Dutton Children's Books

Kyber, Manfred
  The Three Candles of Little Veronica
  Celestial Arts

Maestro, Betsy and Giulio
  The Story of Religion
  Clarion Books

McFarlane, Marilyn
  Sacred Myths: Stories of World Religions
  Sibyl Publications

Miles, Miska
Annie and the Old One
Little, Brown

Millman, Dan
*Secret of the Peaceful
Warrior*
Starseed Press, H. J. Kramer

Pullman, Philip
The Golden Compass
Alfred A. Knopf

Rain, Mary Summer
*Mountains, Meadows and
Moonbeams*
Hampton Roads Publishing

Rylant, Cynthia
Missing May
Orchard Books

Rylant, Cynthia
The Van Gogh Cafe
Harcourt Brace

Sasso, Sandy
But God Remembered
Jewish Lights Publishing

White Deer of Autumn
The Great Change
Beyond Words Publishing

Wilber, Jessica
*Totally Private and Personal
Journaling Ideas for Girls*
Free Spirit Publishing

Index

Index of First Lines to Aphorisms, Poems, and Prayers

About the Authors

MIMI WALCH DOE holds a master's in education from Harvard. She has changed the way hundreds of adults interact with children through her workshops and seminars. *Drawing Angels Near*, coauthored by Mimi, has charmed children and adults of all ages, and *Concert in Angel-Land*, a videotape for young children coproduced by Doe, has been endorsed by Parents' Choice and has won the Angel Award for Excellence and Highest Honors from the Coalition for Quality Children's Media. Mimi lives in Concord, Massachusetts, with her husband and two young daughters.

MARSHA FAYFIELD WALCH is a psychotherapist who works primarily with children and parents. Her experience includes both private and community health center practice. Dr. Walch also serves as a working, clinical consultant to three Head Start centers, offering services to the children, their parents, and their teachers. She has led parenting workshops for preschool teachers, caregivers, social workers, and therapists. Marsha is Mimi's mother and has three other grown children.

To schedule a workshop or lecture in your town, or have a conference/consultation, please write for details.

Mimi Doe
P.O. Box 157
Concord, MA 01742
Fax: 978-369-7188
E-mail: MiDoe@aol.com